# Colorado Legal Research

Carolina Academic Press
Legal Research Series

Tenielle Fordyce-Ruff, Series Editor
Suzanne E. Rowe, Series Editor Emerita

Arizona, Third Edition—Tamara S. Herrera

Arkansas, Second Edition—Coleen M. Barger, Cheryl L. Reinhart & Cathy L. Underwood

California, Third Edition—Aimee Dudovitz, Hether C. Macfarlane & Suzanne E. Rowe

Colorado, Second Edition—Robert Michael Linz

Connecticut—Jessica G. Hynes

Federal, Second Edition—Mary Garvey Algero, Spencer L. Simons, Suzanne E. Rowe, Scott Childs & Sarah E. Ricks

Florida, Fourth Edition—Barbara J. Busharis, Jennifer LaVia & Suzanne E. Rowe

Georgia—Nancy P. Johnson, Elizabeth G. Adelman & Nancy J. Adams

Idaho, Second Edition—Tenielle Fordyce-Ruff & Kristina J. Running

Illinois, Second Edition—Mark E. Wojcik

Iowa, Second Edition—John D. Edwards, Karen L. Wallace & Melissa H. Weresh

Kansas—Joseph A. Custer & Christopher L. Steadham

Kentucky, Second Edition—William A. Hilyerd, Kurt X. Metzmeier & David J. Ensign

Louisiana, Third Edition—Mary Garvey Algero

Massachusetts, Second Edition—E. Joan Blum & Shaun B. Spencer

Michigan, Third Edition—Pamela Lysaght & Cristina D. Lockwood

Minnesota—Suzanne Thorpe

Mississippi—Kristy L. Gilliland

Missouri, Third Edition—Wanda M. Temm & Julie M. Cheslik

New York, Third Edition—Elizabeth G. Adelman, Theodora Belniak, Courtney L. Selby & Brian Detweiler

North Carolina, Second Edition—Scott Childs & Sara Sampson

North Dakota—Anne Mullins & Tammy Pettinato

Ohio, Second Edition—Sara Sampson, Katherine L. Hall & Carolyn Broering-Jacobs

Oklahoma—Darin K. Fox, Darla W. Jackson & Courtney L. Selby

Oregon, Fourth Edition—Suzanne E. Rowe & Megan Austin

Pennsylvania, Second Edition—Barbara J. Busharis, Catherine M. Dunn, Bonny L. Tavares & Carla P. Wale

Tennessee, Second Edition—Scott Childs, Sibyl Marshall & Carol McCrehan Parker

Texas, Second Edition—Spencer L. Simons

Washington, Second Edition—Julie Heintz-Cho, Tom Cobb & Mary A. Hotchkiss

West Virginia, Second Edition—Hollee Schwartz Temple

Wisconsin—Patricia Cervenka & Leslie Behroozi

Wyoming, Second Edition—Debora A. Person & Tawnya K. Plumb

# Colorado Legal Research

Second Edition

**Robert Michael Linz**

Tenielle Fordyce-Ruff, Series Editor
Suzanne E. Rowe, Series Editor Emerita

Carolina Academic Press
Durham, North Carolina

Library of Congress Cataloging-in-Publication Data

Names: Linz, Robert M., author.
Title: Colorado legal research / by Robert Michael Linz.
Description: Second edition. | Durham, North Carolina : Carolina Academic Press, LLC, [2018] | Series: Legal research series | Includes bibliographical references and index.
Identifiers: LCCN 2018030258 | ISBN 9781531010126 (alk. paper)
Subjects: LCSH: Legal research--Colorado.
Classification: LCC KFC1875 .L56 2018 | DDC 340.072/0788--dc23
LC record available at https://lccn.loc.gov/2018030258

e-ISBN 978-1-5310-1013-3

Carolina Academic Press, LLC

700 Kent Street
Durham, North Carolina 27701
Telephone (919) 489-7486
Fax (919) 493-5668
www.cap-press.com

Printed in the United States of America.

*For Max, Kathy, Andrew, Anne, Peter, and Jane*

*Ad Deum qui laetificant juventutem meam*
*Psalm 42*

# Summary of Contents

# Contents

# List of Tables and Figures

## Tables

## Figures

# Series Note

The Legal Research Series published by Carolina Academic Press includes titles from many states around the country as well as a separate text on federal legal research. The goal of each book is to provide law students, practitioners, paralegals, college students, laypeople, and librarians with the essential elements of legal research in each jurisdiction. Unlike more bibliographic texts, the Legal Research Series books seek to explain concisely both the sources of legal research and the process for conducting legal research effectively.

# Foreword to the Second Edition

It's no secret that Colorado has one of the fastest-growing populations and economies in the nation in 2018. The latest *Annual Report of the Colorado Supreme Court*, Office of Attorney Regulation Counsel reveals that the number of registered attorneys in Colorado is up 10 percent from five years ago, and that Colorado experienced a 30 percent increase in Uniform Bar Exam Score Transfer and On Motion applications from out-of-state attorneys seeking to practice here in 2017. Many active, private-practice attorneys in Colorado are solo or small-firm lawyers, who are often without the benefit of law librarians in their workplaces.

In addition to many new Colorado attorneys, there continue to be paralegal students and Colorado citizens who show up daily to consult with librarians and use legal resources at Colorado's public, academic, and court libraries. A gridlocked Congress is encouraging Colorado state and local governments to lead the way on issues of public interest, such as climate change, fracking, marijuana, and immigration. As state and local agencies make more resources available online, and as the number and sophistication of proprietary research databases increases, even seasoned Colorado law librarians are finding it challenging to keep up. The publication of this Second Edition of Robert Linz's *Colorado Legal Research* satisfies an important need to bring the legal community and the public up-to-speed, and to provide accurate, clear instruction on the methods, analysis, and tools of legal research in Colorado.

There are other reasons to embrace this new edition. An expanded *Chapter 4 — Researching Legislative History* — addresses the Colorado General Assembly's efforts to make more documents, committee testimony, and floor debate accessible on its websites, and the Chapter offers useful tables and images to clarify how a bill winds its way through the legislature, and what documents and publications are generated at each juncture. An expanded *Chapter 5 — Researching Administrative Law* — concludes with a new Administrative Law Research Checklist that neatly summarizes what questions to ask when navigating the cumbersome and separate processes of locating and updating Colorado regulations, agency decisions, and Attorney General opinions. The addition of *Chapter 7 — Updating Law with a Citator* — is a useful complement to the book's thorough treatment of case research. It walks the reader step-by-step through the critical skill of using a citator to determine if a case, statute, or regulation is still good law in Colorado, and it includes several tables, screenshots, and checklists to illustrate important distinctions among the four major citator products.

Author Robert Linz has been my close colleague at the University of Colorado Law School's William A. Wise Law Library for 10 years. Our law school and library director have been leaders in defining and developing legal research pedagogy, most notably through organization of the annual Boulder Conference on Legal Information for legal research educators. Robert continues to study and innovate his teaching methods (lectures, in-class demos, hands-on group exercises) and class materials for an annual course in Colorado Legal Research, which he began offering around the time he published the first edition of this book. Many CU Law students have used and provided feedback on this book. Student course evaluations confirm what I have learned in working with Robert: that he is a highly effective researcher and teacher, who is passionate about educating others on the Colorado legal system and the research competencies explored in *Colorado Legal Research*.

Jane Thompson
Associate Director of Faculty Services and Research
William A. Wise Law Library
University of Colorado at Boulder

# Foreword to the First Edition

Every state in the U.S. has its own legal system, shaped by its pioneers and continuing to evolve today. Colorado, the "Centennial State," is no exception. Colorado's colorful legal history includes its early geographic partition among at least five nations and then four U.S. states, and multiple attempts at forming governments on its own (with some success in its miners' courts and the Territory of Jefferson). The result is an ever-changing landscape of state-specific legal resources that bears the mark of these previous jurisdictions.

Legal research, a skill fundamental to a legal education and the practice of law, varies with the jurisdiction. Because each state has its own legal system and corresponding resources, law students, lawyers, and other legal researchers must learn the methods and sources of researching in that state to practice their professions competently. Teaching Colorado's unique legal resources is the subject of this book.

Legal research is more than learning the sources, the "bibliography," of the jurisdiction, however. Legal research is a cyclical process of identifying issues, choosing the correct resources to consult, analyzing results, and then refining issues to research. Resources may be in print, microform, or electronic formats; their authority needs to be assessed, their rules and guidance analyzed, updated, and applied. The process changes with each problem, and a thorough knowledge of the resources of the jurisdiction into which the problem falls is essential. Colorado Legal Research offers guidance on the research process as well as its sources.

Robert Linz is well positioned to explain the intricacies of Colorado legal research. He has studied the Colorado system, and knows its ins and outs well. He has carried out legal research projects in support of the justices and judges of Colorado's appellate court system and the faculty and students of the University of Colorado at Boulder School of Law. He has taught legal research to beginning and advanced law students. His attention to detail and his commitment to legal research education are evident on every page of this book.

*Colorado Legal Research* provides the roadmap for its readers to steer through the intricacies of legal research in Colorado. Colorado legal researchers are indebted to Robert for this work.

Barbara Bintliff
Nicholas Rosenbaum Professor of Law
Director, William A. Wise Law Library
University of Colorado at Boulder

# Preface and Acknowledgments

In recent years, Colorado has gained national attention for pushing the boundaries of the law in controversial areas. In 2000, the people of Colorado passed a referendum to legalize medical marijuana. In the 2009 and 2010 legislative sessions, the Colorado General Assembly enacted legislation to create a scheme in which medical marijuana patients could exercise this right while curbing potential abuses. In 2012, the people of Colorado again amended their Constitution and again over marijuana. By a wide margin, the voters approved Amendment 64 which legalized marijuana for recreation use. The constitutional amendment called for a statutory and regulatory scheme through which citizens could consume marijuana or marijuana products. In 2013, the Colorado General Assembly responded by creating the Colorado Retail Marijuana Code. It empowered the Colorado Department of Revenue to create regulations to implement the Retail Marijuana Code. Local governments were also involved in these groundbreaking laws. Local governments now play a role in permitting or prohibiting businesses from selling marijuana in their jurisdictions. As is always the case, the Colorado courts are slower to contribute to the legal developments surrounding marijuana. Simply, the courts speak to matters when asked to do so. While there are few cases regarding medical marijuana, and certainly criminal cases involving marijuana, there is not yet case law regarding recreational marijuana. But those cases will surely be coming.

The example of Colorado marijuana law is instructive for the legal researcher. For one to research the law well and thoroughly, the researcher will need (1) to know the branches of government; (2) the law they produce; (3) the relationship of the branches to one another and to the citizens of Colorado; (4) in what sources that law is published; and (5) how to find that law. While the Colorado law of marijuana enjoys a certain freshness that helps researchers more clearly see answers to these questions, this general understanding is necessary to perform research successfully for any legal area.

The goal of this book is to help researchers understand the nature of Colorado legal institutions, the law they produce, and how to find that law. It is written for the law student and attorney unfamiliar with Colorado law and legal research. It is also written to help members of the public who do not have the benefit of legal training to become appropriately acquainted with legal research methods and sources so that they can research Colorado law. While locating the law may be difficult, understanding and applying the law to a particular situation can be quite difficult. This text is not intended to provide legal advice but rather to help the researcher locate authority by which he or she can draw his or her own legal conclusions.

To reach this goal, the book contains several helpful features. These include checklists, flowcharts, tables, and graphics. The text book also includes sample problems through which the researcher will see how to navigate the materials to find the law. Finally, the book includes resources for additional information.

The book contains two parts. In Part One, the researcher will find information about the design, resources, and techniques for researching particular types of law. For example, Chapter Two introduces the researcher to the organization of Colorado statutory law and which print and online resources contain the various forms of statutory publication. The researcher will learn about the organization of the current statutory code but also about historical codes and features of these publications which improve research. In Part Two, the researcher will find step-by-step examples with illustrations on how to research particular types of law. In Chapter Fourteen, for example, the researcher will see examples of how to use contextual tools to narrow a list of statutory code sections to the ones most relevant to the researcher's research question.

While the researcher can open to any chapter to learn how to research that area of law, the best approach for the novice legal researcher would be to read first Chapter One on the structure of Colorado government and the various types of authority. This chapter is foundational. It provides the groundwork for understanding how governments derive authority to issue law, and the other types of authority that help the researcher determine where to research and what to find. Beyond Chapter One, researchers will want to turn to chapters in Part One for concepts and resources and to Part Two for specific examples and guidance on research methods.

This book is not designed to provide a comprehensive listing of Colorado legal resources. It is a manual on how to use resources to find Colorado law. For such a comprehensive bibliography, I draw the reader's attention to a companion volume to this text, *Colorado Legal Resources: An Annotated Bibliography*, published by the William S. Hein Company.

While writing involves hours of solitary work, it is also a team sport. I want to thank my co-authors Peter Kersten and Nick Harrell for making this second edition particularly useful for researchers. These authors bring their experience from law practice, research assignments and classroom instruction to provide research solutions to common Colorado legal research questions. I also want to thank my students who used and commented on the first edition and the drafts of the second edition. I also want to thank Suzanne Rowe and Tenielle Fordyce-Ruff for their review of the manuscript. I especially would like to thank Steve Elder at the University of Colorado Law Library for his careful review and proofreading of the manuscript. Finally, I would be remiss not to thank my family for their continued support including especially my parents.

I hope researchers find this manual to be helpful guide for legal research. I encourage feedback and would welcome any of your suggestions.

Robert Michael Linz
Boulder, Colorado
July 2018

# Part I

# Concepts and Resources

## Chapter 1

# Structure of Colorado Government and Authority

Colorado became a state in 1876 during the 100th anniversary of the Declaration of Independence. For this reason, it is known as the Centennial State. The state capitol is located in Denver, which houses the heads of the three branches of Colorado government and a number of state administrative agencies of particular importance to the legal researcher, such as the State Archives.

## I. Colorado Government

Colorado government is structured like other state governments in the United States. The government is composed of a legislative, executive, and judicial branch.[1] The legislative branch, the General Assembly, is bicameral, and consists of a Senate and House of Representatives. Senators are elected to a term of four years while representatives are elected to a term of two years. Term limits apply, limiting senators to no more than two consecutive terms in the senate and representatives to no more than four consecutive terms in the house.[2] Currently, the General Assembly is composed of thirty-five senators and sixty-five representatives. The General Assembly makes law in the form of statutes.

The head of the executive branch is the governor. He is elected every four years, and may not serve more than two consecutive terms of office. The other executive branch officers include the lieutenant governor, secretary of state, state treasurer, and attorney general. Their terms of office are also similarly restricted as that of the governor.[3] As with other chief executives, the governor's

1. Colo. Const. Art. III. The Constitution refers to these branches as "departments."
2. Colo. Const. Art. V, Sec. 3.
3. Colo. Const. Art. IV, Sec. 1.

duties are to ensure the laws are faithfully executed[4] and to serve as commander-in-chief of the state militia,[5] among other duties. He has the power to grant pardons,[6] convene and adjourn sessions of the General Assembly,[7] and veto legislation passed by the General Assembly.[8] He oversees the state's administrative agencies which are limited to twenty departments[9] although each department may be composed of multiple divisions, sections or units. The executive branch makes law in the form of regulations, executive orders, attorney general opinions and agency decisions.

The judicial branch is composed of both appellate and trial courts. The constitution creates a supreme court, district courts, county courts, and a probate and juvenile court for the City and County of Denver.[10] There are two appellate courts in Colorado: the Colorado Supreme Court and the Colorado Court of Appeals. The Colorado Supreme Court is established by the constitution; the Colorado Court of Appeals, however, is created by statute.[11] The court of appeals has an interesting history, having been established and abolished by the General Assembly at different times in Colorado legal history.[12] Colorado is divided into twenty-two judicial districts and each district is served by its own district court. Each county is served by its own county court and municipalities by their own municipal court. The appellate courts make law in the form of judicial opinions. The trial courts issue orders. In Colorado, researchers can find the appellate court opinions, but trial court documents have limited availability.

Local governments exist at the county and municipal level although there are several forms of local government, all of which are provided for by the Colorado Constitution or statutes. Colorado contains sixty-four counties and 271 municipalities. Denver and Broomfield are a hybrid city-county government. County and municipal governments can either be statutory or home-rule. Home-rule governments enjoy more freedom to manage their government for their citizens. Local governments make law in the form of ordinances and in the case of home rule governments, a charter.

---

4. Colo. Const. Art. IV, Sec. 2.
5. Colo. Const. Art. IV, Sec. 5.
6. Colo. Const. Art. IV, Sec. 7.
7. Colo. Const. Art. IV, Secs. 9 and 10.
8. Colo. Const. Art. IV, Secs. 11 and 12.
9. Colo. Const. Art. IV, Sec. 22.
10. Colo. Const. Art. VI, Sec. 1.
11. CRS 13-4-101.
12. Linz, Robert M. and Munger, Claire E., "The Early History of the Colorado Court of Appeals." *Colorado Lawyer* 37 (Nov. 2008): 91.

## II. Law and Legal Research

### A. Primary Authority

The law that governments create is known as *primary law*—constitutions, statutes, regulations, cases, ordinances and court rules. These are primary because they derive from elected or appointed government officials acting in their official capacity or from the people. Ultimately, legal research is the search for primary law. In this context, law is also referred to as authority, so researchers may be directed to search for *primary authority*. This text uses the term authority.

### B. Secondary Authority

There is another type of authority—*secondary authority*, sometimes called *secondary law*. But it is not law at all. It is commentary about the primary law, or primary authority. It serves two useful purposes for the legal researcher.

First, it helps the researcher understand the primary authority. Laws can be difficult to interpret. Law evolves over time. Language used by lawmakers is sometimes obscure or technical. The law or the language used to express it may be difficult to comprehend, further complicated by multiple laws working together to define an area of law. Novice legal researchers may be overwhelmed in deciphering the various laws to discern a rule of law for a particular legal problem. Secondary authority helps researchers with this problem. Written by legal experts, secondary authority provides explanations about the law. These explanations can vary from broad and general, serving as good overviews of an area of law; or they can be quite narrow and detailed. These are descriptive explanations of the law. Legal experts also offer prescriptive explanations, in that they give advice and opinion on how the law should develop. This advice can also be useful in suggesting how the law can develop to create a more just or equitable legal framework in society. Secondary authority is found in a variety of publications, such as treatises (books about the law written by experts), legal encyclopedia articles, law journal articles, practice manuals, and other documents.

Next, secondary authority serves another useful purpose. It directs researchers to the primary authority. Legal writers discuss the law. Their work derives from the law. Lawyers are trained to cite the law they are discussing. They are trained to develop their legal arguments from the judicial decisions, statutes, constitutional provisions, regulations and other primary authority generated by government. To be credible, the authors provide citations to that primary authority and any relevant secondary authority. Some secondary authority is richly referenced. It is not uncommon, for example, that a law journal article contains hundreds of detailed footnotes. Even short summaries of the law are likely to provide a few citations to key primary and secondary authority. Legal researchers can leverage that fertile ground of citation to fully research an area of law.

## C. Mandatory and Persuasive Authority

Researchers also need to be aware of another distinction on legal authority. In addition to being divided into primary and secondary, law is also binding or persuasive. *Binding authority*, sometimes referred to as mandatory authority, is legal authority which is required to be followed in a particular jurisdiction. (A jurisdiction refers to the geographic boundaries controlled by a government, such as the city of Pueblo or the state of Colorado.) It is law that must be followed—if it applies to the particular legal problem. Within Colorado, binding authority includes the Colorado Constitution, statutes enacted by the Colorado General Assembly, Colorado agency regulations, Colorado judicial opinions and local government ordinances. But authority can also be *persuasive*. By subtraction, it is authority that need not be followed. For example, statutes or cases issued by another state's government need not be followed in Colorado. Colorado courts may look to them for guidance, but need not decide similar matters the same way. Primary authority can be binding or persuasive. All secondary authority is persuasive, as none of it carries the force of law in any jurisdiction.

## D. Publications and Authority

Primary and secondary authority are collected by type and published in various print and online publications. For primary authority, cases are published in reporters, statutes in session law volumes and codes, and regulations in registers and codes. Secondary authority is published in a wide variety of publications. For example, law periodical articles are published in journals, reviews or newsletters. Legal encyclopedias, restatements of the law and American Law Report annotations are separate publications. All of these publications are available as print resources or online databases. The task of the legal researcher is to find authority by consulting these various publications of authority.

In addition to sorting primary authority by type (i.e., cases, statutes, regulations, etc.), publishers sort or publish legal authority by jurisdiction. Colorado case law, for example, will be published in Colorado case law reporters or a Colorado case law database. Colorado statutory law is published in the *Colorado Revised Statutes*. This sorting by jurisdiction is necessary and helpful so that researchers can locate the *primary, binding authority* that applies to the *jurisdiction* of the legal problem being researched. To be clear, this means that researchers need citations to Colorado statutes, cases, and regulations when arguing before or persuading Colorado courts and lawmakers. Colorado courts are not required to follow the law of other jurisdictions but are required to follow the law of their own jurisdiction.

There is one other class of publications quite helpful to legal researchers. These are called *finding aids*, or *finding tools*. These includes indexes, citators, and digests. Finding tools are neither primary nor secondary authority. Indeed, they are not authority at all. They simple constitute pointers to primary and secondary authority. Consider an index in a book. Researchers use indexes to find a discussion of the indexed entry within the book. The book index is a finding aid. In legal research, publishers produce entire volumes of indexes to point to the law. As with primary and secondary authority, finding aids are available as print and online resources.

## III. Legal Research and the Structure of Legal Information

The goal of legal research is to find primary authority, but more particularly, all of the primary authority dealing with the particular legal problem that is binding on citizens and government officials of a particular jurisdiction in effect at a certain point in time. Legal publishers are aware of this goal. Legal publications reflect a structure that enables researchers to achieve this goal. In particular, researchers can utilize three properties of legal publications that can simplify legal research.

One property of legal publication is connectivity of legal resources. While not unique to legal publications, connectivity is an important feature of legal publications because it helps researchers locate all of the law that applies to the particular legal problem being researched. For instance, with finding tools, researchers can use the citations to locate primary authority or additional secondary authority. Connectivity is achieved through editor-added citations from one publication to another publication addressing the same issue or area of law.

A second property is that publications organize law topically. Because researchers need to find all of the law on a particular topic, legal publishers will collect all of a particular type of law on a subject and publish it together. Statutory and regulatory law is organized by subject and published in a code. Local government ordinances can also be codified. While judicial decisions are not published topically, a type of publication exists, called a *digest* that organizes case law by topic and provides a citation to the case itself. These organizational schemes greatly simplify legal research. As with connectivity, legal researchers can use the topicality of publication to locate all relevant law. For example, researchers needing to find statutes pertaining to landlord-tenant relations could turn to the chapter in a statutory code that contains those laws.

Third, law is also published *chronologically*. While this makes law more difficult to research, it is useful for two purposes. First, new law can be published quickly. When new statutes are enacted, regulations promulgated or cases decided, legal information consumers need to know the law and how it impacts them. Publishing law topically is time-consuming, as the new law must be integrated into the existing code or digest and then republished. Chronological publication is quite fast, as new law is published to a website or pushed to subscribers electronically. Researchers need to be aware of new laws and pending laws in areas of law they are researching.

The second useful purpose of chronological publication is to aid in historical legal research. The chronological publications are static; once published they are not updated or overwritten with newly developed law. Researchers can retrieve the chronologically publication to determine what the law was at any particular point in time. This feature is particularly necessary when lawyers are trying to determine what law was in effect at the time an incident arose.

As legal research is conducted, legal researchers should keep these three properties—connectivity, topical publication and chronological publication—in mind. These properties will simplify access to unlocking the vast amount of legal information in legal publications.

## IV. Summary

Legal research is about the search for authority. There are two types of authority—primary and secondary. Primary authority is created by elected or appointed officials acting in their official capacities. Primary authority includes the constitution, statutes, regulations, cases, local government ordinances and court rules. Secondary authority serves two purposes. It provides commentary on the primary authority and citations to primary and secondary authority. While authority is categorized into primary and secondary, it is also divided into mandatory and persuasive. Mandatory authority is primary authority that a particular jurisdiction must follow. Persuasive authority need not be followed by law makers. All secondary authority is persuasive authority. Primary authority can be either mandatory if cited in the jurisdiction from which it derived or persuasive if cited in a jurisdiction from which it did not derive. Primary and secondary authority are published in various print publications and online resources by type and by jurisdiction.

Legal researchers use this knowledge of government structure, court hierarchy and the legal system and the publication of law to locate all of the relevant, binding, primary authority applicable to the legal problem being researched. Furthermore, legal researchers leverage the properties of the legal publishing system to simplify their research. These properties include the connectivity of resources one to another, the topical publication, and the chronological publication of law. By utilizing this conceptual framework and tools, researchers can efficiently and effectively research and find the law.

# Chapter 2

# Researching Colorado Statutes

## I. Introduction

The Colorado General Assembly meets annually in regular session from early January until early May.[1] The first session of the Colorado legislature convened in November 1876, shortly after the Colorado constitution was ratified. In the early years of statehood, the General Assembly met every other year. Starting in 1951, the General Assembly started to meet annually in a regular session which spans two calendar years. The odd-numbered years are the first regular session while the even-numbered years are the second regular session. The governor or two-thirds of the members of each house of the General Assembly can also convene a special or extraordinary session of the General Assembly to ask it to craft legislation on subjects specified in the request for the extraordinary session.[2] The most recent special session was convened in 2012.

The General Assembly produces primary authority as statutes. Statutes are both reactionary and anticipatory. Often, they are crafted by legislators at the

---

1. Colo. Const. Art. V, Sec. 7. This provision states that the General Assembly shall convene a session starting no later than the second Wednesday of January of each year and that the session shall last no longer than 120 calendar days. When this change was made in 1951, in even-numbered years the General Assembly was restricted to consider only bills regarding revenue, appropriations, or on subjects designated by the governor. This restriction was entirely removed by legislation passed during the 1982 General Assembly by Senate Concurrent Resolution No. 1.

2. Colo. Const. Art. IV, Sec. 9 states that the governor can call an extraordinary session of the General Assembly by proclamation. This power is also cited in Colo. Const. Art. V, Sec. 7 which further provides that two-thirds of the members of each house of the General Assembly may also call a special session. In either case, the General Assembly may only consider legislation on subjects specified in the request for the extraordinary session.

advocacy of citizens or interest groups to fix a problem in society. At the same time, statutes serve to create a scheme to solve a problem that has not yet arisen. Legislative bodies collect information from many sources as they craft legislation and the statutes often represent a compromise among the various interests and approaches to solving a problem. As the people's chamber, legislation holds a high place among primary authority, and if the legislature has enacted a statutory scheme to address a problem, courts give deference to the intention of the legislature. This chapter explores the process of creating statutory law, into what resources such law is published, and how to find such law in its current and historical form.

## II. The Organization of Colorado Statutory Law

### A. Session Laws

Throughout a session of the General Assembly, bills are introduced, debated, amended, and enacted. Once a bill becomes law, it is published as a *slip law*.[3] The current practice is to publish each slip law, or *session law*, on the General Assembly's website.[4] At the close of the session, the session laws are collected and published into printed session law volumes. Since 1975, these session laws are assigned chapter numbers based on the date of enactment and published in chronological order.[5] In recent sessions, these laws have been published in three volumes. In addition to the acts themselves, each session law set includes the following parts:

1. a certification of authenticity signed by the president of the senate and the speaker of the house,
2. a listing of members of the General Assembly and the officers of Colorado state government,

3. Before online publication became widely available, acts were initially published as slip laws. These law "pamphlets" were the first publication of the statutory law, were published quickly, likely separately paginated and made available at the state house. At the close of the legislative session, these slip laws were gathered and published into session law volumes, which were consecutively paginated and bound. As publication of statutory law has moved online to legislature websites, this distinction may not exist as the statute is published immediately as a session law and appropriately cited.

4. Website of the Colorado General Assembly, http://www.leg.state.co.us/.

5. Prior to 1975, the session laws were assigned chapter numbers by subject of the bill, and organized alphabetically by subject heading.

3. the appropriations acts,
4. any initiatives or referenda approved during the previous election,
5. resolutions and memorials adopted during the legislative session,
6. an index of bills, resolutions, and memorials,
7. a subject index, and
8. a table of bills introduced during the session that were enacted into law.

The session laws are also accompanied by separate publication called the *Red Book*. This single, slim volume alerts researchers to which existing statutory code sections have been impacted by laws enacted during the session of the General Assembly. On the General Assembly's website this information is published simultaneously with the newly published session laws.[6]

The session laws are typically printed and published in August, although the General Assembly's website is updated continuously throughout the legislative session.

## B. Colorado Revised Statutes

### 1. Organization

While each session law enacts law on a single subject, the organization of these laws are by date of enactment, as noted above. There is no effort made within the session law volumes to gather or cross reference all Colorado statutory law on a particular subject. This step is called *codification* and is extremely important for statutory research as codification enables the researcher to find all statutory law on a particular topic relatively easily.

The official code of Colorado statutory law is the *Colorado Revised Statutes* (CRS). It is hierarchically arranged into titles, articles, and sections. The forty-five titles are the broadest levels of organization, covering major topics or subjects. (See Figure 2-1.) There are titles on insurance, state government, professions and occupations, domestic relations, education, taxation, utilities, water and crimes, to name a handful of the forty-five titles of the CRS. Each title is further subdivided into articles. Titles can have any number of articles. Finally, the articles can be divided into parts and sections. Each of these further divisions organizes the statutory law into logical categories all dealing with a particular topic of law. (See Figure 2-2.)

---

6. The list of available Colorado session laws and red books are available on the General Assembly's website, https://leg.colorado.gov/session-laws.

**Figure 2-1. Colorado Revised Statutes**

| | | | |
|---|---|---|---|
| Title 1 | Elections | Title 24 | Government—State |
| Title 2 | Legislative | Title 25 | Public Health and Environment |
| Title 3 | United States | Title 25.5 | Health Care Policy and Financing |
| Title 4 | Uniform Commercial Code | Title 26 | Human Services Code |
| Title 5 | Consumer Credit Code | Title 27 | Behavioral Health |
| Title 6 | Consumer and Commercial Affairs | TItle 28 | Military and Veterans |
| Title 7 | Corporations and Associations | Title 29 | Government—Local |
| Title 8 | Labor and Industry | Title 30 | Government—County |
| Title 9 | Safety—Industrial and Commercial | Title 31 | Government—Municipal |
| Title 10 | Insurance | Title 32 | Special Districts |
| Title 11 | Financial Institutions | Title 33 | Parks and Wildlife |
| Title 12 | Professions and Occupations | Title 34 | Mineral Resources |
| Title 13 | Courts and Court Procedure | Title 35 | Agriculture |
| Title 14 | Domestic Matters | Title 36 | Natural Resources—General |
| Title 15 | Probate, Trusts and Fiduciaries | Title 37 | Water and Irrigation |
| Title 16 | Criminal Proceedings | Title 38 | Property—Real and Personal |
| Title 17 | Corrections | Title 39 | Taxation |
| Title 18 | Criminal Code | Title 40 | Utilities |
| Title 19 | Children's Code | Title 41 | Aeronautics: Aircraft and Airports |
| Title 20 | District Attorneys | Title 42 | Vehicles and Traffic |
| Title 21 | State Public Defender | Title 43 | Transportation |
| Title 22 | Education | Title 44 | Revenue—Regulation of Activities |
| Title 23 | Postsecondary Education | | |



Citations to the code sections take the form of title-article-section. A citation to CRS 15-12-406 is a reference to a code section titled "formal testacy proceedings—contested cases" and is located in Title 15 (dealing with probate, trusts and fiduciaries) and in Article 12 (dealing with probate of wills and administration).

**Figure 2-2. Articles, Parts, and Sections of Title 15**

Title 15. Probate, Trusts, and Fiduciaries ☆ Add to Favorites

Includes current version of Colorado statutes, constitution & court rules. Browse Table of Contents below or search above.

Effective Date: 03/09/2016 Go ☑ Specify Content to Search

Select all content | No items selected | Clear Selection

**Fiduciary**

- Article 1. Fiduciary
- Article 1.1. Uniform Prudent Investor Act
- Article 1.5. Colorado Uniform Custodial Trust Act

**Powers of Appointment**

- Article 2. Powers of Appointment [Repealed]
- Article 2.5. Uniform Powers of Appointment Act

**Colorado Probate Code**

- Article 10. General Provisions, Definitions, Jurisdiction
- Article 11. Intestate Succession and Wills
- Article 12. Probate of Wills and Administration
  - 15 CO ST Colorado Probate Code, Art. 12, Refs & Annos
  - Part 1. General Provisions
  - Part 2. Venue for Probate and Administration; Priority to Administer; Demand for Notice
  - Part 3. Informal Probate and Appointment Proceedings
  - Part 4. Formal Testacy and Appointment Proceedings
  - Part 5. Supervised Administration
  - Part 6. Personal Representative; Appointment, Control, and Termination of Authority
  - Part 7. Duties and Powers of Personal Representatives
  - Part 8. Creditors' Claims
  - Part 9. Special Provisions Relating to Distribution
  - Part 10. Closing Estates
  - Part 11. Compromise of Controversies
  - Part 12. Collection of Personal Property by Affidavit and Summary Administration Procedure for Small Estates
  - Part 13. Determination of Heirs, Devisees, and Property Interests by Special Proceeding
  - Part 14. Colorado Uniform Estate Tax Apportionment Act
- Article 13. Ancillary Administration
- Article 14. Persons Under Disability—Protection
- Article 14.5. Uniform Adult Guardianship and Protective Proceedings Jurisdiction Act
- Article 15. Nonprobate Transfers on Death
- Article 16. Trust Administration
- Article 17. Effective Date—Transition



Article 12 is actually composed of fourteen parts all of which address the subject of administration of estates (See Figure 2-2.). Part 4 of Article 12 (where 406 is located) is titled "formal testacy and appointment proceedings" but all parts deal with some aspect of probate administration. (See Figure 2-3.) Again, the part numbers are not listed in the citation but they give the researcher a sense of the organizational scheme of the code.

## Figure 2-3. CRS 15-12-406

COLORADO REVISED STATUTES

*** This document reflects changes current through all laws passed at the First Regular Session of the Seventieth General Assembly of the State of Colorado (2015) ***

TITLE 15. PROBATE, TRUSTS, AND FIDUCIARIES
COLORADO PROBATE CODE
ARTICLE 12. PROBATE OF WILLS AND ADMINISTRATION
PART 4. FORMAL TESTACY AND APPOINTMENT PROCEEDINGS

C.R.S. 15-12-406 (2015)

15-12-406. Formal testacy proceedings -- contested cases

(1) In a contested case in which the proper execution of a will is at issue, the following rules apply:

(a) If the will is self-proved pursuant to section 15-11-504, the will satisfies the requirements for execution without the testimony of any attesting witness, upon filing the will and the acknowledgment and affidavits annexed or attached to it, unless there is evidence of fraud or forgery affecting the acknowledgment or affidavit.

(b) If the will is notarized pursuant to section 15-11-502 (1) (c) (II), but not self-proved, there is a rebuttable presumption that the will satisfies the requirements for execution upon filing the will.

(c) If the will is witnessed pursuant to section 15-11-502 (1) (c) (I), but not notarized or self-proved, the testimony of at least one of the attesting witnesses is required to establish proper execution if the witness is within this state, competent, and able to testify. Proper execution may be established by other evidence, including an affidavit of an attesting witness. An attestation clause that is signed by the attesting witnesses raises a rebuttable presumption that the events recited in the clause occurred.

**HISTORY:** Source: L. 73: R&RE, p. 1576, § 1. C.R.S. 1963: § 153-3-406.L. 2009: Entire section amended, (HB 09-1287), ch. 310, p. 1687, § 16, effective July 1, 2010.

Cross references: For provisions relating to the time of taking effect or the provisions for transition of this code, see § 15-17-101.

COMMENT

2008 Revisions. This section, which applies in a contested case in which the proper execution of a will is at issue, was substantially revised and clarified in 2008.

Self-Proved Wills: Paragraph (1) provides that a will that is self-proved pursuant to Section 2-504 satisfies the requirements for execution without the testimony of any attesting witness, upon filing the will and the acknowledgment and affidavits annexed or attached to it, unless there is evidence of fraud or forgery affecting the acknowledgment or affidavit. Paragraph (1) does not preclude evidence of undue influence, lack of testamentary capacity, revocation, or any relevant evidence that the testator was unaware of the contents of the document.

Notarized Wills: Paragraph (2) provides that if the will is notarized pursuant to Section 2-502(a)(3)(B), but not self-proved, there is a rebuttable presumption that the will satisfies the requirements for execution upon filing the will.

Witnessed Wills: Paragraph (3) provides that if the will is witnessed pursuant to Section 2-502(a)(3)(A), but

## 2. Research Value

The CRS is an annotated code.[7] In addition to the statutory language, each code section may be followed by citations called *annotations* to judicial decisions, law review articles or other authority which applies, interprets or references the statutory code section. Not all code sections contain annotations, and sometimes annotations may be located at the beginning of an article or part. Nevertheless, annotations are tremendously helpful for the researcher. They help the researcher find relevant authority on the topic of the statute. The research references are an application of the connectivity discussed in Chapter 1.

## 3. Parts of a Statute in an Annotated Code

Each part of a statute in an annotated code can be identified and searched separately using LexisNexis, Westlaw and other online services. The parts, called fields or segments, include the citation; caption, or section and rule; preliminary or heading; text; credits; and history. The citation is the statutory citation of the code section. The caption or section and rule is name of the code section. The preliminary or heading identifies the location of the code section within the hierarchical arrangement of the code. The text is the text of the statutory language itself. The credits and history refer to the source notes or historical development of the code section. Researchers can typically also search just through the annotations and research references following the code section. Using these parts in research can greatly increase the efficiency and effectiveness of the research.

## 4. Other Content

In addition to containing the Colorado statutory law currently in effect at the date of publication of the code, the CRS contains some additional helpful information. It republishes the United States Constitution and Declaration of Independence. This version of the Constitution is not annotated. It also contains a copy of the Colorado Constitution which is annotated. The CRS also

7. Not all statutory codes are annotated. The *United States Code*, for example, which is the official statutory code publication of federal statutory law, is not annotated. While unannotated codes are poor tools for doing research, they have the advantage of brevity. As the unannotated code contains only the statutory text, it is a much shorter publication than for example the *United States Code Annotated*, an annotated commercial version of the *United States Code* published by Thomson Reuters.

contains court rules and related forms. These are the entire set of rules issued by the Colorado Supreme Court to regulate conduct in Colorado courts and to manage other matters of discipline and procedure in the Colorado judiciary (See Figure 2-1 for the contents listing of the CRS).

## 5. Sources of the Colorado Revised Statutes

LexisNexis is the official publisher, but the CRS is created and edited under authority of the Committee on Legal Services by the Colorado Revisor of Statutes and the Office of Legislative Legal Services. Thomson Reuters also publishes a version of the Colorado Revised Statutes under the title of the *Colorado Revised Statutes Annotated* (CRSA).[8] While it does not enjoy official status, it contains the same statutory language as the official CRS. It too is an annotated code. The annotations, however, are produced by lawyer-editors at Thomson Reuters. These annotations may vary from those of the code published by LexisNexis. As with the LexisNexis version, the CRSA contains the United States Constitution, Declaration of Independence, Enabling Act, Colorado Constitution, and Colorado court rules and forms.

The CRS is published in print and online. As noted, LexisNexis is the printer and distributor of the CRS. A new edition is published each September, after the close of the session of the Colorado General Assembly and after the Revisor of Statutes and other staff members have updated or amended the code with new laws and deleted repealed laws. LexisNexis provides online access to the CRS without charge. It is available through the General Assembly's website but can be accessed directly.[9] The statutory text and annotations of the online version are an exact replica of the print version of the code, modified only in format for the online environment. LexisNexis also publishes an online version of the CRS on its subscription-based services, Lexis Advance. Likewise, Thomson Reuters makes its online version of the CRS available on its subscription-based services, Westlaw.

The CRS is also available online from various online legal information providers. For Colorado lawyers, the most relevant of these services is Casemaker. Members of the Colorado Bar Association, a voluntary bar, are provided free access to Casemaker as part of their membership.[10]

8. West's *Colorado Revised Statutes Annotated*. Eagan, MN: Thomson Reuters, c1989–.

9. The website address is http://www.lexisnexis.com/hottopics/colorado/.

10. For more information, visit the Colorado Bar Association's website at http://www.cobar.org/index.cfm/ID/1749/DPMEM/Casemaker/.

# III. Researching Statutory Law

## A. Finding Statutes

Researchers have a variety of options to find a statute. The options depend on whether the researcher is using the print or online version of the CRS. Regardless of format, however, the researcher will ultimately obtain a citation and use it to locate the statutory text.

### 1. Print Research

Researchers using one of the print versions can employ one of three methods to locate a relevant code section. First, they can consult the index. The index is contained in one or two volumes and generally shelved at the end of the set. It is organized alphabetically by topic and subtopic, and contains an appropriately rich vocabulary of index terms to direct the researcher to the appropriate code section, or redirect the researcher to another part of the index. Second, researchers can utilize the tables of Short Titles and Popular Names, or Words and Phrases to locate a code section. The table of Short Titles and Popular Names is particularly useful for those situations in which researchers have the popular or common name for an act but do not know the citation. For example, if a researcher is asked to locate the Charter Schools Act, he will find an entry in the table pointing him to CRS 22-30.5-101. In the Words and Phrases table, researchers can locate code sections that have defined words and phrases. Often, legislation uses words and phrases in precise ways. To avoid confusion with the common usage of those terms, the act will define the word or phrase. Researchers can use this table to find those technical definitions.

Finally, researchers can use the organizational structure of the code to find relevant code sections. In this approach, the researcher surveys the titles and articles of the code, and based upon the likely topic of the code section, opens to the title and article table of contents to scan the code section entries and choose the most appropriate one. While this method may sound inefficient, it takes advantage of an important research technique for statutory research, which will be addressed in the next section.

### 2. Online Research

Researchers using an online version of the code have a broader set of search options. First, researchers may be able to use the same research techniques as in print if the online service contains those features. The subscription-based services from LexisNexis and Thomson Reuters provide the ability to search in an index, a popular name table, and a table of contents. In the CRSA on

Westlaw, researchers may search for words and phrases defined in the statutes. Neither Lexis Advance, the free version of the CRS from LexisNexis, nor the version available from Casemaker provide this type of searching. All of these services, however, do permit researchers to search hierarchically through a table of contents of titles and articles.

Second, the online services provide the ability to search by keyword. This research method is most familiar to current researchers who are accustomed to entering a few search terms into a search box to find relevant content in a database. Typically, the researcher need not use any special search connectors between the terms, although that feature is available as "Terms and Connectors" searching, and is addressed in Chapter 11. Keyword searching relieves the problem of "decoding" the terms used by the indexer when developing the index. However, it forces researchers to be more careful in sifting through results generated by search terms. Online services can improve the basic keyword searches by allowing those terms to be searched within parts or fields of the documents. This approach can greatly improve the effectiveness and efficiency of the search. Fields exist for statutory text, titles, citations, and annotations, but researchers should consult online help to determine what fields are available and how to search them. Chapter 13 addresses this type of research as well.

The biggest challenge with keyword searching of online statutes is knowing that the correct statutory section has been retrieved. To address this problem, researchers need to learn how review results and read statutes.

### 3. Reviewing Results and Identifying Statutes

As researchers delve into the body of statutory law, they may feel overwhelmed and uncertain with the search results. This discomfort may be particularly acute with keyword searching as the search engine may return results in which those keywords appear in the statutory title, text or annotations. Consequently, the code sections may not all be relevant. Furthermore, the same keywords can appear in many different parts of the CRS. But not all of those code sections will come from the same article or title and therefore not deal with the same subject. In planning searches and reviewing research results, researchers need to keenly sort the results to discard irrelevant code sections. This sorting can be accomplished if the researcher recalls that the code is hierarchical and subject-oriented. And, if the researcher has an idea of the type of subject under which this law will fall.

To do this, the researcher should identify the code section within the context of the code. This first occurs when reviewing the list of citations. By reading the citations, and noting the title of the code section, the researcher can immediately identify the general subject dealt with by the code section. If helpful, the researcher can then retrieve and review the code section itself. The researcher should read the title of the code section and skim the statutory language to determine what problem the code section is addressing. The researcher should then locate the code section within the overall article. In print, this is done by locating the page where the article is outlined. Online, researchers may be able to refer to an online table of contents. In most online statutory displays, a hierarchical breadcrumb trail is provided for the code section. Each level of hierarchy is linked typically, and the researcher can click on the article level. The researcher is looking for the overall structure of the article, other topics addressed in the article, and the topics of the sections immediately preceding and following the retrieved code section. By taking the time to establish context, researchers will gain confidence in their results and save time in research missteps.

## 4. Updating Statutes

Once appropriate code sections have been located, the researcher needs to ensure that the code section has not been changed since its publication. As noted previously, a code is a subject organization of law in effect at the time the code is produced. Later sessions of the Colorado General Assembly may change the language of the code section. Researchers have several different ways to check on the currency of the code section. Before proceeding, the researcher should be aware that the General Assembly meets in session from early January to early May. Therefore, if the research is conducted after that time period, and the researcher is using the code from the most recent session of the General Assembly, the legislature cannot create new legislation to modify the code.

Updating will depend on what format of the CRS the researcher is using. Updating authority is an essential part of the legal research process.

### *a. Print Codes*

The two print versions of the code are updated in slightly different ways. Currently, LexisNexis publishes the CRS in softbound volumes. At the close of each legislative session, the complete CRS is reprinted reflecting changes made in the mostly recently concluded session of the General Assembly. If the research is occurring at a time when it is possible that the statutory language can change, the researcher will need to go the General Assembly's website and locate the current session information. As noted, the General Assembly publishes recently enacted laws on its website. The researcher will need to review those laws to determine if one of them has changed the code section begin researched. To aid in this process, the legislature publishes the "Red Book." In print, the book's cover is red and therefore a link is provided to the "red book" online. Whether using the print or online version, the "red book" works the same way. It lists each code section that has been modified or created during the session of the General Assembly. Researchers should consult this list for the relevant code section. The "red book" also contains a "reverse" table ordered by house and senate bill number.

Thomson Reuters publishes its version of the CRS as hardbound volumes. These volumes are updated with annual "pocket part" supplements containing changed laws and new annotations. The pocket part is located in the back of each volume, in a pocket affixed inside the back cover of the hardbound volume. To use a pocket part, the researcher first consults the hardbound volume for the code section, and then consults the pocket part for changes. The pocket part is organized by code section, like the hardbound volume. Pocket parts are published once a year, approximately in September. During the legislative session, Thomson Reuters publishes two interim softbound statutory supplements known as the advance legislative service. These supplements contain new laws enacted during the current session of the General Assembly, a table listing code sections affected by newly enacted bills, and amended court forms and court rules. The first of these two supplements is published in March and the second after the close of the session. Therefore, after researchers have checked the hardbound volume and the pocket part, they then check these legislative session pamphlets. Finally, researchers can consult the General Assembly's website as explained above.

#### *b. Online Codes*

Researchers may think that the online codes are automatically updated as new law is enacted by the General Assembly. Indeed, that might be true, but the researcher should verify it by consulting the database information page. Typically, the service will provide a link to this page either at the top or bottom of each code or next to the title of the database. The link will either be termed as "currentness" or "currency" or may be denoted by the letter 'I' enclosed in a circle. The service will either give a date through which the statute is current, or the last enacted law in the session of the legislature.

If the service does not update the statutory language immediately after new law is enacted, the researcher may need to consult other sources. Some services provide a separate database of session laws. These copies contain mark-up language that indicate which language has been added or amended. Typically, new text is denoted in ALL CAPS or underlined, and deleted text by striking through the old language.

## IV. Historical Statutory Research and Territorial Laws

In as much as it is important to update statutory research to ensure the researcher is using the most current language, there are times when the researcher needs to locate an older version of the code section. Parties are judged under the law in effect at the time of the incident or when the document was drafted. The incident or drafting may have occurred many years ago. In other cases, a researcher may wish to see how the statutory language evolved over time. For either application, the researcher needs to locate an earlier, pre-amended version of the statute. The first step in this process is to be aware of the prior versions of Colorado statutory law.

### A. Code Editions

The current edition of the code was issued in 1973. That is to say, it reflects the organizational scheme developed for the 1973 edition of the Colorado Revised Statutes. The current edition is organized by topic, article, and section. And it is organized into broad subject areas which are assigned to a title number. While new editions of the code contain new and amended laws, each annual publication still organizes that law into the scheme develop in 1973.

But there are other ways to organize statutory law. Colorado has had eight previous statutory codifications. Table 2-1 contains a list of those previous editions.

A statutory code section may appear in one or more of the previous editions of the code. Researchers need a method to efficiently trace the development of a code section. The various editions of the code provide three different methods: source notes, comparative tables, and the index.

### B. Source Notes

Sources notes provide the history of the code section. They indicate when it was originally enacted and when amended thereafter. The source note immediately follows the code section. In the LexisNexis version of the CRS, they are denoted in boldface type as "Source." In the Thomson Reuters version of the CRS they appear in a smaller typeface and are also explained in section titled "Historical and Statutory Notes," both following the statutory text. They also appear in all online versions of the code.

Source notes provide the statutory history by noting either the session law year in which the legislation was created or amended, or the earlier edition of

**Table 2-1. Colorado Statutory Compilations**

| Title | Citation |
|---|---|
| *Revised Statutes of Colorado* (1868) | R.S. p. ___, § ___. |
| *General Laws of Colorado* (1877) | G.L. § ____. |
| *General Statutes of Colorado* (1883) | G.S. § ____. |
| *Revised Statutes of Colorado* (1908) | R.S. 08: § ___. |
| *Compiled Laws of Colorado* (1921) | C.L. § ___. |
| *Colorado Statutes Annotated* (1935) | CSA: C. ___, § ___. |
| *Colorado Revised Statutes* (1953) | CRS 53: § ___. |
| *Colorado Revised Statutes* (1963) | C.R.S. 1963: § ___. |
| *Colorado Revised Statutes* (1973) | C.R.S. |

the code in which it appeared. Publishers can use different symbols to denote changes to the code section. In the official LexisNexis version, earlier session laws are indicated with an "L" followed by the year and in recent years the bill number the legislation is based on. The CRS also uses abbreviations for the previous editions of the code. The front matter of each volume of the CRS contains a complete listing of source note symbols as well as an explanation of how to interpret them.

Using the source notes, the researcher can locate an earlier version of the code section as it appeared in either the session laws or in an earlier edition of the statutory codes.

## C. Comparative Tables

While it is an easy task to locate older session laws, it may be more difficult to trace the development of a code section through the statutory codes. When researching backwards, to find an earlier version of the code section, the source should direct the user to the appropriate code section. But if researchers need to find how a code section evolved forward into a later edition of the code, they will need to consult a comparative table. Located toward the end of the statutory code volumes, these tables list where existing code sections appear in the last edition of the code. For example, the code preceding the 1973 code was issued in 1963. When the 1973 code was issued, it contained a table listing where each code section of the 1963 code appeared in the 1973 code. These tables are typically organized by the older code section, but may appear as a reverse table and be organized by the newer code section. Comparative tables are also used within an edition of a code to indicate where code sections may have moved if parts of the code have been reorganized. Likewise, there may be a "reverse" table that indicates where current code sections appeared in earlier editions of the code. The researcher is advised to carefully look at the pages of comparative tables to see what is available.

## D. Index

Comparative tables first appeared in the 1921 code. If researchers need to conduct this type of statutory research in the earliest state codes, they will need to use the index and search for the subject of the law. Because this approach lacks the one-to-one editor-provided relationship between newer and older code section, the researcher should take care to ensure the code sections really are the same code section and that one evolved from the other. To do this, the researcher would consult the index using the same subject matter search terms as the newer code section. She would then open to those code sections in the older edition and note the statutory language. It should be similar in form and similar in content as the newer language. The researcher will need to use good judgment to determine that the older code section was indeed the predecessor to the newer code section.

## E. Territorial Session Laws

Colorado became a state in 1876, but the territorial government existed from 1861 through the Spring of 1876. During that time, the territorial legislature enacted law to govern the new region. Session laws were published in 1861 and the even numbered years between 1862 through 1876. Law libraries should contain a copy of those codes, but they are also available online and in microfiche. The University of Colorado Law Library has digitized the entire collection of territorial session laws and made them available on its website.[11] The website is the easiest way to retrieve these old laws. Researchers can find the law either by citation, title search, keyword search, or by index entry.

11. The website address is http://lawlibrary.colorado.edu/colorado-session-laws.

## V. Summary

Statutes are law created by the legislative branch of government. The Colorado General Assembly sits in session between early January and early May of each year. Statutory law is initially released as a slip law on the General Assembly's website as each bill is enacted into law. At the close of each legislative session, the slip laws are collected and published together in session law volumes. This collection arranges the law by date of enactment. The session laws are then organized by subject and put into a code, which is a topical organization of statutory law. The official code of Colorado statutory law is the Colorado Revised Statutes. This publication is updated at the close of each legislative session as new laws are added and existing laws are amended or repealed. All changes are reflected in the code. The Colorado Revised Statutes is an annotated code, which means it contains references to cases, regulations and secondary authority that are relevant to the code section being researched.

Researchers should use one of the two print annotated codes or one of the several online codes for their Colorado statutory research. In addition to finding statutes, the code also publishes the Colorado Constitution. Researchers have several options for researching codes. These include keyword searches, field or segment searches, and index searches. Researchers can also use one of several tables including tables of contents, popular name tables or words and phrases tables. Researchers should make sure they have located a code section in the proper part of the code and make sure they have checked for the latest updates to the statutory language.

**Statutory Research Checklist**

- ❑ Do I have a citation? What keywords can I use in the index or as keywords?
- ❑ Do I have a common name of the act? Could I use the popular name table?
- ❑ Am I trying to see how a particular word or phrase has been defined and used?
- ❑ Is this code section located in the right part of the code? What Title is it located under?
- ❑ Do I understand the context of this code section in relation to the surrounding code sections?
- ❑ When did the events in my legal problem take place? Was this code section in effect at the time of the incident or do I need to locate an earlier version?
- ❑ Did I update my code section? Is the Colorado General Assembly in session?
- ❑ Did I check the pocket part or interim update for changes to my code section? Did I check on the General Assembly's website? Did I check the Red Book?
- ❑ Did I check the currency link if using an online code?
- ❑ Did I remember to check the annotations? Did I note relevant cases and law review article citations?

## Chapter 3

# The Colorado Constitution

## I. Introduction

A constitution is the fundamental and organic law of a nation or state. It establishes the organization and powers of the government and the rights of citizens. It represents the will of the people, living now and in the past, and as such provides continuity of legal cultural identity through the generations. The Colorado constitution is published along with the Colorado statutes and statutory research methods apply equally to constitutional research. This chapter provides the history of Colorado's constitution, the resources in which it can be researched, and additional sources for understanding its provisions.

## II. History of the Constitution

The Colorado constitution was adopted on March 4, 1876. Its passage was the third attempt at statehood by the citizens of the Territory of Colorado.

As large numbers of settlers began arriving in Colorado in the late 1850s to mine gold and other metals, the need to establish government grew. At that time, Colorado was part of the Kansas Territory. When Kansas became a state in 1860, its boundaries did not include what is now the eastern portion of Colorado. In order to settle property claims and provide for civil government, residents of Colorado engaged in various forms of self-government, but without lasting success. For example, in 1860 some Colorado residents drafted a constitution for the "State of Jefferson," but lacking authority, the attempt at self-rule failed.

In light of this need for government, Congress passed the Organic Act of 1861, establishing the Territory of Colorado.[1] This Act gave the residents of Colorado the structure of government under the authority of the federal government. In 1864, Congress passed an Enabling Act to authorize the creation of the State of Colorado.[2] This passage resulted in a constitutional convention in 1865, which produced a constitution but failed to secure its adoption by the residents of the Territory of Colorado. In 1875, Congress passed a second enabling act.[3] Again, a constitutional convention was convened in Denver in 1875, which completed a draft of a constitution in March 1876. This constitution was approved by the citizens of the Territory of Colorado on July 1, 1876. With President Ulysses S. Grant's proclamation of August 1, 1876, Colorado became the nation's 38th state.[4] As Colorado became a state on the 100th anniversary of the Declaration of Independence, it is known as the Centennial State.

## III. Structure of the Constitution

The Colorado Constitution lists twenty-nine articles, two of which have been repealed.[5] The third, fourth, fifth, and sixth articles create the fundamental structure of government in an executive, legislative, and judicial branch. Other articles address issues such as education (Article IX), finances (Article X and XI), corporations (Article XV), and local government (Article XX). Table 3-1 lists the twenty-nine articles in Colorado's constitution.

Article II of the constitution contains Colorado's Bill of Rights. As with the other provisions, Colorado's constitution lists these rights in far greater detail

1. Act of Feb. 28, 1861, An Act to provide a temporary Government for the Territory of Colorado, 12 Stat. 172 (1861).

2. Act of March 21, 1864, An Act to enable the People of Colorado to form a Constitution and State Government, and for the Admission of such state into the Union on an equal Footing with the original States, 13 Stat. 32 (1864).

3. Act of March 3, 1875, an act to enable the people of Colorado to form a constitution and state government, and for the admission of the said state into the Union on an equal footing with the original states, 18 Stat. 474 (1875).

4. A Proclamation by the President of the United States of America, No. 6, Aug. 1, 1876, 19 Stat. 665 (1876).

5. The constitution also included a schedule, appended to the end of the document, which provides information on the transition of territorial government to state government.

than does the federal constitution. Colorado's Bill of Rights is composed of thirty-four sections. It includes those protections guaranteed by the original

**Table 3-1. List of the Constitution's Articles**

| | |
|---|---|
| Article I | Boundaries |
| Article II | Bill of Rights |
| Article III | Distribution of Powers |
| Article IV | Executive Department |
| Article V | Legislative Department |
| Article VI | Judicial Department |
| Article VII | Suffrage and Elections |
| Article VIII | State Institutions |
| Article IX | Education |
| Article X | Revenue |
| Article XI | Public Indebtedness |
| Article XII | Officers |
| Article XIII | Impeachments |
| Article XIV | Counties |
| Article XV | Corporations |
| Article XVI | Mining and Irrigation |
| Article XVII | Militia |
| Article XVIII | Miscellaneous |
| Article XIX | Amendments |
| Article XX | Home Rule Cities and Towns |
| Article XXI | Recall from Office |
| Article XXII | Intoxicating Liquors (Repealed) |
| Article XXIII | Publication of Legal Advertising (Repealed) |
| Article XXIV | Old Age Pensions |
| Article XXV | Public Utilities |
| Article XXVI | Nuclear Detonations |
| Article XXVII | Great Outdoors Colorado Program |
| Article XXVIII | Campaign and Political Finance |
| Article XXIX | Ethics in Government |

federal Bill of Rights as well as those additional rights deemed necessary by the people of Colorado since 1876. For example, Colorado's constitution explicitly guarantees equality between the sexes.[6] It also declares English to be the state's official language.[7]

Like other state constitutions, Colorado's has been amended numerous times. The means to amend the constitution are contained in Section 1 of Article V and in Article XIX. The first method, in Article V, enables citizens to propose a constitutional amendment through the initiative and referendum process. The Legislative Council, a non-partisan research arm of the General Assembly, collects and publishes these ballot initiatives preceding an election. These initiatives are distributed in the "Blue Book" to citizens prior to an election.[8] The second method, contained in Article XIX, allows amendments to be proposed in the General Assembly. Throughout the years, various individuals have called for a more comprehensive rewriting of the State's constitution but have not succeeded.[9]

## IV. Sources of the Text

### A. Print

The original constitution is housed at the Colorado State Archives in Denver. Access to the document is limited. However, researchers can obtain a digitized version of that document at the State Archive's website.[10]

Most researchers will access the text of the constitution by consulting an annotated statutory code. Both the CRS[11] and CRSA[12] contain the text of the

6. Colo. Const. art II, sec. 29.

7. Colo. Const. art II, sec. 30a.

8. Ballot initiatives and additional information about this process are available on the Legislative Council's website at www.colorado.gov/cs/Satellite/CGA-Legislative Council/CLC/1200536134742?rendermode=preview.

9. *See* Harry Neil Hayes, *A New or Revised Constitution for Colorado*, 11 Dicta 303 (1933–34); Hubert D. Henry, *Should We Have a Constitutional Convention in Colorado?*, 26 Dicta 258 (1949). The latest effort occurred during the State's Centennial in 1976. *See* Report of the Citizen's Assembly on the State Constitution, *The Colorado Constitution: Is it Adequate for the Next Century?*, Boulder, CO (August 27–29, 1976).

10. Colorado State Archives, 1876 State Constitution, Colorado Department of Personnel and Administration, www.colorado.gov/dpa/doit/archives/history/constitution/index.htm.

11. *Colorado Revised Statutes* (LexisNexis 2017).

12. *Colorado Revised Statutes Annotated* (Thomson Reuters 2017).

constitution and research references to cases and other related sources. In each publication, the Constitution is printed at the beginning of the first volume of the set. This practice continues a tradition of the earliest compilations of Colorado statutes, which published key federal documents pertaining to Colorado's existence. In the territorial codes, one finds the publication of the Organic Act establishing the Territory of Colorado. Likewise, in all earlier editions of the Colorado statutes, one finds the Colorado Constitution and Enabling Act.

### B. Online

The constitution can be found on various online sources, too. The primary online source is provided through the Colorado General Assembly's website.[13] This online version is a reproduction of the copy located in the *Colorado Revised Statutes*. As with the print edition, this version includes case annotations and references to additional research resources. Complementing their print products, both LexisNexis and Westlaw publish the Colorado Constitution through their online services. A search of the Internet will uncover other websites publishing the Colorado constitution. As with any online resource, be sure to check the website's currency and credibility.

## V. Researching Constitutional Issues

A researcher may be drawn to constitutional research through a number of different avenues. Invariably, the researcher will be investigating whether the civil rights of his client have been violated or the government has acted outside the scope of the authority granted to it by the constitution.

To research a constitutional law issue, the researcher will start by locating and reading the constitutional text in either of the Colorado annotated codes. After consulting the text, the researcher can review the annotations following the text to locate cases and other materials impacting the constitutional provision. This approach will give the researcher a lead into the body of research materials tied to the Colorado constitution.

To begin to research in the *Colorado Revised Statutes*, the researcher can consult the index, consult the constitution's table of contents, or directly turn

---

13. Colorado General Assembly, www.leg.state.co.us.

to the provision. The constitution does not have a separate index, but its topics appear in the set's multivolume general index. The constitution is preceded by its own table of contents. CRS also publishes a table of changes to the constitution adopted at general elections since 1980.

As with the CRS, the researcher using the CRSA can access the constitutional provisions through an index, through the table of contents, or by opening directly to the provision. As in the CRS, the editors of the CRSA have indexed the constitution's topics within the set's multi-volume general index. However, the CRSA also contains an index specifically for the constitution; it is located in the last volume containing the constitution.

If using the online versions of the constitution, research options may vary. On both LexisNexis and Westlaw, the researcher may approach the material as in the print, consulting the table of contents or index (if provided) or even opening directly to a particular provision. However, the researcher can also use a terms and connectors search. As with online statutory research, the researcher should be certain to check the context of the provision in which the search terms are contained within the overall statutory scheme.

A researcher may want or need to take another approach to researching Colorado constitutional issues. While the annotated codes will direct the researcher to cases interpreting or applying the constitutional text, the researcher may access those cases directly using the *Colorado Digest*. This research approach will be discussed in greater detail in Chapter 6. Briefly, the digest empowers the researcher to locate cases by topic. Reading a relevant case will direct the researcher to the appropriate constitutional provision.

A researcher may opt to pursue yet a third research approach: consult a treatise. Oesterle and Collins have written a comprehensive treatise on the Colorado Constitution.[14] Current through the 2000 election, this text provides a history of the constitution along with analysis and commentary of each provision. The authors include citations to cases, statutes, and other materials interpreting each constitutional provision.

Finally, the researcher should check the law journal literature for relevant articles. These articles may contain history and analysis of particular provisions as well as various policy arguments. The annotated codes will cite relevant law journal articles, but these articles may also be found by consulting a periodical index at the local law library. Researching periodicals is explained in Chapter 9.

---

14. Dale A. Oesterle and Richard B. Collins, *The Colorado State Constitution: A Reference Guide* (Greenwood Press 2002).

## VI. Researching Colorado Constitutional History

When researching a constitutional issue, researchers may be confronted with the need to investigate the history of the provision for several reasons. First, as with other written materials, the plain meaning of the textual language may not always be clear. Research may reveal that alternative language was considered and rejected, and that rejected language can help clarify the meaning of the adopted language. Second, researchers may seek the historical legal and societal context in which this language was adopted. Researchers hope that by understanding the problems citizens were attempting to solve at the time, they can clarify the current language.

Third, a researcher may garner a new insight into the meaning and application of a provision by exploring the debates at the constitutional convention. For example, the interaction of state and religion and its expression in the Colorado constitution were hotly debated at the 1875 convention. The final document reflects the compromise of the three major factions at the convention.

In approaching this historical research, the researcher can turn to a few different sources. One source is the second Enabling Act passed by Congress in March 1875, authorizing the citizens of Colorado to form a state. Among other things, this document set parameters on the type of government to be formed, provides for certain rights of the citizens, and specifies the procedure to obtain statehood. The Enabling Act is published in the annotated codes preceding the text of the constitution as well as in the *United States Statutes at Large.*[15]

Researchers interested in the legislative history and proceedings of the Constitution have three sources available to them. The first source was issued by the convention itself and was distributed with the finished constitution: the *Address to the People of Colorado.* It is a statement by the convention delegates summarizing the various provisions of the constitution and presenting arguments why citizens should adopt this constitution.

Researchers can delve more deeply into the details of the convention by consulting the *Proceedings of the Constitutional Convention.*[16] This volume was issued by the Colorado Secretary of State pursuant to an Act by the General Assembly "[t]o publish and bind in book form all records of the constitutional

15. *See* note 3 above.

16. *Proceedings of the Constitutional Convention* (The Smith-Brooks Press 1907).

convention of Colorado, Held in 1876."[17] This single volume is a reprint of the text of the original manuscript minute-book of the convention proceedings. It provides a daily account of the formal debates of delegates and reports of committees surrounding the text of the various constitutional provisions. Researchers will also find in this book the Enabling Act of 1875, the *Address to the People*, the constitution as adopted, and finally the proclamation of President Ulysses S. Grant admitting Colorado as a state.

For a broader view of the development of the constitution, researchers should consult Hensel's history of the Colorado constitution.[18] This well-written narrative relies on contemporary reports of the convention published in local Denver newspapers. Unlike the *Proceedings of the Constitutional Convention*, this account provides more detail into the motivation, politics, and societal pressures surrounding the various issues. This well-documented text includes ten appendices covering such areas as biographies of the delegates to the convention, photographs of some of the delegates, a list of the standing committees of the convention, and the votes of the delegates and counties on ratification of the constitution.

Other treatises examine the documents and debates surrounding the creation of the Constitution. Researchers can start their research by examining collections by Jensen[19] and Elliot.[20] The Law Library of Congress also publishes these types of documents on its website.[21]

## VII. Summary

The Colorado constitution establishes the structure of Colorado government and the fundamental rights of Colorado citizens. It is published along with

17. 1907 Colo. Sess. Laws Ch. 135.

18. Donald Wayne Hensel, *A History of the Colorado Constitution in the Nineteenth Century* (unpublished Ph.D. thesis, U. of Colo. 1957) (copy on file at the U. of Colo. Law Library).

19. *The Documentary History of the Ratification of the Constitution* Merrill Jensen, ed. (State Historical Society of Wisconsin 1976).

20. Jonathon Elliot, *The Debates in the Several State Conventions on the Adoption of the Federal Constitution* (2d ed., 1888). The first edition of this work was published in 1830.

21. See generally (www.loc.gov/law). Particular documents regarding the history and creation of the document can be found on the Library of Congress's website at https://www.loc.gov/collections (visited: August 28, 2018).

the Colorado statutes in the CRS and CRSA, and can be researched and read as a statute, utilizing case annotations and research references available in annotated codes. For a historical understanding of the Constitution, researchers can turn to one of two resources that provide some insight into the compromises and intent of the document's drafters.

**Constitution Research Checklist**

- ❑ Does this legal problem likely invoke a provision of the Colorado constitution?
- ❑ Have you developed search terms that can be used in a Colorado statutory compilation index?
- ❑ On locating a relevant provision, did you consult the case annotations and research references?
- ❑ For historical context, did you consult the two sources that might aid in that understanding?

# Chapter 4

# Researching Legislative History

## I. Introduction

At some point, the legal researcher will need to interpret ambiguous statutory language. This need may arise because the researcher is relying on particular language from a statutory section or wanting an overall understanding of the legislation. While legislators intend that the statutory language be clear, it is not always so. In these situations, judges and lawyers draw upon a toolbox of settled statutory interpretation techniques. These approaches are codified at CRS 2-4-203.[1] One of these techniques is to locate and read the documents created during the legislative process. The concept is these documents will contain statements of what legislators intended when they were drafting the legislation and, thus, allow the researcher to look behind the language of the statute. This process of locating the documents created during the legislative process is known as compiling a legislative history. In Colorado, researchers look to documents created by the Colorado General Assembly during its legislative process. This chapter will provide an overview of the legislative process, identify the documents created during the process, and provide a research strategy for locating them.

1. The statute reads in its entirety: "Ambiguous statutes—aids in construction (1) If a statute is ambiguous, the court, in determining the intention of the general assembly, may consider among other matters: (a) The object sought to be attained; (b) The circumstances under which the statute was enacted; (c) The legislative history, if any; (d) The common law or former statutory provisions, including laws upon the same or similar subjects; (e) The consequences of a particular construction; (f) The administrative construction of the statute; (g) The legislative declaration or purpose."

## II. The Legislative Process

Legislation begins with an idea. The idea may come from a legislator but may also come from citizens, businesses, or advocacy groups. The idea may arise to solve a new problem or to remedy existing legislation. In either case, the idea is transformed into a written document called a bill. The bill is the first document created during the legislative process.

A legislator agrees to sponsor the bill and becomes the bill's primary sponsor. The bill will have a sponsor in both the House and Senate. A bill may have additional sponsors as well, but the primary sponsor is responsible for guiding the bill through the legislative process.

The bill will then be introduced into the chamber of the General Assembly of the legislator and assigned a bill number. Senate bills start with the number 001 while House bills start with the number 1001. Bill numbers are prefaced with a two-letter abbreviation of the chamber in which the bill originated, and since 1990, the bill number is also prefaced with the year of the legislation session. So, the third bill introduced into the House for 1999 would be numbered HB 99-1003 and for the third senate bill, the number would be SB 99-003.

The bill is then assigned to a committee for evaluation. This assignment is made by the Speaker of the House or President of the Senate, as appropriate for the chamber. The House and Senate each have ten standing committees, known as committees of reference. Each focuses on a particular subject area. (See Table 4-1.) The committee receiving the bill will then research the bill, collect information, hold hearings, and consider testimony of interested parties. Using this information, the committee may amend the bill language. At the conclusion of its work, the committee will either favorably recommend the bill with or without changes to the originally introduced bill, refer it to another committee, table it for later in the legislative session, or kill it.

If the committee favorably recommends the bill, the committee sends it to the full chamber, known as the committee of the whole, to consider it. The bill is calendared for second reading at which time the bill can be debated by the legislators and changes made to the bill language. These changes are offered in the form of amendments to the bill and need approval of the members of the chamber. If approved, the changes are incorporated into the text of the bill, and the bill is calendared for a third reading. While further amendments may be made at the third reading, typically these do not occur. At the third reading, a vote on the bill is taken and recorded. If the bill passes, it must be sent to the other chamber for review and approval. The process is repeated in the other chamber, starting with submission to the appropriate committee.

**Table 4-1. Committees of Reference**

| Senate Committees | House Committees |
|---|---|
| Agriculture, Natural Resources & Energy | Agriculture, Livestock & Natural Resources |
| Appropriations | Appropriations |
| Business, Labor & Technology | Business Affairs & Labor |
| Education | Education |
| Ethics | Finance |
| Finance | Health & Human Services |
| Health & Human Services | Judiciary |
| Judiciary | Local Government |
| Local Government | State, Veterans & Military Affairs |
| Senate Services | Transportation & Energy |

Ultimately, both chambers must pass identical versions of the bill. If the chambers have not done so, they can agree to send the bill to a conference committee. This committee is composed of three members of each chamber. The conference committee's goal is to forge a consensus bill. If successful, the consensus bill is then sent to the committee of the whole for each chamber. Once the legislation is approved by each chamber, it is signed by the Speaker of the House and President of the Senate, and sent to the governor for review.

The governor has three options. The first is to sign the bill into law. Second, he can permit the bill to become law by not signing it within ten days of receiving the bill during the legislative session or thirty days following the end of the session. Finally, he can veto the bill. If he vetoes the bill, it can still become law by a two-thirds majority vote of both chambers of the legislature. The General Assembly has created an illustration of these legislative process steps in Figure 4-1.

# Figure 4-1. How a Bill Becomes Colorado Law*

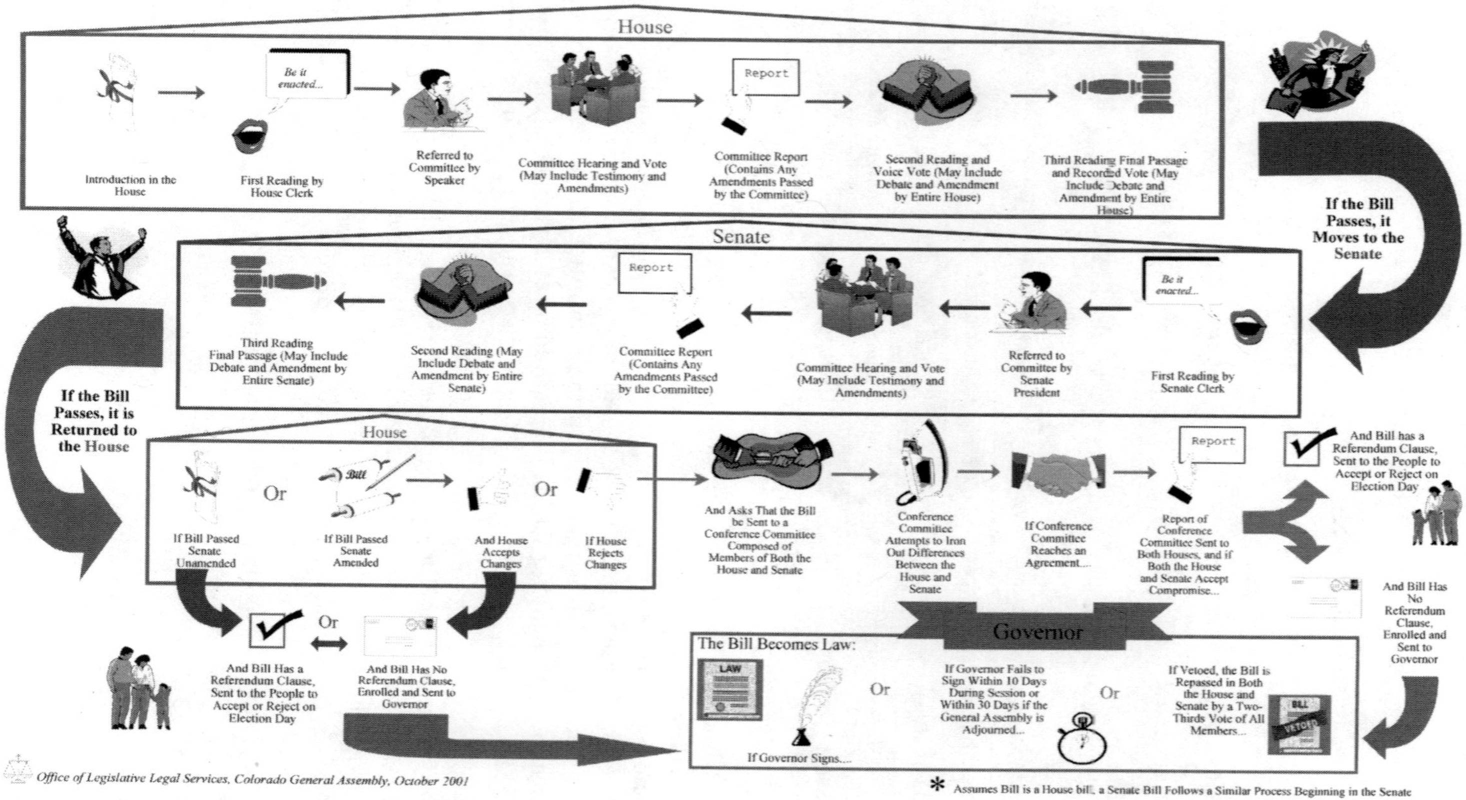


Source: https://leg.colorado.gov/sites/default/files/bill_becomes_law_chart.pdf.

## III. Legislative History Research

Throughout this process, documents are created. Researchers locate these documents to decipher legislative intent. These documents include (1) the various versions of the bill, (2) committee reports, (3) testimony from hearings, and (4) floor debates. The final document created by the process is the session law (See Chapter 2 for more details on session laws).

### A. Bills

As noted, legislation begins with a bill and the bill contains the language legislators agreed on as the legislation worked its way through the legislative process. Therefore, a researcher will want to obtain the various versions of the bill as the changed language may suggest something about intent.

There are six different bill versions. These are the (1) introduced bill, (2) engrossed bill, (3) reengrossed bill, (4) revised bill, (5) rerevised bill, and (6) enrolled bill.

(1) The *introduced* bill is the original version of the bill introduced in the legislative session. This version will be sent to the committee assigned to consider the bill and is also called the *printed* bill.

(2) The *engrossed* bill is the version passed by the first chamber after the second reading of the bill. It will include any revisions from the committee as well as any amendments adopted by that chamber on second reading.

(3) The *reengrossed* bill contains all changes adopted by the first chamber after the third reading of the bill. It is this version of the bill that is sent to the other chamber for consideration.

(4) The *revised* bill is the version of the bill passed by the second chamber with any amendments adopted after the second reading by that second chamber.

(5) The *rerevised* bill is the bill with amendments passed by the second chamber after the third reading of the bill.

(6) The *enrolled* bill is the version of the bill passed by both legislative chambers. This version is signed by the President of the Senate and the Speaker of the House and the Governor. This version of the bill is the session law.

Researchers should obtain each version of the bill, if possible. Tracking the changes to the language can help researchers to determine legislative intent. Used in conjunction with committee reports, researchers may be able to piece together a "legislative" intent.

The Colorado General Assembly website provide bills back to the 1997 session of the General Assembly.[2] However, the website provides multiple versions of the bill dating back to only 2000. For years 1997 through 1999, the website provides the final version of the bill at the close of the legislative session. This final version may be the enrolled bill/session law if enacted into law. From 2000 until 2003, the General Assembly posts a single "compiled changes" version of the bill in which changes from both the House and Senate are noted on the same bill document. Since 2004, the General Assembly has made available the various versions of the bill as separate documents although each successive version of the bill contains notation indicating the prior changes to the bill during legislative session. Bill versions are available for bills both enacted into law and those killed during the legislative process.

The bills may also be obtained through various other institutions including the Colorado State Archives[3] and Colorado law libraries. Researchers should contact these institutions to determine their holdings.

## B. Committee Reports

The work of the committee is often foundational in understanding the intent of the legislation. It is the committee that calls witnesses, gathers testimony of knowledgeable individuals about the legislation and collects and reviews studies about the legislation. The typical committee report shows what language was amended as a result of the committee's work, but little else. The report provides no information about why the committee amended the bill as it did; however, the committee may submit a summary of its work on each bill. This brief summary contains scant detail about the committee's work on the bill and is very factual in its content. The summary may be accompanied by reports collected by the committee and also by the vote tallies of the committee members on the bill.

Researchers can locate these committee reports in two places. First, they are published within the Colorado House and Senate journals. These two pub-

2. See http://www.leg.state.co.us/clics/cslFrontPages.nsf/PrevSessionInfo?OpenForm.

3. The website address for the Colorado State Archives legislative records information is located at https://www.colorado.gov/pacific/archives/legislative-records/.

lications record the daily proceedings of the respective chambers during the legislation session. The House and Senate journals have been printed since the first legislative session of 1876 and are available online starting with the 1998 legislative session. The State Archives and Colorado law libraries may also contain copies of the committee reports.[4]

Second, the committee reports are available as separate documents on the Colorado General Assembly's website. These reports are included along with the other information pertaining to the bill and start with the 2004 legislative session.

In addition to reports, researchers can locate committee summaries on the General Assembly's website starting with the 2000 legislative session. At the State Archives the summaries are available in print starting with the 1973 legislative session when the General Assembly began creating committee summaries.

## C. Testimony

As committees research the bill, they can hold hearings calling to the General Assembly various experts to testify about the bill. While transcripts are not created of this testimony, starting in 1973, the General Assembly has been recording committee hearings. While the process of listening to the audio recordings can be tedious and time-consuming, it does provide direct access to testimony of experts before the committee.

Access to these audio recordings varies. Researchers will access audio recordings from 1973 through 2011 at the State Archives. The earliest recordings were made on reel-to-reel tapes. Due to the fragility of both tapes and the equipment needed to play the recordings, the State Archives has limited access to the equipment. Researchers should consult the State Archives' website to ascertain how to retrieve content from the tapes.[5] Starting with the 2012 legislative session, audio recordings are available on the General Assembly's website.

4. The University of Colorado Law School William A. Wise Law Library has digitized the complete collection of Colorado House and Senate Journals. This collection is accessible at http://lawcollections.colorado.edu/colorado-house-and-senate-journals/.

5. This FAQ on the State Archives' website provides current details—https://www.colorado.gov/pacific/archives/legislative-audio-faq. Essentially, the researcher will submit a request for a committee hearing and a staff member will retrieve the recording. The State Archives charges a fee for this service.

## D. Floor Debates

After a bill is voted favorably out of committee, it is sent to the floor of the chamber. Legislators may debate and amend the bill during both the second and third reading of the bill. As with committee hearings, these debates have been recorded since the 1973 session of the General Assembly. Also as with the committee hearings, researchers need to contact the State Archives for audio recordings produced from 1973 through 2011 but can access floor debates after 2011 on the General Assembly's website. Again, the process of listening to the debates can be cumbersome and time-consuming. The online audio recordings somewhat simplify the process by allowing researchers to jump to the point in the audio recording where the bill is being discussed. However, there are no shortcuts for listening to the recordings for what legislators were intending in amending and passing this legislation.

## E. Other Sources of Legislative Intent

Due to the relative paucity of documents indicating a legislative intent, researchers may look to extra-legislative sources for assistance. These include Colorado Legislative Council research reports, notes of individual legislators, interviewing legislators, judicial opinions, and law journal articles and news reports.

### 1. Legislative Council Research Reports

The Colorado Legislative Council is the research arm of the Colorado Legislative Assembly. In this role, it researches issues of concern to the General Assembly and produces written reports on its work. One type of report is the Research Report.

Also, in addition to the committees of reference, there are other committees. These include standing committees, ad hoc committees, and commissions. The General Assembly can request one of these other committees to research a specific issue. This committee will investigate the problem, engage in fact finding, and collect testimony. At the conclusion of its research, the committee will issue a report reviewing what it has done and what conclusions it has drawn about the problem. This report may include proposed legislation with some explanation about its rationale for the legislation. This legislation may then be submitted as a bill in a future session of the General Assembly. While these types of reports are not common, researchers should look for them.

These reports are available from the Legislative Council and on the University of Denver's law library website.[6]

### 2. Legislator's Notes

While infrequent, a legislator may deposit his or her notes about the legislation with the State Archives. These notes could include the legislator's observations about the legislation. To access such notes, if they exist, the researcher should check with the State Archives.

### 3. Interviewing Legislators

A similar and perhaps better approach than looking for legislator's notes would be to interview legislators involved in drafting legislation. The first point of contact would likely be the bill's primary sponsors, but other contacts could be the members of the committees who reviewed the legislation.

### 4. Court Cases

If the legislation has been litigated and appealed, a court may have interpreted the statute in question. Researchers have a few different methods to find these cases. One approach is to consult the annotations in the Colorado Revised Statutes for the legislation. Another approach is to search Colorado case law for the name of the act or the CRS citation. More detail about case law searching is provided in Chapter 6.

### 5. Journal Articles and News Reports

The final avenue is to check journal articles or news reports about the legislation. Some author may have written an article discussing this new piece of legislation in context of existing law, particularly if the topic is novel, controversial, or has broad impact. This type of article is most likely to be found in *The Colorado Lawyer*, but may also be found in legal newspapers and perhaps even one of the journals from the state's two law schools. Researchers may also check the archives for *The Denver Post* and now-defunct *Rocky Mountain News* for possible articles.

---

6. This collection is available at http://www.law.du.edu/forms/library/clcsearch.cfm.

## IV. Putting It All together — The Research Process

Given these sources of information, researchers will need to follow a process to locate the various documents. After researchers have identified the need to perform a legislative history, they should follow this process:

1. Review the statute in the Colorado annotated codes,
2. Review the session law and locate the bill number,
3. Locate the various versions of the bill,
4. Locate the House and Senate Journals entries discussing the bill, or any committee reports or summaries of committee reports,
5. Locate and listen to the audio recordings, if available, and
6. Check the various extra-legislative sources.

For each step in the process, Table 4-2 lists what sources to consult and what information to look for in that source.

### A. Step 1: Review the statute in the Colorado annotated codes

The starting point for conducting a legislative history is the statutory language in question. Typically, the research begins when the researcher needs to interpret vague language uncovered while reading a statute. However, the researcher may also be pursuing a more general request to research the legislative history of an act. In either case, the researcher should start the process with the Colorado annotated code. The researcher will likely start with the current code but consulting an older edition of the code may be appropriate for historical statutory research.

In addition to reviewing the language, the researcher will need to note when the code section was modified by the General Assembly by reviewing the source note following the legislation (See Chapter 2). The source note will indicate when the legislation was enacted or amended using the symbol 'L' followed by a year. The researcher then records these citations and uses them to locate the session laws for the code section. The researcher should investigate the legislative history for all the years in which the legislation was created or amended as is appropriate to the research question. If the code section was modified in multiple years, the researcher will need to go through the remaining steps in the legislative history research process for each year.

The source note might also contain another valuable piece of information; the bill number of the legislation that created or amended the statutory code

**Table 4-2. Steps in the Legislative History Research Process**

| Steps | Where to Look | Why Look for It | What to Look for |
|---|---|---|---|
| 1 | Colorado Revised Statutes, or prior versions | Statutory language, Act or code section or subsection containing ambiguous language to be researched | Search Source Notes for Bill Number and/or Session Law citation(s) |
| 2 | Colorado Session Laws | Contains final version of bill language at conclusion of legislative session | Bill markups of changed or deleted or new language.<br>The bill number, if the researcher did not find the bill number in the CRS. |
| 3 | Colorado General Assembly website; State Archives; Colorado law libraries | Contains online or print versions of the bills, or bill summaries | Changes in language in bill versions |
| 4 | House and Senate Journals; Reports | Provides key information about the bill in the legislative process including bill sponsors, committee assignments and reports, dates when the bill was reviewed and amended and vote counts | Tables located in Index in print versions or Status Sheet in online version indicating dates and/or page numbers when the bill was amended |
| 5 | State Archives, General Assembly's website | Provides access to audio recordings of floor debates and committee hearings | Contact State Archives for necessary information; on General Assembly's website, look for Audio and Video Broadcasts under Session Information. |
| 6 | State Archives; case law collection; journal or newspaper databases | Explore these options to find extra-legislative sources of legislative intent | Any documents discussing the legislation and indicating intent, purpose, or effect. |

section. These bill numbers have been included in the sources notes starting with the 2009 edition of the Colorado Revised Statutes. This bill number is used to complete the legislative history research process.

## B. Step 2: Review the session law and locate the bill number

The researcher's next step is to consult the session law. Researchers are looking for two pieces of information. First, the researcher should read the statute as enacted by the General Assembly. This version of the law contains the language as enacted before codification and may include a "Purpose" or "Legislative Declaration" section which indicates what the legislation is about. Second, the session law will include the bill number of the legislation. As noted, this number is essential for completing the remaining steps in the legislative history research process. The bill number will be located on the first page of the act toward the top of the page.

## C. Step 3: Locate the various versions of the bill

With the bill number in hand, the next step is to locate the various versions of the bill. While this is relatively easy to do for legislation enacted since 2000, it is more challenging for older legislation. As noted in Section III.B above, the researcher should consult the General Assembly's website, the State Archives, and local law libraries.

## D. Step 4: Locate the House and Senate Journal entries discussing the bill and Committee Reports

The House and Senate journals will indicate when the bill was discussed by those two chambers during the legislative process. Researchers obtain this information by consulting a table for the legislation. In the print editions, this table is in an appendix at the back of the last volume for session. The table is organized by the house bill number and the senate bill number. These tables indicate where the bill is discussed in the House or Senate journals at each stage of the legislative process. The table will also direct the researcher to a page number and/or date. The researcher can then use this information to turn to the page in the House or Senate journal volume to see what action the legislators took on the bill at that time. To expedite the research process, the tables in the print volumes mark those pages and dates in which the legislation was amended with an asterisk (*). Researchers can then focus their efforts on looking at only entries in which the legislation was amended. These entries include committee reports, such as they are in Colorado. Researchers may also find committee summaries on the General Assembly's website.

If the researcher is researching online, the researcher will consult the Status Sheet for the year of the legislative session being researched. The Status Sheet will provide a date with which the researcher will then consult the Journals online calendar. Dates in which some action took place will be active links. The researcher will then click on the date and link to a .pdf copy of the journal page.

The journals provide access to the changed bill language and are also provide the dates in which the committee of reference or committee of the whole discussed the bill. This information about the amending process is in turn used to locate the audio recordings.

### E. Step 5: Locate and listen to the audio recordings, if available

As noted, audio recordings have been made of committee hearings and floor debates of legislation enacted since the 1973 session of the General Assembly. For recordings earlier than 2012, researchers will need to contact the State Archives, and should be ready to provide their staff with the bill number, year, and possible date of committee or floor action. For legislation enacted since 2012, researchers will find these recordings on the General Assembly's website. As of 2016, the audio recordings are organized by session, and then by House or Senate Chamber, House or Senate committee. Researchers will need to know the type of audio recording they seek (i.e., floor debate or committee testimony) and the date of the recording. Once located, researchers will need to listen to the recording and take notes.

### F. Step 6: Check the various extra-legislative sources

The final step in the Colorado legislative history process is to consult extra-legislative sources for possible indication of legislation intent. While information located from these sources is not an "official" part of the legislative record, it may help the researcher obtain a better understanding of what problem the General Assembly was attempting to solve it enacted the legislation.

## V. Reading Legislative History

While consulting and collecting the various documents, researchers can attempt to determine if the General Assembly as a legislative body spoke to the language or statute in question. Often, the legislator is less concerned with particular language and more concerned with the broader problem to be solved. At any rate, at the conclusion of this process, the researchers will be confident they have located the documents indicating legislative intent.

## VI. Summary

Conducting legislative history research is not particularly complicated but does require somewhat time-consuming examination of documents created during the legislative process. To succeed, researchers should be aware of the legislative process, the documents created during that process and the sources containing those documents. Both happily and unhappily for the researcher, Colorado legislative histories are scant on the type of rich detail and textures one hopes to uncover when determining legislative intent. Nonetheless, legal researchers may attempt to unearth what little may be available as a supplement to or substitute for the other approaches of statutory interpretation.

**Legislative History Research Checklist**

- ❑ Did I locate the statue in an annotated edition of the Colorado statutes?
- ❑ Did I consult the source note for the code section(s) of the legislation to determine when the legislation was enacted or amended? Does the source note contain the bill number?
- ❑ Have I read the session law enacting this legislation? Did I obtain the bill number from the session law?
- ❑ Did I locate the table of House or Senate bills in the appendix of the House and Senate journals? Did I consult both the House and Senate journals for the appropriate year?
- ❑ If using the General Assembly's website, did I consult the status sheet to determine when the legislation was modified during the legislative process?
- ❑ Was this legislation enacted before or after 1973? Will I be able to listen to audio recordings? Will these be available at the State Archives (prior to 2012) or on the General Assembly's website (since 2012)?
- ❑ Did the Colorado Legislative Council issue a research report on this topic?
- ❑ Are there are any law journal articles or news reports about this legislation? Did I search *The Colorado Lawyer* for any bar journal articles?
- ❑ Do any of these sources discuss the statute in question, either the specific language or the general intent?

## Chapter 5

# Researching Administrative Law

## I. Introduction

As the legislative branch enacts statutes and the judicial branch issues cases, so too does the executive branch generate primary law. In Colorado, both the state constitution and Title 24 of the Colorado Revised Statutes define the nature and extent of executive branch authority. The executive department includes the governor, lieutenant governor, secretary of state, state treasurer, and attorney general.[1] Reporting to the governor, the executive branch is limited to twenty departments, which are composed of a number of divisions[2] (See Table 5-1). The executive branch issues law in the form of *regulations*, also called *rules*, and administrative decisions.

Despite the size of the executive branch, administrative agencies and the regulations they issue are subordinate to and derive authority from statutes. The statutes serve to authorize the creation of the executive agencies but more directly enable the agencies to issue regulations. Specifically, while statutes provide legislative policy in a particular area, agency regulations provide the procedures to implement that policy. In order for the executive branch to issue these regulations, however, the statute must enable an agency to create those regulations.

Though regulations are authorized generally by statute, administrative agencies must provide specific notice to the public of proposed regulations. This notice and other requirements governing the creation and publication of regulations are contained in the State Administrative Procedures Act.[3] In particular, Section 103 outlines what an agency must do. Figure 5-1 outlines the process.

1. Colo. Const. art. IV, § 1.
2. Colo. Const. art. IV, § 22.
3. Colo. Rev. Stat. § 24-4-101 (LexisNexis 2017).

## Table 5-1. Organizational Chart of Colorado State Government

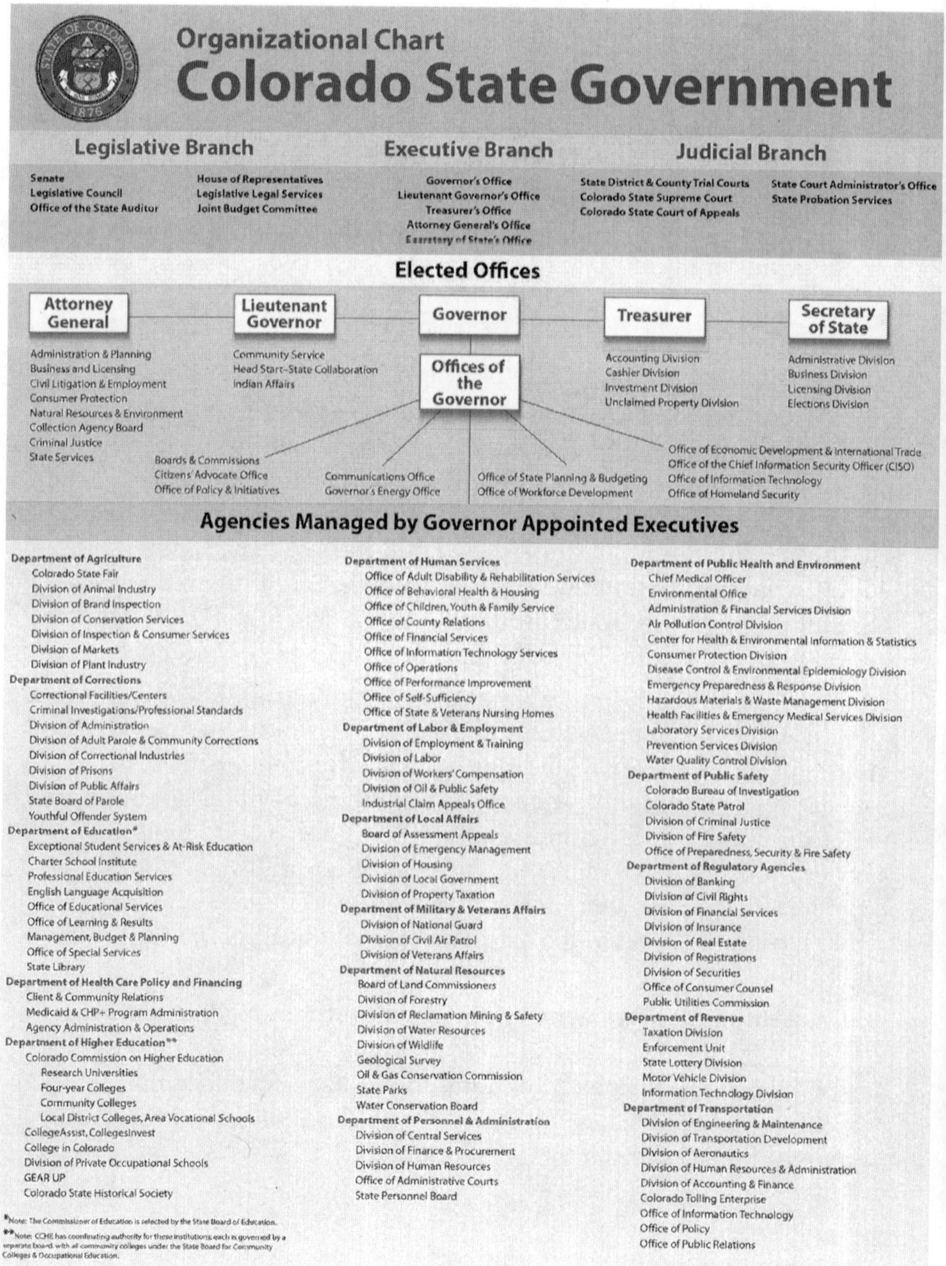


Source: https://www.sos.state.co.us/pubs/CCR/files/perm_rulemaking_process_flowchart.pdf.

**Figure 5-1. Permanent Rulemaking Process**

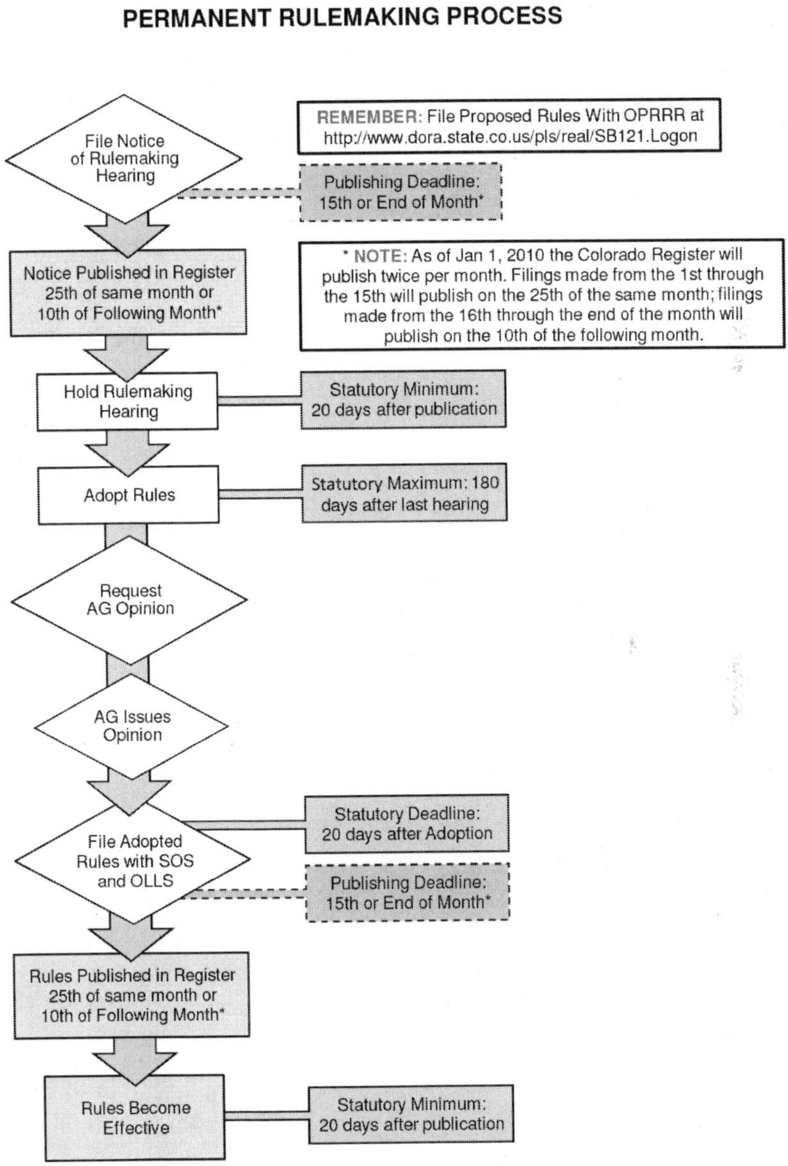


Colorado Secretary of State • Administrative Rules Program • 1700 Broadway, Suite 300 • Denver CO 80290 • 303-894-2200 • www.sos.state.co.us

The applicable procedure includes publishing notice of a proposed rule,[4] holding a public hearing about the rule,[5] submitting the final rule to the attorney general for review,[6] and publishing the final rule. Both proposed and final regulations are published, as explained in Part II of this chapter.

In addition to creating regulations, agencies can also adjudicate disputes arising from application of an agency's regulations. These disputes are heard by administrative law judges (ALJ) who issue their decisions in a form similar to judicial opinions. These decisions are reviewable by the Colorado Court of Appeals. The agency decision is published and can be located from a variety of sources; this research is explained below in Part III.

Finally, the attorney general's office is also part of the executive branch. As the state's attorney, this office issues advisory opinions on the legality of agency regulations and other matters when requested by the executive branch agencies.

This chapter reviews the resources and research methods for agency regulations, administrative law decisions, and attorney general opinions.

## II. Regulations

### A. Sources

In Colorado, administrative regulations are published in two sources: *The Colorado Register* (CR) and the *Code of Colorado Regulations* (CCR). Both publications were created by statute.[7] Together, these two publications serve as the official source for proposed and final agency regulations, notices of rule making, and attorney general's opinions relating to such regulations. These are both printed online and in print.

When an agency proposes a new rule or amends an existing rule, the agency is required to publish that proposed rule in the CR. Along with the rule, the agency must also give notice to invite public comment on the rule. This published notice indicates the date, time, and location of that meeting. All of this information is found in the CR.

4. Colo. Rev. Stat. §24-4-103(3) (LexisNexis 2017).
5. Colo. Rev. Stat. §24-4-103(4) (LexisNexis 2017).
6. Colo. Rev. Stat. §24-4-103(8)(b) (LexisNexis 2017).
7. Colo. Rev. Stat. §24-4-103(11)(a) (LexisNexis 2017).

After the agency meeting, the final version of the rule is again published in the CR as a permanent rule, adopted, and made part of the *Code of Colorado Regulations*. As with other codes, the CCR organizes all of the regulations currently in force by subject. In this case, the CCR is organized by department. Figure 5-2 shows the correlation between CCR numbers and Colorado agencies. A researcher uses the CCR to locate all of the currently active regulations promulgated by an agency. In this regard, the relationship between the CR and CCR is similar to the relationship between the Colorado session laws and the Colorado Revised Statutes; the former publishes chronologically while the latter publishes topically.

The CR is published twice each month by the Secretary of State's office and is available both online and in print. The online version is the official version.[8] Researchers can subscribe to an email notification alerting them when a new issue of the CR is published.[9] Subscribers will also receive notifications of meetings and other news items from the Secretary of State's office. The CCR is also published in both print and online versions. The online version is the official version as of July 1, 2007.[10]

## B. Researching Regulations

To locate a regulation, the researcher needs a CCR citation. This citation is a combination of numbers representing the volume number, major department, agency or division, and specific regulation number. Figure 5-3 reproduces a portion of a regulation from the Division of Motor Vehicles, a division of the Department of Revenue. The citation for this regulation is 1 CCR 204-13. It is the 13th regulation (denoted by the 13 in the citation) issued by this division (denoted by the "04" in "204") in this department (denoted by "2" in "204") and is found in volume 1 of the CCR set. Regulations can be found in the online version of the CCR by searching with the citation, or by browsing the structure of the code. Chapter 15 provides a comprehensive review of methods to locate current, superseded, and pending regulations.

---

8. Colorado Online Register, www.sos.state.co.us/CCR/RegisterHome.do. The print version is published by LexisNexis.

9. Colorado Register Free Email Notification Service, www.sos.state.co.us/CCR/EmailSubscription.do.

10. Colorado Secretary of State, Code of Colorado Regulations, www.sos.state.co.us/CCR/Welcome.do.

**Figure 5-2. Code of Colorado Regulations**

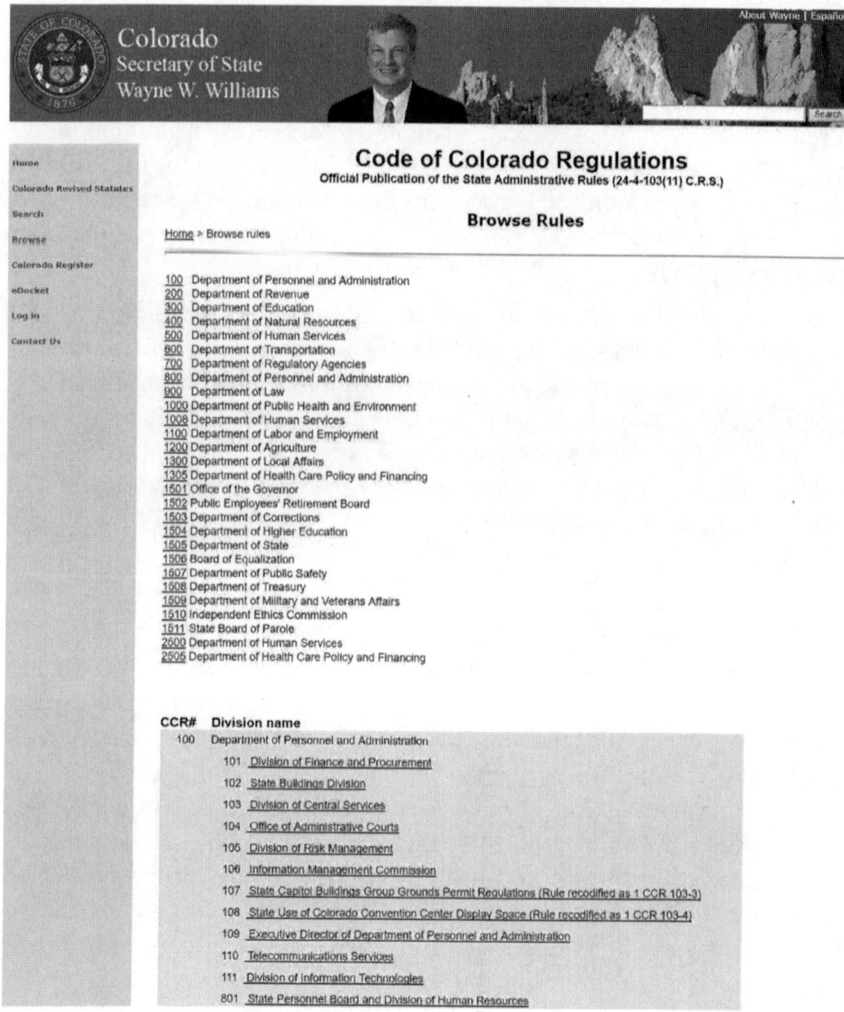


Source: www.sos.state.co.us/CCR/NumericalDeptList.do.

## III. Agency Decisions

In addition to promulgating regulations, agencies also engage in a quasi-judicial function. Agencies are empowered to adjudicate matters relating to agency regulations or actions. Colorado created an administrative court system through which administrative law judges (ALJ) decide matters relating to

## Figure 5-3. Partial reprint of 1 CCR 204-13

 

Basis, Purpose and Statutory:

The statutory basis for this regulation are 24-4-103, 24-72.1-103, 42-1-204, 42-2-107 and 42-2-302 CRS.

The department is responsible for the application process for obtaining Colorado driver's licenses and identification cards. The purpose of this regulation is to set forth guidelines for the type of documents that the department will use as proof of the applicant's lawful presence in the United States, identity and age. This rule is required for the preservation of public health, safety or welfare and noncompliance with the requirements of this section would be contrary to the public interest.

**1.0 Definitions**

1.1 Age—The length of time in full years since a person's date of birth.

1.2 Applicant—Any natural person applying to the department for a Colorado license or identification card.

1.3 Department—The Colorado Department of Revenue.

1.4 Document—An original document certified by the issuing agency, an amended original document certified by the issuing agency, or a true copy certified by the issuing agency, excluding miniature, wallet sized, or photocopy documents.

1.5 Exception Processing—Review of documentary evidence presented by an applicant when it appears that the applicant cannot provide the documents otherwise required to prove the applicant's age, identity, lawful presence, and/or residency. This process is detailed more fully in section 5.0 below.

1.6 Full Legal Name –The applicant's full legal name is the name on the applicant's birth certificate, unless it has been changed by court order, marriage, divorce, or adoption.

1.7 Hearing—Hearing before a department administrative hearing officer.

1.8 Identification Card—A photo identification document issued by a Department of Motor Vehicles or its equivalent that contains the bearer's full legal name and date of birth, but that does not confer upon the bearer the right to operate a motor vehicle.

1.9 Identity—Full legal name of the applicant.

1.10 Incomplete Application—Any application for license or identification card submitted with insufficient proof of identity, age, or lawful presence, as required by these rules.

1.11 Lawful Presence—Demonstration of citizenship in the United States or the lawful entry of an alien into the United States for an authorized period of time after inspection and authorization by an immigration officer.

1.12 License—A driver's license, commercial driver's license, minor driver's license, or instruction permit.

1.13 Notice of Denial—Notice of formal denial of application for a license or identification card.

1.14 Notice of Incomplete Application—Written notice of the documents provided and the documents required to complete an application for a license or identification card.

worker's compensation, human services, licensing, and other administrative cases. Parties may appeal the decision of an ALJ to the Court of Appeals. Agency decisions appear in form as judicial opinions (See Figure 5-4).

Locating agency decisions can be quite problematic. One source for some agency decisions is the website for the Colorado Office of Administrative Courts.[11] This site selectively publishes only a handful of worker's compensation decisions. To locate other types of decisions, researchers may review the websites of the administrative agency involved in the proceeding. If the website does not contain the decisions, the researcher should call the agency to determine whether decisions are available.

## IV. Attorney General Opinions

The attorney general serves as the state's attorney. In this capacity, he or she represents the state in legal matters but also gives legal advice to state agencies. In this latter role, the attorney general issues two types of advisory opinions: those relating to proposed regulations and those addressing general issues brought to his or her office.

When agencies propose new regulations, the attorney general is required to review the regulations. This review ensures that each new rule is compliant with existing law. This regulatory opinion is published in the *Colorado Register* along with the new regulation. For the online version of the CR, a link to the opinion is provided along with the new rule. In print, the filing directions suggest that these opinions be filed at the end of the set of binders. (See Figure 5-5).

The attorney general also issues opinions on other matters as requested by the governor or one of the executive branch agencies. The primary source for these formal opinions is the attorney general's website,[12] which lists opinions by year starting in 2001.[13] Casemaker offers attorney general opinions starting with 1984, and researchers can also consult a microfiche set containing attorney general opinions starting in 1964 as well as check on Lexis Advance and Westlaw.

---

11. Colorado Department of Personnel and Administration, www.colorado.gov/dpa/oac.

12. Colorado State Attorney General, www.coloradoattorneygeneral.gov.

13. AG Opinions, Colorado State Attorney General, coag.gov/resources/formal-ag-opinions.

**Figure 5-4. Agency Decision**

<table>
<tr><td>STATE OF COLORADO<br>OFFICE OF ADMINISTRATIVE COURTS<br>633 17th Street, Suite 1300 Denver, Colorado 80202</td><td rowspan="2">▲ COURT USE ONLY ▲</td></tr>
<tr><td rowspan="2">KENT LAMBERT,<br>Complainant,<br><br>vs.<br><br>RITTER INAUGURAL COMMITTEE, INC. and BILL RITTER FOR GOVERNOR,<br>Respondents.</td></tr>
<tr><td>CASE NUMBER:<br><br>OS 20080010</td></tr>
<tr><td colspan="2">ORDER GRANTING MOTIONS TO DISMISS AND AGENCY DECISION</td></tr>
</table>

On April 21, 2008 Kent Lambert (Complainant) filed a complaint against the Ritter Inaugural Committee, Inc. (Inaugural Committee) and Bill Ritter for Governor (Candidate Committee), collectively "Respondents", with the Secretary of State (Secretary) alleging violations of Colorado's campaign finance laws. Complainant filed an amended complaint with the Secretary on April 22, 2008. On April 22, 2008, the Secretary referred the complaint to the Office of Administrative Courts (OAC) as required by Colo. Const. art. XXVIII, § 9(2)(a). The case was assigned to the undersigned Administrative Law Judge (ALJ). A status conference was scheduled on May 1, 2008 and a hearing was scheduled on May 7, 2008 in Denver, Colorado. Complainant was represented in this proceeding by Scott Gessler, Esq. The Inaugural Committee was represented by Michael D. Plachy, Esq. and Alex C. Myers, Esq. The Candidate Committee was represented by Mark G. Grueskin, Esq. and Theresa L. Corrada, Esq.

On May 1, 2007 Messrs. Gessler, Grueskin, and Plachy appeared by telephone for the status conference. During that conference, Respondents' counsel represented that they would be filing Motions to Dismiss the complaint and requested that the May 7 hearing date be vacated. The request to vacate the hearing was unopposed by Complainant's counsel. The ALJ granted the request to vacate the May 7 hearing and established a briefing schedule for receipt of motions, responses and reply briefs. *See*, May 2, 2008 Order Vacating Hearing and Procedural Order. Respondents filed their motions on May 1, 2008. Complainant filed his response on June 2, 2008. The Candidate Committee filed its reply on June 9, 2008. The Inaugural Committee requested a one-day extension to file its reply. The Inaugural Committee filed its reply on June 10, 2008. The ALJ grants the Inaugural Committee's request to file its reply brief on June 10, 2008.

**Figure 5-5. Attorney General Regulatory Opinion**

CYNTHIA H. COFFMAN
Attorney General
DAVID C. BLAKE
Chief Deputy Attorney General
MELANIE J. SNYDER
Chief of Staff
FREDERICK R. YARGER
Solicitor General

STATE OF COLORADO
DEPARTMENT OF LAW

RALPH L. CARR
COLORADO JUDICIAL CENTER
1300 Broadway, 10th Floor
Denver, CO 80203
Phone 720-508-6000

Office of the Attorney General

Tracking Number: **2016-00668**

**OPINION OF THE ATTORNEY GENERAL RENDERED IN CONNECTION WITH THE RULES ADOPTED BY THE Division of Liquor Enforcement ON 02/23/2017**

**1 CCR 203-2**
**LIQUOR CODE**

The above-referenced rules were submitted to this office on 02/24/2017 as required by section 24-4-103, C.R.S. This office has reviewed them and finds no apparent constitutional or legal deficiency in their form or substance.

**March 13, 2017 14:02:37 MST**

Frederick R. Yarger

CYNTHIA H. COFFMAN
Attorney General
by FREDERICK R. YARGER
Solicitor General

Source: www.sos.state.co.us/CCR.

# V. Summary

Administrative agencies produce primary authority as regulations. Agencies derive their authority to issue regulations from statutes, and in this regard serve to implement legislative policy by specifying the details of how legislation is implemented. In Colorado, agencies are required to give notice of proposed regulations and to solicit public comment before finalizing and implementing regulations. These requirements are set forth in the State Administrative Procedures Act located in Article 4 of Title 24 in the CRS. Regulations are published in two publications: the *Colorado Register* and the *Code of Colorado Regulations.* The CR is published twice a month and includes proposed and emergency regulations, meeting notices, attorney general regulatory opinions and final regulations. The CCR publishes final regulations only and does so by organizing them by agency. Both of these publications are available on the Colorado Secretary of State's website which also publishes pending regulations. Historical regulatory research is somewhat more complicated and requires researchers to consult regulatory source notes, online and in some cases print resources. In addition to regulations, administrative law research may also involve locating agency decisions, attorney general opinions, and other helpful information such as licenses and guidance documents. Generally, these documents are harder to locate but researchers are advised to start with the agency's website.

**Administrative Law Research Checklist**

- ❑ Does the agency have statutory authority to issue this regulation? What is the citation to the authority?
- ❑ Is the regulation final or do you need to locate a pending regulation?
- ❑ Do you have a regulatory citation or will you need to search by keyword or department?
- ❑ Do you need to locate an earlier version of the regulation? Is that version earlier than 2007 requiring you to use print or afterwards allowing you to use the online code?
- ❑ Did you check the regulation's website for pending regulations?
- ❑ Do you need to locate agency decisions? Did you check the agency's website?
- ❑ Do you need to find an attorney general opinion? Is it available on the attorney general's website or do you need to consult another source which has older opinions?

# Chapter 6

# Researching Judicial Decisions

## I. Introduction

As discussed in Chapter 1, primary law is generated by the three branches of government. The judicial branch produces judicial opinions, or cases. The case is a written record of the decision reached by the court on the matter before it. It includes a recitation of the facts in the dispute, the law that applies to the matter, the legal reasoning the court uses to arrive at its decision, and the decision itself, which is also called the holding. Not all courts issue written decisions, and even courts that generally do issue them may not do so in all matters. In Colorado, appellate courts write judicial opinions, whereas trial courts will issue orders. While trial court orders and other documents are becoming more available, case law research mostly involves searching for appellate court opinions.

This chapter examines how to research cases. It begins by explaining both the state and federal court system in Colorado. Then, it discusses how to research Colorado appellate court opinions.

## II. The Court System in Colorado

### A. State Courts in Colorado

As with other states and the federal government, Colorado's court system is composed of trial courts and appellate courts. Figure 6-1 provides a chart of the system. Colorado's court system was created by Article VI of the state constitution and is further articulated in Title 13 of the Colorado Revised Statutes.[1] Generally, the trial court is the starting point of court actions for

1. See generally Title 13 of the Colorado Revised Statutes.

almost all cases.[2] In Colorado, there are five types of trial courts: county courts, district courts, water courts, municipal courts, and the Denver court system. These courts differ in jurisdiction, or the power to hear certain types of cases. Researchers look to the trial courts for orders, motions, and other trial documents.

### 1. County Courts

County courts are courts of limited jurisdiction. They handle civil cases in which the amount in controversy is less than $15,000, misdemeanors, traffic infractions, felony complaints, restraining orders, and small claims actions.[3] For even lesser controversies, the General Assembly has created "small claims" courts as a division within the county courts.[4] These small claims courts implement simplified and more relaxed rules of procedure as the courts are intended to allow citizens to represent themselves *pro se*, or without an attorney.

### 2. District Courts

District courts are courts of general jurisdiction. They hear civil cases in any amount,[5] as well as domestic relations, criminal, juvenile, probate, and mental health cases.[6] The Colorado judicial system is divided into twenty-two districts covering the state.[7]

### 3. Water Courts

Colorado also has a system of seven water courts following the drainage patterns of Colorado main river basins. These courts have exclusive jurisdiction

---

2. Colorado Constitution Article VI, Section 3 vests the Colorado Supreme Court with original jurisdiction in a handful of matters.

3. Colo. Const. Art. VI, Sec. 17; Colo. Rev. Stat. § 13-6-103 (LexisNexis 2017); Colo. Rev. Stat. § 13-6-104 (LexisNexis 2017); and Colo. Rev. Stat. § 13-6-106 (LexisNexis 2017).

4. Part 4 of Article 6 in Title 13 of the Colorado Revised Statutes sets forth the statutory authority, jurisdiction and other matters related to small claims courts. See Colo. Rev. Stat. § 13-6-401 *et seq.* (LexisNexis 2017).

5. As the jurisdiction for district and county courts may overlap, attorneys are required to consult the jurisdictional statutes to determine into which court to bring their action.

6. Colo. Const. Art. VI, Sec. 9(1).

7. Colo. Const. Art. VI, Sec. 10(1) and Colo. Rev. Stat. § 13-5-101 (LexisNexis 2017).

**Figure 6-1. The Court System in Colorado**

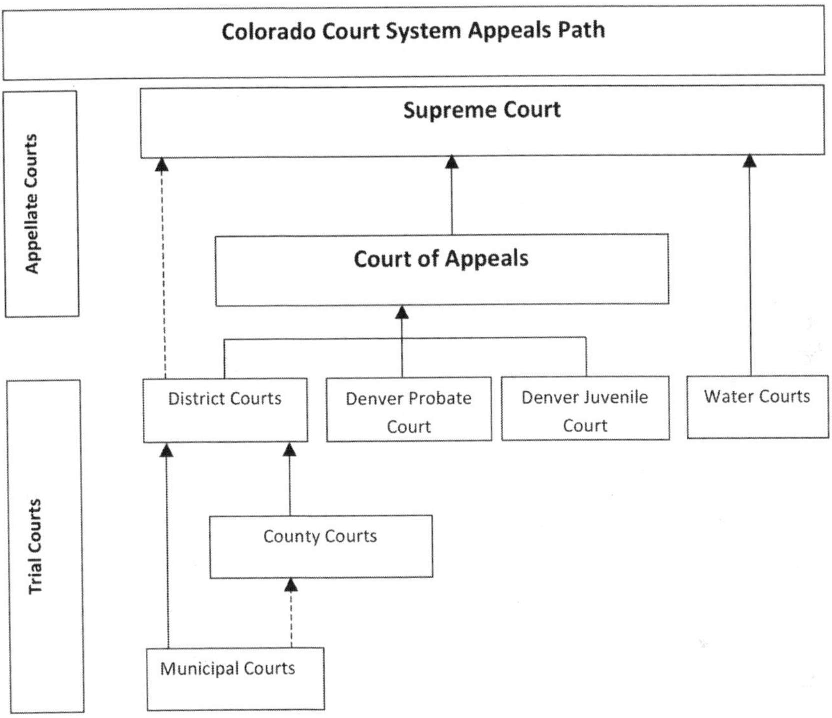


**Notes:**

This diagram describes the general appeals process in Colorado. The researcher should consult the Colorado Constitution and Colorado Revised Statutes for details.

If the matter originates in the County Courts, the appeal goes to the District Court and then the Supreme Court. Most matters originating in the District Courts are appealed to the Court of Appeals.

If the Municipal Court is a court of record, the appeal goes to the District Court. Otherwise, the matter is tried anew in the County Court.

over cases relating to the determination of water rights, use, and administration of water, and all other water matters.

### 4. Municipal Courts

Municipal courts hear violations of municipal ordinances. While municipal courts are locally funded, appeals from them can end up in the state court system. If the municipal court is a court of record,[8] litigants can appeal its decision to the district court. If it is not a court of record, the matter is sent to the county court for a new trial.

### 5. Denver Courts

The Denver court system differs somewhat from the rest of the state's courts. Denver is a combined city-county government. While other district courts hear probate and juvenile matters, Denver assigns these functions to a separate probate court and juvenile court. The Denver county court serves as a municipal court by adjudicating violations of municipal ordinances while also retaining the jurisdiction of other state county courts.

### 6. Appellate Courts

Colorado also contains two appellate courts.[9] Article VI of the state constitution vests a supreme court with appellate jurisdiction over all matters arising from Colorado state courts. The Supreme Court sits in Denver and is composed of seven justices.[10] Colorado has also created an intermediate court of appeals.[11] The court's jurisdiction is broad but does have limitations.[12] The court sits in Denver and is composed currently of twenty-two judges who hear cases in three-judge panels.[13] The Supreme Court publishes all of its judicial opinions. The Court of Appeals publishes many of its opinions. However, the Court of Appeals marks certain opinions as unpublished.[14] While the published opinions can be found in case reporters and online services, the unpublished opinions must be requested from the Court.[15]

Almost all case law research is concerned with finding the opinions of these courts. Appellate courts decide issues of law whereas the trial courts determine

---

8. A court of record is a court that keeps a record of its proceedings. CRS 13-1-111 specifies which Colorado courts are courts of record.

9. For an excellent treatment of the Colorado's appellate courts and practice, see Ralph Ogden, *Colorado Appellate Advocacy Deskbook* (Bradford Publishing Co. 2007).

10. Colo. Const. art. 6, § 5.

11. Colo. Rev. Stat. § 13-4-101 (LexisNexis 2017).

12. Colo. Rev. Stat. § 13-4-102(1) (LexisNexis 2017).

13. Colo. Rev. Stat. § 13-4-106(1) (LexisNexis 2017).

14. Colo. App. R. 35(f).

15. Currently, unpublished opinions can be requested from the Colorado Judicial Branch website at www.courts.state.co.us/Courts/Court_of_Appeals/Opinion_Request.cfm.

the facts and apply law to those facts to settle the outcome of the matter before the court. Therefore, appellate court decisions make law and establish precedent. For these reasons, case law research is primarily concerned with finding appellate court decisions.

### B. Federal Courts in Colorado

As with the Colorado court system, the federal court system includes trial courts and appellate courts. In the federal system, the trial courts are called district courts. While many states may contain multiple federal district courts, in Colorado there is one federal district court based in Denver and called the District of Colorado. The district courts are courts of general jurisdiction and can hear nearly all federal cases of both a civil and criminal nature. Bankruptcy cases are heard in federal bankruptcy courts. Colorado houses a federal bankruptcy court, also seated in Denver.

A losing party may appeal the decision of the federal district court to the intermediate appellate court in its region. The federal court system contains thirteen intermediate appellate court circuits.[16] The circuits are numbered one to eleven and also include the Federal Circuit and District of Columbia Circuit, both located in Washington, D.C. Colorado is in the Tenth Circuit, which also includes the states of Wyoming, Utah, New Mexico, Kansas, and Oklahoma. The Court of Appeals for the Tenth Circuit is based in Denver.

Decisions of the circuit courts can be appealed to the Supreme Court of the United States. Located in Washington, D.C., it is the court of last resort for federal issues and some state issues. The Court selects very few cases to hear each year, choosing only those cases critical to resolve a constitutional issue or a *circuit split*, a conflict between the decisions of appellate courts in different circuits.

## III. Publication of Cases

Colorado state courts will hear issues of state law while federal courts will hear issues of federal law. While the publication and finding of cases is similar for all judicial opinions, the rest of this chapter focuses on Colorado state court opinions. Judicial opinions are published in case reporters. The reporters can publish the decisions from a single court or multiple courts. Judicial opinions

16. 28 U.S.C. § 1291 (2012).

are also published electronically. These cases can be obtained both from commercial publishers and increasingly through the courts' websites.

When doing case law research in Colorado, the researcher will almost exclusively be searching for appellate court cases. After an appellate court reaches its decision, it initially publishes the case as a slip opinion (See Figure 6-2). Slip opinions are found on the court's website[17] for both the Colorado Supreme Court and Court of Appeals. These slip opinions are also made available to West and other publishers. These commercial publishers will then make the opinions available on their online services, generally within twenty-four hours.

Cases are also still printed. West will also publish the cases in "advance sheets," which are softbound pamphlets that update their hardbound case reporters, explained later in this chapter. In addition to putting the opinion on Westlaw, West also publishes the opinions in the *Pacific Reporter*, a unit of its National Reporter System, explained in the next section. Colorado has designated the *Pacific Reporter* as the official reporter for state opinions.[18] West also publishes Colorado cases in a set titled *Colorado Reporter*. This set is designed to provide researchers and practitioners with only the Colorado cases published in the *Pacific Reporter*. It is paginated exactly like the *Pacific Reporter*, and cases found in the *Colorado Reporter* are cited with the *Pacific Reporter* citation.

Historically, Colorado published its own set of reporters. The opinions of the Supreme Court were published in the *Colorado Reports*. The court published its cases in this official reporter from 1864 until 1980. Likewise, the Court of Appeals published its cases in the *Colorado Court of Appeals Reports*. The publication history of the *Colorado Court of Appeals Reports* is somewhat varied, tracking the history of the court itself. Initially, the Court of Appeals existed from 1891 to 1905.[19] It was then reformed in 1911 and existed another four years until 1915, when it was once again disbanded.[20] The court was then re-

---

17. These opinions are located currently under the link for "Case Announcements" on the landing pages for the Colorado Supreme Court (https://www.courts.state.co.us/Courts/Supreme_Court/) and for the Colorado Court of Appeals (https://www.courts.state.co.us/Courts/Court_Of_Appeals/).

18. Colo. Rev. Stat. § 13-2-124 (LexisNexis 2017); *Annual Report of the Colorado Judiciary*, July 1 1982 to July 2, 1983, pg. 10.

19. The court was established by 1891 Colo. Sess. Laws at pg. 118 (S.B. 98).

20. Robert M. Linz & Clare E. Munger, *The Early History of the Colorado Court of Appeals*, 37 Colo. Law. 91 (Nov. 2008); Jeannie Towle Millinger & Molly Wingate, *The Colorado Court of Appeals: History of Colorado's Intermediate Appellate Court* (Continuing Legal Education in Colorado, Inc. 2008).

## Figure 6-2. *Clancy Systems v. Salazar* Case Slip Opinion

Opinions of the Colorado Supreme Court are available to the public and can be accessed through the Court's homepage at http://www.courts.state.co.us/supct/supctcaseannctsindex.htm Opinions are also posted on the Colorado Bar Association homepage at www.cobar.org.

ADVANCE SHEET HEADNOTE
February 19, 2008

**06SC698, Clancy Systems International, Inc. v. Salazar: Uniform Commercial Code - Displacement - Common Law - Register a Transfer of a Security - Removal of Restrictive Legend**

Clancy Systems International petitioned the supreme court for review of the court of appeals' published opinion reversing the district court's summary judgment against Salazar. The district court ruled that Salazar's common law tort claims, for losses caused by Clancy's insistence upon placing a restrictive legend on a stock certificate issued to Salazar, had been displaced by provisions of Colorado's Uniform Commercial Code. The court of appeals disagreed, holding that even if the code provides specific relief for Salazar's loss, it does not also preempt his common law claims.

The supreme court reversed and remanded, holding that by imposing liability on an issuer for unreasonable delay in registering a transfer of securities, section 4-8-401(b) of the revised statutes not only imposes liability on the issuer for loss resulting from its unreasonable delay in removing a

Source: Colorado Judiciary website, www.courts.state.co.us/Courts/Supreme_Court/opinions/2006/06SC698.pdf

established in 1970 by the Colorado legislature.[21] Consequently, the researcher will find a run of cases from 1891 to 1915 published in volumes 1 to 27 of the *Colorado Court of Appeals Reports*. The set continues in 1970 with volume 28 and terminates in 1980 with volume 44.

The publication of Colorado cases in West's *Pacific Reporter* does not completely overlap the publication in the official reporters. In the *Pacific Reporter*, West began its publication with the 1883 case of *Morrell v. Ferrier*,[22] which is printed in volume 7 at page 22 in the *Colorado Reports*. Therefore, the researcher searching for a print copy of a Colorado case published in an earlier volume of the *Colorado Reports* will need to locate it in the official state reporter.[23] Westlaw does contain the complete collection of Colorado appellate court cases, as does LexisNexis, Casemaker, and Bloomberg Law.

In addition to the print and electronic sources, Colorado appellate opinions are published by the Colorado Bar Association (CBA).[24] Beginning in November 1971, the CBA published both case summaries and full opinions from both the Colorado Supreme Court and the Colorado Court of Appeals in its monthly journal, *The Colorado Lawyer*. Starting with opinions published in January 1996, the Colorado Bar Association made those opinions available online at its website. Additionally, the Colorado Bar Association offers access to a commercial, online legal research service called Casemaker. A free service to bar members, Casemaker contains Colorado Supreme Court cases from 1864 and Court of Appeals cases from 1891.

## A. The National Reporter System

The *Pacific Reporter*, published by West, is part of a larger organization of case law called the National Reporter System. Developed in the 1880s by John B. West, the National Reporter System is a way to organize judicial

---

21. 1969 Colo. Sess. Laws Ch. 106. See also *Report to the General Assembly: Intermediate Court of Appeals for Colorado*, Colorado Legislative Research Publication No. 138 (Nov. 1968).

22. *Morrell v. Ferrier*, 7 Colo. 22, 1 P. 94 (1883).

23. In addition to the *Colorado Reports*, there existed a publication called *The Colorado Law Reporter*. It purported to publish "rulings and adjudications of the highest judicial authority" from Colorado as well as from the other state supreme courts and the United States Supreme Court "primarily in the hope of realizing a profit" but also to confer "a substantial benefit upon the legal profession." The title was published from 1880 to 1884.

24. The Colorado Bar Association is a non-profit voluntary member organization. For more information, visit its website at www.cobar.org.

opinions of the states and federal government into logical groupings. The National Reporter System reports published cases from state supreme and intermediate appellate courts as well as federal appellate courts and district courts.

The state opinions are published in one of seven regional reporters. These regional reporters are the *Atlantic, North Eastern, North Western, South Eastern, South Western, Southern,* and *Pacific.* Because these regions were developed initially in the 1880s, the placement of some states into the regions does not always seem to make sense. For example, the *North Western Reporter* does not contain the cases from the states of Washington or Oregon but rather Minnesota and Michigan, states that were considered part of the northwest in the late 19th century. Similarly, the *South Eastern Reporter* includes the states of Georgia and North Carolina, but cases from Florida, Alabama, Mississippi, and Louisiana are reported in the *Southern Reporter* series. And cases from Oklahoma, Montana, Wyoming, and Colorado are published in the *Pacific Reporter.*

The judicial opinions of the federal courts are published in various West reporters. Supreme Court opinions are published in the *Supreme Court Reporter*, Courts of Appeals opinions in the *Federal Reporter*, and district courts opinions in the *Federal Supplement.* West also publishes the opinions of the Bankruptcy Court, Military Court, and various other courts in their own reporter sets.

## B. Online Sources of Colorado Case Law

### 1. Commercial Publishers

Court opinions are also available online. Westlaw, LexisNexis, Bloomberg Law, and Casemaker contain the complete run of Colorado Supreme Court opinions (beginning in 1877) and Court of Appeals opinions (beginning in 1891). Additionally, Westlaw provides access to Supreme Court of Colorado Territory opinions from 1864 to 1876.

### 2. No Fee Solutions

The Colorado judiciary also publishes its opinions, but only for cases decided since 2000. Researchers can also find Colorado cases using Google Scholar's case law search. The collection is limited to cases published since 1950.[25]

---

25. Google Scholar is available at http://scholar.google.com. Coverage information is available at https://scholar.google.com/intl/en/scholar/help.html#coverage/.

Table 6-1 sets out the content of each of these services related to Colorado.

**Table 6-1. Colorado Case Law Availability**

| Case Reports | | |
|---|---|---|
| Publication | Courts | Dates |
| *Colorado Reports* | Colorado Supreme Court | 1877 to 1980 |
| *Colorado Court of Appeals Reports* | Colorado Court of Appeals | 1891 to 1905, 1911 to 1915, 1970 to 1980 |
| *Pacific Reporter* | Supreme Court<br>Court of Appeals | 1883 to Present<br>1891 to Present |
| *Colorado Reporter* | Same as *Pacific Reporter* | |
| Westlaw | Supreme Court<br>Court of Appeals<br>Territorial Supreme Court | 1877 to Present<br>1891 to Present<br>1864 to 1876 |
| LexisNexis | Colorado Supreme Court<br>Colorado Court of Appeals | 1864 to Present<br>1891 to Present |
| Casemaker | Colorado Supreme Court<br>Colorado Court of Appeals | 1864 to Present<br>1970 to Present |
| *The Colorado Lawyer* | Colorado Supreme Court<br>Colorado Court of Appeals | 1970 to 2005<br>Case summaries 2006 to Present |
| Bloomberg Law | Colorado Supreme Court<br>Colorado Court of Appeals | 1864 to Present<br>1891 to Present |
| Google Scholar | Colorado Supreme Court<br>Colorado Court of Appeals | 1950 to Present<br>1950 to Present |
| Colorado Judiciary Website | Both Appellate Courts | 2000 to Present |
| **Case Digests** | | |
| *Colorado Digest* | All three digests publish headnotes from Colorado appellate cases and federal cases interpreting Colorado state law. | |
| *Pacific Digest* | | |
| *Decennial Digest* | | |

# IV. The Digest System

## A. About the Digest

Despite—and perhaps because of—this breadth of coverage of case law in the reporters, there is a research problem with case law publication. As with session laws, cases are published in these reporters by jurisdiction but also in chronological order according to the date in which the opinion was decided. While a particular reporter volume will include a table of cases and subject index, the reporter sets themselves do not contain an overall index in which to find all of the case law on the particular subject that is relevant to the legal matter. For legislation, researchers solve this problem with a code. For case law, researchers have a similar organizational tool: a digest.

A *digest* is a subject organization of case law; in that sense, it is similar to a code. However, a digest differs from a code in that the digest does not reprint the cases found in the reporters, as a code will reprint the statutes found in the session law volumes. Rather, a digest prints a summary of the point of law discussed in the case. The summary is a brief paragraph.

The most famous and most widely used digest is produced by West, and it is called the American Digest System. In the 1880s, building from work by other individuals, West classified American law. It divided the vast body of American case law into seven broad subject areas. These areas are persons, property, contracts, torts, crimes, remedies, and government. These overarching categories are subdivided into topics. These topics include citizens, civil rights, compromise and settlement, negligence, damages, perjury, and liens, among many others. In fact, the digest system now includes over 400 topics. The topics are further subdivided into subtopics. Each subtopic represents a particular point of law. Each point of law is identified by a key symbol and a number, and hence are called key numbers.

When researchers refer to "key numbers," they are really referring to topics and key numbers. The key number, to be meaningful, has to be preceded by a topic designation. As particular key numbers are found in multiple topics, a researcher will not be able to locate the proper points of law without the topic as well. When researching online, note that West has also assigned numbers to the topics. These topics and key numbers are important when doing Westlaw research.

The digest entries, of course, are drawn from cases. Those same digest entries are also published at the beginning of the case as headnotes. Therefore, a researcher has a complete system to tie in a case to a topic and key number, and then to digest entries which are cited back to that and other related cases. Figure 6-3 illustrates how a headnote in a case is reprinted in the digest.

The same headnote can appear in two different locations in the digest. This occurs when the editor determines that the point of law fits into two different but related topics. Occasionally, the editors may reclassify the topic and key numbers, and even move a headnote from one classification to another. In Figure 6-4, a headnote from the *Clancy Systems* case that originally appeared under the topic of Common Law was later moved to the topic of Statutes. When this shift occurs, the editors provide a note indicating where the headnote was formerly classified. In print, a general note appears under the former topic indicating where else similar headnotes might appear. As Figure 6-5 shows, on Westlaw the editors include a cross-reference in the headnote indicating where this headnote formerly appeared.

## B. Digest Benefits

To review, the digest system is a topic-based organization of case law. The value of this approach is that when the researcher identifies a particular case in a particular area of law, the researcher will be able to locate all of the other cases that have discussed that same point of law using the digest and headnotes.

### 1. Comprehensive Coverage

One benefit is comprehensive coverage. Every point of law from every published case from all American jurisdictions is classified in the American Digest System. Thus, the system is comprehensive. West publishes digests for most of the regional reporters; for example, the *Pacific Digest* covers cases published in the *Pacific Reporter* series. West publishes a digest for all federal cases, the *Federal Practice Digest.* West also publishes a digest for state case law, for example, the *Colorado Digest.* It publishes digests for specialty case law, for example, the *Bankruptcy Digest* for cases reported in the *Bankruptcy Reporter.* And it publishes a comprehensive digest for all cases published in the United States. This digest is the *Decennial Digest* which is published in several hardbound volumes each year. Though unwieldy, it is comprehensive and with it the researcher could find every single American case that discusses some point of law within its time-frame of coverage.

### 2. Cross-Jurisdictional Searching

This last point also signifies another benefit of the digest system. It uses the same organizational topics and key numbers throughout the system.

Figure 6-3. Case Publication and the American Digest System

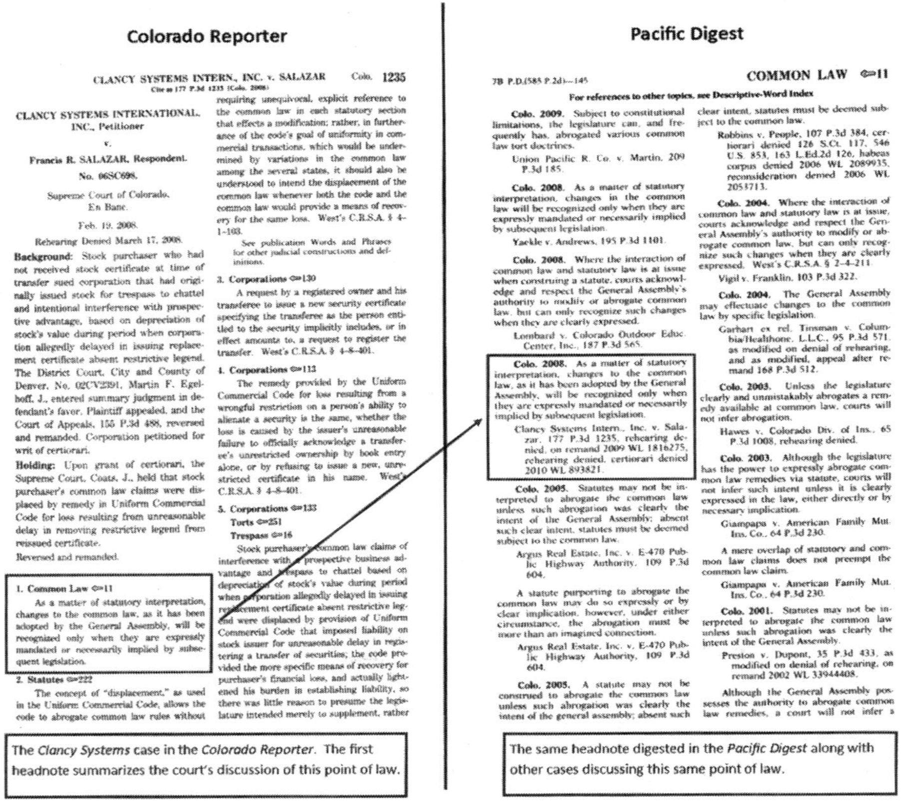

**Colorado Reporter**

CLANCY SYSTEMS INTERN., INC. v. SALAZAR Colo. 1235
Cite as 177 P.3d 1235 (Colo. 2008)

CLANCY SYSTEMS INTERNATIONAL, INC., Petitioner

v.

Francis R. SALAZAR, Respondent.

No. 06SC698.

Supreme Court of Colorado, En Banc.

Feb. 19, 2008.

Rehearing Denied March 17, 2008.

**Background:** Stock purchaser who had not received stock certificate at time of transfer sued corporation that had originally issued stock for trespass to chattel and intentional interference with prospective advantage, based on depreciation of stock's value during period when corporation allegedly delayed in issuing replacement certificate absent restrictive legend. The District Court, City and County of Denver, No. 02CV2391, Martin F. Egelhoff, J., entered summary judgment in defendant's favor. Plaintiff appealed, and the Court of Appeals, 155 P.3d 488, reversed and remanded. Corporation petitioned for writ of certiorari.

**Holding:** Upon grant of certiorari, the Supreme Court, Coats, J., held that stock purchaser's common law claims were displaced by remedy in Uniform Commercial Code for loss resulting from unreasonable delay in removing restrictive legend from reissued certificate.

Reversed and remanded.

**1. Common Law** ⇔11

As a matter of statutory interpretation, changes to the common law, as it has been adopted by the General Assembly, will be recognized only when they are expressly mandated or necessarily implied by subsequent legislation.

**2. Statutes** ⇔222

The concept of "displacement," as used in the Uniform Commercial Code, allows the code to abrogate common law rules without requiring unequivocal, explicit reference to the common law in each statutory section that effects a modification; rather, in furtherance of the code's goal of uniformity in commercial transactions, which would be undermined by variations in the common law among the several states, it should also be understood to intend the displacement of the common law whenever both the code and the common law would provide a means of recovery for the same loss. West's C.R.S.A. § 4-1-103.

See publication Words and Phrases for other judicial constructions and definitions.

**3. Corporations** ⇔130

A request by a registered owner and his transferee to issue a new security certificate specifying the transferee as the person entitled to the security implicitly includes, or in effect amounts to, a request to register the transfer. West's C.R.S.A. § 4-8-401.

**4. Corporations** ⇔113

The remedy provided by the Uniform Commercial Code for loss resulting from a wrongful restriction on a person's ability to alienate a security is the same, whether the loss is caused by the issuer's unreasonable failure to officially acknowledge a transferee's unrestricted ownership by book entry alone, or by refusing to issue a new, unrestricted certificate in his name. West's C.R.S.A. § 4-8-401.

**5. Corporations** ⇔133
**Torts** ⇔251
**Trespass** ⇔16

Stock purchaser's common law claims of interference with a prospective business advantage and trespass to chattel based on depreciation of stock's value during period when corporation allegedly delayed in issuing replacement certificate absent restrictive legend were displaced by provision of Uniform Commercial Code that imposed liability on stock issuer for unreasonable delay in registering a transfer of securities; the code provided the more specific means of recovery for purchaser's financial loss, and actually lightened his burden in establishing liability, so there was little reason to presume the legislature intended merely to supplement, rather

The *Clancy Systems* case in the *Colorado Reporter*. The first headnote summarizes the court's discussion of this point of law.

**Pacific Digest**

7B P.D.(585 P.2d)—145 COMMON LAW ⇔11

For references to other topics, see Descriptive-Word Index

**Colo. 2009.** Subject to constitutional limitations, the legislature can, and frequently has, abrogated various common law tort doctrines.

Union Pacific R. Co. v. Martin, 209 P.3d 185.

**Colo. 2008.** As a matter of statutory interpretation, changes in the common law will be recognized only when they are expressly mandated or necessarily implied by subsequent legislation.

Yackle v. Andrews, 195 P.3d 1101.

**Colo. 2008.** Where the interaction of common law and statutory law is at issue when construing a statute, courts acknowledge and respect the General Assembly's authority to modify or abrogate common law, but can only recognize such changes when they are clearly expressed.

Lombard v. Colorado Outdoor Educ. Center, Inc., 187 P.3d 565.

**Colo. 2008.** As a matter of statutory interpretation, changes to the common law, as it has been adopted by the General Assembly, will be recognized only when they are expressly mandated or necessarily implied by subsequent legislation.

Clancy Systems Intern., Inc. v. Salazar, 177 P.3d 1235, rehearing denied, on remand 2009 WL 1816275, rehearing denied, certiorari denied 2010 WL 893821.

**Colo. 2005.** Statutes may not be interpreted to abrogate the common law unless such abrogation was clearly the intent of the General Assembly; absent such clear intent, statutes must be deemed subject to the common law.

Argus Real Estate, Inc. v. E-470 Public Highway Authority, 109 P.3d 604.

A statute purporting to abrogate the common law may do so expressly or by clear implication, however, under either circumstance, the abrogation must be more than an imagined connection.

Argus Real Estate, Inc. v. E-470 Public Highway Authority, 109 P.3d 604.

**Colo. 2005.** A statute may not be construed to abrogate the common law unless such abrogation was clearly the intent of the general assembly; absent such clear intent, statutes must be deemed subject to the common law.

Robbins v. People, 107 P.3d 384, certiorari denied 126 S.Ct. 117, 546 U.S. 853, 163 L.Ed.2d 126, habeas corpus denied 2006 WL 2089935, reconsideration denied 2006 WL 2053713.

**Colo. 2004.** Where the interaction of common law and statutory law is at issue, courts acknowledge and respect the General Assembly's authority to modify or abrogate common law, but can only recognize such changes when they are clearly expressed. West's C.R.S.A. § 2-4-211.

Vigil v. Franklin, 103 P.3d 322.

**Colo. 2004.** The General Assembly may effectuate changes to the common law by specific legislation.

Garhart ex rel. Tinsman v. Columbia/Healthone, L.L.C., 95 P.3d 571, as modified on denial of rehearing, and as modified, appeal after remand 168 P.3d 512.

**Colo. 2003.** Unless the legislature clearly and unmistakably abrogates a remedy available at common law, courts will not infer abrogation.

Hawes v. Colorado Div. of Ins., 65 P.3d 1008, rehearing denied.

**Colo. 2003.** Although the legislature has the power to expressly abrogate common law remedies via statute, courts will not infer such intent unless it is clearly expressed in the law, either directly or by necessary implication.

Giampapa v. American Family Mut. Ins. Co., 64 P.3d 230.

A mere overlap of statutory and common law claims does not preempt the common law claim.

Giampapa v. American Family Mut. Ins. Co., 64 P.3d 230.

**Colo. 2001.** Statutes may not be interpreted to abrogate the common law unless such abrogation was clearly the intent of the General Assembly.

Preston v. Dupont, 35 P.3d 433, as modified on denial of rehearing, on remand 2002 WL 33944408.

Although the General Assembly possesses the authority to abrogate common law remedies, a court will not infer a

The same headnote digested in the *Pacific Digest* along with other cases discussing this same point of law.

## Figure 6-4. The Same *Clancy Systems* Headnote Now Classified under Statutes

**⚩1206(1) STATUTES** 26A Colo D 2d—382

**For later cases, see same Topic and Key Number in Pocket Part**

**Colo.App. 2011.** The General Assembly has the authority to abrogate the common law.

Hamill v. Cheley Colorado Camps, Inc., 262 P.3d 945, certiorari denied 2011 WL 4448977.

**Colo.App. 1992.** Common-law principles must yield to state statutes governing same subject.

State for Use of Dept. of Corrections v. Pena, 837 P.2d 210, certiorari granted, affirmed in part 855 P.2d 805.

**Colo.App. 1976.** Common law prevails in state, but legislature may repeal any part of common law either expressly or by passage of inconsistent legislation.

Shoemaker v. Mountain States Tel. & Tel. Co., 559 P.2d 721, 38 Colo.App. 321.

**⚩1206(2). Plain, literal, or clear meaning of statute; ambiguity.**

**C.A.10 (Colo.) 2001.** Under Colorado law, absent clear legislative intent, the common law prevails in any conflict with statutory law.

Doering ex rel. Barrett v. Copper Mountain Inc., 259 F.3d 1202.

**D.Colo. 1991.** When Congress enacts statute that creates or recognizes rights, general rule is that existing common-law rights are not thereby replaced, absent clear and unequivocal statement by Congress.

Federal Deposit Ins. Corp. v. Isham, 777 F.Supp. 828.

**D.Colo. 1981.** Though it has adopted common law of England, the Colorado Legislature may at any time by a legislative act, repeal any part of the common law, either expressly or by passage of an act inconsistent therewith on any particular subject. C.R.S.1973, 2–4–211.

Morton v. Allied Stores Corp., 90 F.R.D. 352.

**Colo. 2012.** When common law claims preexist a statute, the statute must express a clear legislative intent to negate the preexisting common law right.

Capital Securities of America, Inc. v. Griffin, 278 P.3d 342, rehearing denied.

**Colo. 2012.** Where the interaction of common law and statutory law is at issue, the court respects the General Assembly's authority to modify or abrogate the common law, but can only recognize such changes when they are clearly expressed.

Wal-Mart Stores, Inc. v. Crossgrove, 276 P.3d 562, rehearing denied.

**Colo. 2011.** The Supreme Court construes alterations made to the common law by the General Assembly strictly, and will only recognize changes that the General Assembly has expressly mandated or necessarily implied by subsequent legislation. West's C.R.S.A. § 2–4–211.

Oram v. People, 255 P.3d 1032, as modified on denial of rehearing.

**Colo. 2008.** As a matter of statutory interpretation, changes in the common law will be recognized only when they are expressly mandated or necessarily implied by subsequent legislation.

Yaekle v. Andrews, 195 P.3d 1101.

**Colo. 2008.** Where the interaction of common law and statutory law is at issue when construing a statute, courts acknowledge and respect the General Assembly's authority to modify or abrogate common law, but can only recognize such changes when they are clearly expressed.

Lombard v. Colorado Outdoor Educ. Center, Inc., 187 P.3d 565, appeal after remand 266 P.3d 412, certiorari denied 2012 WL 2237470.

**Colo. 2008.** As a matter of statutory interpretation, changes to the common law, as it has been adopted by the General Assembly, will be recognized only when they are expressly mandated or necessarily implied by subsequent legislation.

Clancy Systems Intern., Inc. v. Salazar, 177 P.3d 1235, rehearing denied, on remand 2009 WL 1816275, rehearing denied, certiorari denied 2010 WL 893821.

**Colo. 2005.** Statutes may not be interpreted to abrogate the common law unless such abrogation was clearly the intent of the General Assembly; absent such clear intent, statutes must be deemed subject to the common law.

Argus Real Estate, Inc. v. E-470 Public Highway Authority, 109 P.3d 604.

**† This Case was not selected for publication in the National Reporter System**

**Figure 6-5. Headnotes on Westlaw Contain References to Previous Classifications**

**West Headnotes (5)**

Change View

**1 Statutes**

As a matter of statutory interpretation, changes to the common law, as it has been adopted by the General Assembly, will be recognized only when they are expressly mandated or necessarily implied by subsequent legislation.

2 Cases that cite this headnote

| | |
|---|---|
| 361 | Statutes |
| 361III | Construction |
| 361III(G) | Other Law, Construction with Reference to |
| 361k1203 | Common or Civil Law |
| 361k1206 | Statutory Alteration or Abrogation of Common Law |
| 361k1206(2) | Plain, literal, or clear meaning of statute; ambiguity (Formerly 85k11) |

| | |
|---|---|
| 361 | Statutes |
| 361III | Construction |
| 361III(G) | Other Law, Construction with Reference to |
| 361k1203 | Common or Civil Law |
| 361k1207 | Statutory adoption of common law (Formerly 85k11) |



Hence, researchers can perform multi-jurisdictional research using the same topic and key number located in their particular state or in the federal or regional digest.

### 3. Language Normalization

The digest method also provides another benefit; namely, it eliminates the variances of language. Different judges can use different terms to express the same concept. Doing a keyword search, a researcher would like to include in the search all of the keywords for that concept. However, the researcher may not know all of the terms, and therefore might miss relevant case law. The digest solves this problem. The placement of a case's points of law is done by an editor. The editor reads the various cases and determines which points of law are discussed in the case. The editor then writes the summary and assigns the appropriate topic and key number to that summary. That summary becomes a headnote in the case. It is also then published in the appropriate digest volumes. Through this manual process, cases are categorized into the appropriate areas of law, regardless of the language used in the case.

West has put this comprehensive research system on Westlaw which will be discussed in the next section. The digest is a powerful and underappreciated research tool. Until recently, most case law research was performed using the digest system. With the advent of online databases and keyword searching, digests and topical, structured approaches to case law research have been largely abandoned.

## V. Researching Cases

Researchers can find cases using a citation, keywords, or the digest. All three approaches will be discussed in this section. But first this chapter will identify the different parts of a case.

### A. Parts of a Case

Courts and publishers have established a common method for drafting judicial decisions. Each case is composed of different parts which help researchers locate important information in the case and also to help find cases. Referring to Figure 6-6, these parts include:

- ❑ Citation—The citation indicates where the case is published. The citation consists of numbers and abbreviations that identify the case in a print reporter or an online database. A case can have multiple citations, and these are called "parallel" citations. For example, a case may be given a public domain citation by the court issuing the opinion, and then also be given a citation by Thomson Reuters referring to its publicationin the National Reporter System. Finally, it may receive a LexisNexis citation as well as a citation to a specialty reporter.
- ❑ Case Name—The case name identifies the parties to the litigation and whether they are plaintiffs/appellants or defendants/appellees. The parties are listed with their full legal names even though the case is referred to by an abbreviation consisting of the first party appellant and first party appellee.
- ❑ Docket Number—The docket number is the identifier the court uses to track the litigation in its court. The number typically identifies the year the matter was filed, the court into which it was filed and the matter number for that year. Docket numbers are unique identifies and can be quite helpful in locating cases.

- Syllabus—The syllabus is a summary of the case, and sometimes referred to as the "summary" of the court's opinion. The syllabus may consist of two parts—the background and the holding. The background provides a brief factual and procedural overview of the case before it reached the current appellate court. The holding is the current court's disposition of the matter. Courts can affirm, reverse, remand or vacate the lower court opinion.
- Headnotes—As discussed earlier in the chapter, headnotes are publisher-provided editorial enhancements. Headnotes identify the various points of law discussed by the court in the case. The text of the headnote is drawn from the text of the case. The headnote is numbered and the number refers to the location in the case where the editor drew that point of law. The location is marked with a bracketed ([]) number corresponding to the headnote number. In a case published by Thomson Reuters, the headnote is composed of two parts—the Topic and the Key Number. These are references to the organization of American case law in the American Digest System. Cases published by LexisNexis online will also contain headnotes to their own classification system. Other vendors and the official court opinions may contain headnotes as well. While headnotes are located toward the top of the case, they are not considered part of the case and should never be cited.
- Attorneys—The attorneys and their firms listed here are the ones that argued the case before the court.
- Judge—The judge listed here is the one who authored the majority opinion, which directly follows. If the case included a concurring or dissenting opinion, the judges who authored those opinions would be listed at the beginning of their concurring or dissenting opinions, which follow the opinion of the court.
- Opinion—The opinion is the discussion and decision of the majority or plurality of the judges on the court hearing the case. The opinion contains a review of the facts of the case, a procedural history, and a discussion of the issues raised by the parties. The opinion addresses the various points or rules of law implicated by the case, and importantly provides a rationale for deciding how the rule of law applies to the current case or why it might be changed by this case. Finally, the opinion provides a "holding" which is the disposition of the case. If there is a concurring or dissenting opinion, these would follow the majority opinion. Concurring and dissenting opinions typically lack

**Figure 6-6. Parts of a Case from *Clancy Systems v. Salazar***

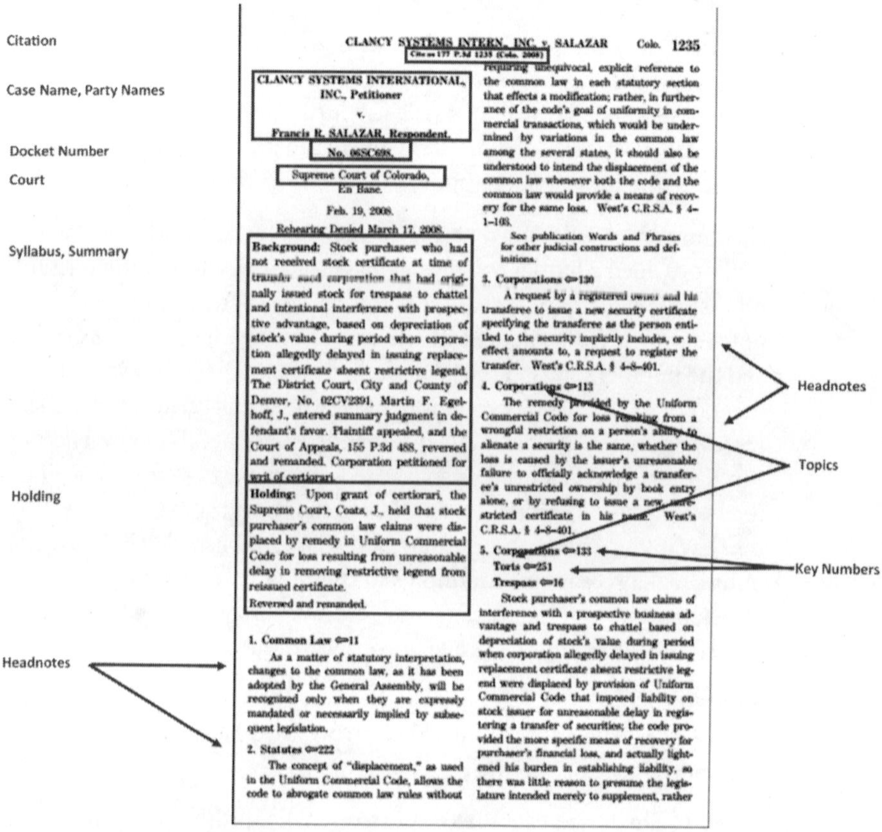


CLANCY SYSTEMS INTERN., INC. v. SALAZAR Colo. 1235

Cite as 177 P.3d 1235 (Colo. 2008)

CLANCY SYSTEMS INTERNATIONAL, INC., Petitioner

v.

Francis R. SALAZAR, Respondent.

No. 06SC698.

Supreme Court of Colorado, En Banc.

Feb. 19, 2008.

Rehearing Denied March 17, 2008.

**Background:** Stock purchaser who had not received stock certificate at time of transfer sued corporation that had originally issued stock for trespass to chattel and intentional interference with prospective advantage, based on depreciation of stock's value during period when corporation allegedly delayed in issuing replacement certificate absent restrictive legend. The District Court, City and County of Denver, No. 02CV2391, Martin F. Egelhoff, J., entered summary judgment in defendant's favor. Plaintiff appealed, and the Court of Appeals, 155 P.3d 488, reversed and remanded. Corporation petitioned for writ of certiorari.

**Holding:** Upon grant of certiorari, the Supreme Court, Coats, J., held that stock purchaser's common law claims were displaced by remedy in Uniform Commercial Code for loss resulting from unreasonable delay in removing restrictive legend from reissued certificate.

Reversed and remanded.

**1. Common Law 🔑11**

As a matter of statutory interpretation, changes to the common law, as it has been adopted by the General Assembly, will be recognized only when they are expressly mandated or necessarily implied by subsequent legislation.

**2. Statutes 🔑222**

The concept of "displacement," as used in the Uniform Commercial Code, allows the code to abrogate common law rules without requiring unequivocal, explicit reference to the common law in each statutory section that effects a modification; rather, in furtherance of the code's goal of uniformity in commercial transactions, which would be undermined by variations in the common law among the several states, it should also be understood to intend the displacement of the common law whenever both the code and the common law would provide a means of recovery for the same loss. West's C.R.S.A. § 4-1-103.

See publication Words and Phrases for other judicial constructions and definitions.

**3. Corporations 🔑120**

A request by a registered owner and his transferee to issue a new security certificate specifying the transferee as the person entitled to the security implicitly includes, or in effect amounts to, a request to register the transfer. West's C.R.S.A. § 4-8-401.

**4. Corporations 🔑113**

The remedy provided by the Uniform Commercial Code for loss resulting from a wrongful restriction on a person's ability to alienate a security is the same, whether the loss is caused by the issuer's unreasonable failure to officially acknowledge a transferee's unrestricted ownership by book entry alone, or by refusing to issue a new, unrestricted certificate in his name. West's C.R.S.A. § 4-8-401.

**5. Corporations 🔑133**
**Torts 🔑251**
**Trespass 🔑16**

Stock purchaser's common law claims of interference with a prospective business advantage and trespass to chattel based on depreciation of stock's value during period when corporation allegedly delayed in issuing replacement certificate absent restrictive legend were displaced by provision of Uniform Commercial Code that imposed liability on stock issuer for unreasonable delay in registering a transfer of securities; the code provided the more specific means of recovery for purchaser's financial loss, and actually lightened his burden in establishing liability, so there was little reason to presume the legislature intended merely to supplement, rather

Reprinted with permission from Thomson Reuters.

the history and procedural background of the majority opinion. In concurring opinions, the judges (and those other judges who join the opinion) agree with the holding of the majority but disagree about the rationale or basis for the holding. In dissenting opinions, the judge (and those other judges who join the opinion) disagree with the holding and the rationale.

## B. Finding Cases with a Citation

### 1. Print

The simplest method to find a case is to use its citation. The citation may be found from an annotated code, secondary authority, or other publication. Regardless of the source, every case citation follows the same basic form. That form is the volume number of the reporter, followed by the reporter title and

**Figure 6-6. Parts of a Case from *Clancy Systems v. Salazar*, continued**

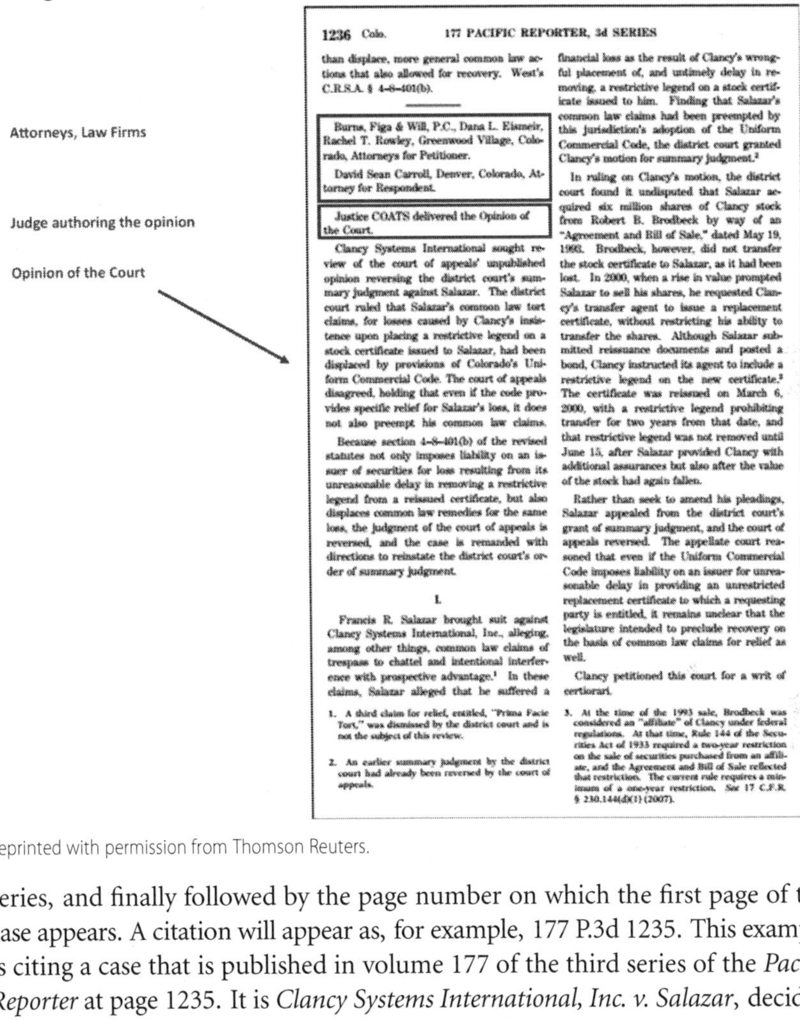


1236 Colo. 177 PACIFIC REPORTER, 3d SERIES

than displace, more general common law actions that also allowed for recovery. West's C.R.S.A. § 4-8-401(b).

Burns, Figa & Will, P.C., Dana L. Eismeir, Rachel T. Rowley, Greenwood Village, Colorado, Attorneys for Petitioner.

David Sean Carroll, Denver, Colorado, Attorney for Respondent.

Justice COATS delivered the Opinion of the Court.

Clancy Systems International sought review of the court of appeals' unpublished opinion reversing the district court's summary judgment against Salazar. The district court ruled that Salazar's common law tort claims, for losses caused by Clancy's insistence upon placing a restrictive legend on a stock certificate issued to Salazar, had been displaced by provisions of Colorado's Uniform Commercial Code. The court of appeals disagreed, holding that even if the code provides specific relief for Salazar's loss, it does not also preempt his common law claims.

Because section 4-8-401(b) of the revised statutes not only imposes liability on an issuer of securities for loss resulting from its unreasonable delay in removing a restrictive legend from a reissued certificate, but also displaces common law remedies for the same loss, the judgment of the court of appeals is reversed, and the case is remanded with directions to reinstate the district court's order of summary judgment.

I.

Francis R. Salazar brought suit against Clancy Systems International, Inc., alleging, among other things, common law claims of trespass to chattel and intentional interference with prospective advantage.[1] In these claims, Salazar alleged that he suffered a financial loss as the result of Clancy's wrongful placement of, and untimely delay in removing, a restrictive legend on a stock certificate issued to him. Finding that Salazar's common law claims had been preempted by this jurisdiction's adoption of the Uniform Commercial Code, the district court granted Clancy's motion for summary judgment.[2]

In ruling on Clancy's motion, the district court found it undisputed that Salazar acquired six million shares of Clancy stock from Robert B. Brodbeck by way of an "Agreement and Bill of Sale," dated May 19, 1993. Brodbeck, however, did not transfer the stock certificate to Salazar, as it had been lost. In 2000, when a rise in value prompted Salazar to sell his shares, he requested Clancy's transfer agent to issue a replacement certificate, without restricting his ability to transfer the shares. Although Salazar submitted reissuance documents and posted a bond, Clancy instructed its agent to include a restrictive legend on the new certificate.[3] The certificate was reissued on March 6, 2000, with a restrictive legend prohibiting transfer for two years from that date, and that restrictive legend was not removed until June 15, after Salazar provided Clancy with additional assurances but also after the value of the stock had again fallen.

Rather than seek to amend his pleadings, Salazar appealed from the district court's grant of summary judgment, and the court of appeals reversed. The appellate court reasoned that even if the Uniform Commercial Code imposes liability on an issuer for unreasonable delay in providing an unrestricted replacement certificate to which a requesting party is entitled, it remains unclear that the legislature intended to preclude recovery on the basis of common law claims for relief as well.

Clancy petitioned this court for a writ of certiorari.

1. A third claim for relief, entitled, "Prima Facie Tort," was dismissed by the district court and is not the subject of this review.

2. An earlier summary judgment by the district court had already been reversed by the court of appeals.

3. At the time of the 1993 sale, Brodbeck was considered an "affiliate" of Clancy under federal regulations. At that time, Rule 144 of the Securities Act of 1933 required a two-year restriction on the sale of securities purchased from an affiliate, and the Agreement and Bill of Sale reflected that restriction. The current rule requires a minimum of a one-year restriction. *See* 17 C.F.R. § 230.144(d)(1) (2007).



series, and finally followed by the page number on which the first page of the case appears. A citation will appear as, for example, 177 P.3d 1235. This example is citing a case that is published in volume 177 of the third series of the *Pacific Reporter* at page 1235. It is *Clancy Systems International, Inc. v. Salazar*, decided by the Colorado Supreme Court in 2008. The first two pages of this case are shown in Figure 6-6. To find the case in print, researchers can find the case in either the *Pacific Reporter* series or the *Colorado Reporter* series, since it is a Colorado case. In either instance, researchers will browse the volumes on the shelf until they locate volume 177 containing cases published in the third series of the *Pacific Reporter*. The researcher will then open to page 1235 to read the case.

## 2. Online

To find a case online, the researcher has at least three choices. For recent cases, the researcher may be able to find the case on the Colorado Supreme

Court or Court of Appeals website. While this version of the opinion will lack editorial enhancements, it does contain the full text of the opinion. Secondly, researchers can locate the case on Google Scholar.

Finally, researchers can also locate the case on the various fee-based online services. There are several methods but if the researcher has a citation the easiest method is to use the default search box and enter the citation to find the case. The services will retrieve and display the case. If a researcher is unsure of the citation format, these services help by offering templates for citation forms or by allowing the researcher to locate the case by party name.

## C. Finding Cases with Keywords

Researchers may not always have a case citation but rather may be called upon to find cases relating to the issue being researched. For these situations, the researcher should develop a list of descriptive keywords and use either Boolean or Natural Language searching techniques, as discussed in Chapter 13. While print case reporters lack indexes, those keywords can be used in print digests. Using keywords for online research is also quite useful. Novice researchers typically enter the keywords into a search box, which will result in a large number of results unrelated to Colorado law. Researchers can use some techniques to improve upon this approach and increase their chances of finding relevant Colorado cases.

One technique is to limit the search to only the case law databases containing Colorado cases. This approach limits the total number of documents searched to those most likely relevant to the research question. A second method is to use those search terms within particular parts of the case. While this cannot be done in print, it is a very effective technique for online databases and is one advantage of directly searching within a case law database instead of generally within the online research platform. It is effective because it limits what parts of the document are being searched, leading to more precise search results. For example, if the researcher knows one of the party names of the case, she can search only the title field for that party name resulting only in cases where the name appears as a party instead of a word located generally within the text of the case. In order to use this technique, researchers need to know the names of the parts of a case. In Westlaw, these parts are called fields whereas in LexisNexis they are called segments. Tables 6-2 and 6-3 list the fields and segments for Westlaw and LexisNexis case databases, respectively, and Figure 6-7 indicates where these parts appear in a case. Each online service will provide some documentation identifying these fields and

**Table 6-2. Selected Westlaw Fields for Case Databases**

| Identifier | Name | Description |
|---|---|---|
| CI | Citation | Opinion citation |
| TI | Title | Title of the opinion (i.e., Smith v. Jones) |
| DN | Docket Number | Docket number assigned by court |
| CO | Court | Court issuing the opinion |
| JU | Judge | Name of judge writing the principal opinion |
| CON | Concurring | Name of judge writing a concurring opinion |
| DIS | Dissenting | Name of judge writing a dissenting opinion |
| AU | Attorney | Names of counsel |
| SY | Synopsis | Summary of case provided by West editors, including background and holding of case. |
| DI | Digest | Searches both headnotes and topic fields. |
| TO | Topic | Contains Topic and Key Numbers |
| HE | Headnotes | Searches headnotes of the case |

the various search options for them, typically located through a "help" link in the system.

In the present example, a researcher could retrieve the *Clancy Systems* case by searching the citation field using the form of CI(177 +3 1235). Researchers can locate cases based on other criteria. These criteria include cases with opinions written by a particular judge, argued by a particular attorney, issued by a particular court, or discussing particular points of law. On Westlaw, this last search criterion implements West's American Digest System.

## D. Finding Cases Using the Digest

### 1. Print

In order to use the digest method to locate cases, the researcher needs a topic and a key number. This information can be located in the headnote of

**Table 6-3. LexisNexis Segments for Cases**

| Segment | Description |
|---|---|
| Attorney | the name of individuals, law firms, or organizations representing a party of interest in the case. |
| Cite | Citation of the case in an official reporter or parallel reference |
| Court | Name of the court that heard the case |
| Disposition | Final decision of the court |
| Headnotes | Searches Lexis headnotes for the case |
| History | Prior and subsequent history of the case |
| Judges | Names of the judges hearing the case |
| Name | Names of all the parties involved in a case |
| Number | Docket number(s) assigned to a case by the court |
| Opinion | Text of the opinion issued by the court. It includes the majority, dissent, and concurrence |
| Summary | Searches both court-provided and LexisNexis-created summaries |
| Written by | Name of the judge(s) authoring the opinion, including the majority, concurrence, and dissent |

Source: *Using Segments on Lexis Advance*, available at https://lexisnexis.custhelp.com/app/lexisadvance.

a relevant case. If the researcher has identified the relevant point of law, he can then take the topic and key number from the appropriate headnote directly to the topic volumes of the digest to locate other cases that discuss the same point of law. A researcher, however, can also turn directly to the digest to locate the appropriate topic and key numbers for a research problem. Each digest has an index, called the Descriptive-Word Index. This multivolume index works much like other indexes. The researcher creates a list of keywords and then looks for each word or phrase in the index. The index will then direct the researcher to the appropriate topics volume or to another entry in the index. The researcher locates the appropriate volume where that topic is treated and then reads the headers for the appropriate key number. The researcher will skim the entries, noting the case reporter citation to read the entire case.

**Figure 6-7. Case Fields and Segments**

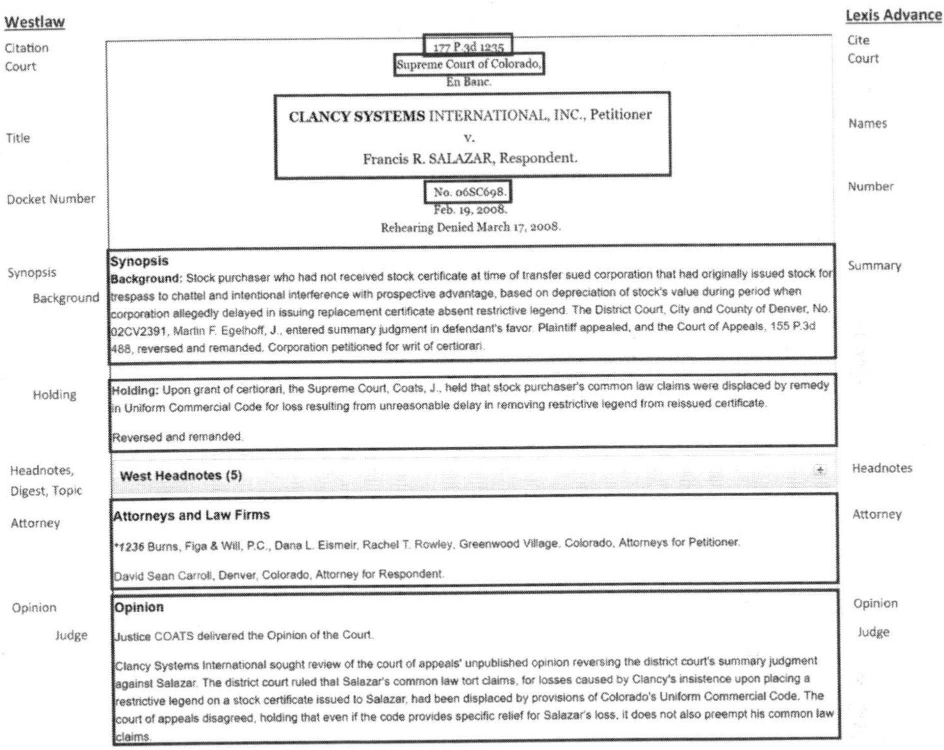


Reprinted from Westlaw with permission of Thomson Reuters.

Print digests are updated with pocket parts. Each pocket part is organized exactly like the hardbound volume. Therefore, a researcher would need to consult the topic in the pocket part to determine if other entries exist for the key number being researched. In print, the researcher can complete the updating by consulting the mini-digests in any reporter advance sheets published after the date of the digest pocket part.

A few other features about the digests deserve mention. Each topic contains coverage notes and a table of contents that lists key numbers under that topic. These features are shown in Figure 6-8. Researchers can use these features to see how extensively the editors have treated the topic. Occasionally, the West editors rearrange and renumber the key numbers within a topic. If this happens, the digest will contain a conversion table noting the new and old key number assignments.

**Figure 6-8. Coverage Notes and Table of Contents**

6 Colo D 2d—389

# COMMON LAW

## SUBJECTS INCLUDED

The body of customary and statutory law recognized and adopted in the several states as the basis of their jurisprudence, not created by express enactment by the legislatures of such states

Presumptions as to its existence and proof of its rules

Its sources, principles and maxims, and its application in general

## SUBJECTS EXCLUDED AND COVERED BY OTHER TOPICS

Jurisdiction of courts, remedies and procedure, distinction between the common-law and other systems of jurisprudence, see ACTION, PLEADING, EQUITY, ADMIRALTY and other specific topics

Particular questions of law, statement and application of governing common-law rules, see specific topics

Statutes modifying the common-law, see STATUTES and specific topics

**For detailed references to other topics, see Descriptive-Word Index**

---

*Analysis*

## 2. Online

### a. Westlaw

West has implemented the digest system on Westlaw through three different methods. First, Westlaw has created an online version of the digest. Accessible through the "Key Numbers" link, the digest can be browsed topically or searched by keywords. By using this latter approach, Westlaw will return those topics and key numbers that match the search terms. This feature saves time and relieves the researcher from having to search through the topics looking for an appropriate one. Once a relevant topic is identified, the researcher can then select the desired case law database and locate all cases using that topic and key number.

Second, researchers can launch into a digest search directly from within a case. If the researcher has already located an on-point case, the researcher can then scan that case's headnotes looking for appropriate topics and key numbers. Westlaw provides a link for each topic and key number in the case. By clicking on one of these links, the researcher can create a "custom digest" by selecting the desired jurisdictional database and even limiting the search by keyword. The custom digest returns all of the cases within that database that contain the headnotes with the topic and key number. The researcher can then sift through the results, reviewing the cases that appear relevant.

Researchers can also directly locate cases using the Digest, Topic, or Headnote field as mentioned earlier in this chapter. In this search, the researcher can either enter a keyword, topic, and/or key number to retrieve relevant cases. Only the Topic and Headnote fields of cases in the selected databases will be searched. A sample search in the Topic field would look like TO(85k11) where "85" is the topic number for Common Law and "k11" is the key number.[26] If the researcher can run that search in the Digest field, he can potentially narrow the search results to more relevant cases. An example of that search would be DI(85k11 and abrogat!) with which the researcher would find cases that discuss abrogation of the common law.

### b. Other Online Services

Other online research services may implement a digest through their own system of headnotes. For example, in Lexis Advance, the researcher may approach this topical research when starting with a case. As with West cases, Lex-

---

26. To simplify searching the digest online, West assigns numbers to the Topics. Researchers can either search topics using the names, if known, or the topic number.

**Figure 6-9. Lexis Headnotes in *Clancy***

▾ LexisNexis® Headnotes

Governments > Courts ▾ > Common Law ▾

Governments > Legislation ▾ > Interpretation ▾

***HN1*** **Courts, Common Law**
Subject to constitutional limitations, the General Assembly is vested with the power to legislate for this jurisdiction, Colo. Const. art. V, § 1. Although it has chosen to give the common law of England full force until repealed by legislative authority, Colo. Rev. Stat. § 2-4-211 (2007), it may therefore selectively modify or abrogate portions of that law, at its choice. The Colorado Supreme Court has long made clear, however, that courts will not lightly presume a legislative intent to do so; and as a matter of statutory interpretation, changes to the common law, as it has been adopted by the General Assembly, will be recognized only when they are expressly mandated or necessarily implied by subsequent legislation. More like this Headnote

*Shepardize* - Narrow by this Headnote

Commercial Law (UCC) > ... > General Provisions ▾ > Policies & Purposes ▾ > Supplemental Principles of Law ▾

***HN2*** **Policies & Purposes, Supplemental Principles of Law**
In adopting the Uniform Commercial Code, the General Assembly has expressly indicated its intent that preexisting principles of law and equity have continuing vitality and be treated as supplementing the code, unless they have been "displaced" by any of its particular provisions, Colo. Rev. Stat. § 4-1-103 (2007). Common law causes of action survive adoption of the code unless they have been explicitly referenced by name. Other jurisdictions have also rejected such a narrow understanding of the code's doctrine of "displacement" and have more fully explained their construction in terms of the code's purposes and structure. More like this Headnote

*Shepardize* - Narrow by this Headnote

Commercial Law (UCC) > ... > General Provisions ▾ > Policies & Purposes ▾ > Supplemental Principles of Law ▾

***HN3*** **Policies & Purposes, Supplemental Principles of Law**
The concept of "displacement," as used in the code, has been described as allowing the code to abrogate common law rules without requiring unequivocal, explicit reference to the common law in each statutory section that effects a modification. Rather, in furtherance of the code's goal of uniformity in commercial transactions, which would be undermined by variations in the common law among the several states, it should also be understood to intend the displacement of the common law whenever both the code and the common law would provide a means of recovery for the same loss. More like this Headnote

Reprinted with the permission of LexisNexis.

isNexis cases contain headnotes, although they are not the same headnotes as those that appear in West cases. Each headnote is categorized into a topic and subtopic, which are links to the topic hierarchy. After identifying a relevant headnote, the researcher can click on a link labeled "More Like this Headnote" to retrieve additional similar cases in the same or another jurisdiction. The researcher can also click on the topic or subtopic links to do further research in the topic hierarchy. Figure 6-9 highlights the first Lexis Advance headnote from the *Clancy* case that corresponds to the first headnote from Westlaw's publication of the same case.

Bloomberg Law has a limited set of headnotes, mostly dealing with transactional topics which it implemented into its online service with the acquisition of the Bureau of National Affairs, Inc. Bloomberg has also implemented a "headnote" system called "Points of Law." Using a computer-algorithm and not a human editor, Bloomberg will scan all of its case law to identify points of law within the cases and give researchers the ability to locate other similar cases based upon the results of this algorithm.

Casemaker lacks a digest or headnotes, as do the rest of the online services.

### E. Updating Case Law Research

The citator is the principal method for updating case law. As discussed in Chapter 7 the citator will list cases that have cited the case in hand, indicating whether the case is strengthened or weakened by later authority. Researchers must check the status of each relevant case uncovered during research using either print or online citators.

## VI. Additional Topics

### A. Briefs

In addition to locating a judicial opinion, the researcher may also want to locate the briefs written by the parties for the appeal. Briefs include the arguments of the parties used to persuade the court and can be a good source for locating relevant authorities, legal reasoning, and legal writing.

Both Westlaw and LexisNexis provide limited briefs for Colorado cases, with coverage starting in 2000. If a brief exists for a case, both services will provide a link to it from the case display. Researchers can also search brief databases directly.

In Colorado, the University of Colorado Law Library has collected many Colorado Supreme Court briefs, Colorado Supreme Court certiorari briefs, and Colorado Court of Appeals briefs. The collection of Colorado Supreme Court briefs dates to 1874 while the collection of Colorado Supreme Court certiorari briefs dates to 1970. The Colorado Court of Appeals briefs begins in 1893 and runs through 1915.

The University of Colorado Law Library is digitizing its collection of briefs. The researcher should check the law library's website to determine if the brief being researched is available online.[27]

27. The Colorado Supreme Court Briefs digital collection is located at http://lawcollections.colorado.edu/colorado-supreme-court-briefs/.

## B. Oral Arguments

Increasingly, courts are recording oral arguments and making them available on their website. The Colorado Judiciary's website publishes both live and archived oral argument recordings.[28] Dating to 2005, these recordings are available for both Supreme Court and Courts of Appeals hearings. The recordings can be selected from a list or searched with keywords. The list of recordings are organized by docket number and date. Case names and topics can be searched using the keyword search function.

## C. Unpublished Opinions

Not all appellate court opinions are published. While all supreme court opinions, at both the state and federal level, will be published, only a fraction of the intermediate appellate court opinions are published. Each intermediate appellate court may exercise its own discretion about which of its opinions it will publish. Generally, this decision is driven by the court's determination whether a case will add value to the doctrine in the jurisdiction.

The Colorado Court of Appeals does not publish all of its opinions. Pursuant to Colorado Appellate Rule 35(f),[29] the court may decide whether to publish its judicial decision. Researchers may request a copy of an unpublished opinion through the Court of Appeals' website. However, the researcher should consider that an unpublished decision will have no precedential impact and may likely not be permitted to be cited.

## D. Trial Court Documents

This chapter has mainly focused on locating appellate court opinions. Case law research is essentially the effort to locate decisions of the appellate courts, whose function it is to decide questions of law. However, researchers may want to find the work product of the trial courts. For instance, locating trial court orders help them understand how a particular judge has ruled on a particular issue.

At the state level, trial court decisions are very difficult to obtain for several reasons. First, the trial court usually does not issue an opinion. Rather, it will issue an order that may or may not contain an explanation. Second, the state

28. Appellate Courts Live Broadcast, available at https://www.courts.state.co.us/Courts/live/.

29. *Supra* n. 14.

trial courts rarely will publish that order. Certainly, it will be made available to the parties and may even be available to the other judges, clerks, and staff attorneys at that particular court, but rarely will it even be available to other members of that state's judiciary.

Despite these conditions, trial courts documents are becoming increasingly available on the online services. Westlaw includes a database of Colorado trial court documents which date back to 2002, but with selective coverage of motions, trial court memoranda, trial pleadings, and other civil trial filings from the Colorado state and federal courts. LexisNexis offers a selection of pleadings and motions from 2000. Bloomberg Law provides selective documents for the Denver and El Paso County district courts.

If these online services do not have the documents, the researcher should call the clerk of the court in which the proceedings took place and request copies, if available. Researchers can find contact information on the Colorado judiciaries' website.

## VII. Summary

Case law research is mainly concerned with finding appellate court opinions. These opinions are available from a wide variety of free-access websites such as the Colorado Judiciary's website and Google Scholar as well as subscription-based databases such as Westlaw, Lexis and similar commercial sources. While finding a case using a case name or docket number is a straight-forward search, to locate a collection of relevant cases, researchers will need to utilize keywords and topical case finding methods. The best of these later methods is West's American Digest System which researchers most frequently encounter when reviewing headnotes of cases published in West reporters or on Westlaw. While trial court documents are becoming more available, these are still more difficult to find. Curious researchers can consult available collections on Westlaw, LexisNexis and Bloomberg as well as call the clerk's office for the court in which the case was tried. Increasingly, briefs and oral arguments for Colorado appellate cases are available on the Colorado judiciary's website and may provide a useful understanding of the case's issues and arguments in support of the positions taken by counsel. All opinions of the Colorado Supreme Court are published but only select opinions of the Colorado Court of Appeals are published. Researchers will need to visit the Colorado Judiciary's website to request these unpublished opinions.

**Case Law Research Checklist**

- ❑ Has an analysis been completed to determine the issue(s), keywords and jurisdiction of the problem to be researched?
- ❑ Have appropriate search phrases been formulated for use in online case law databases?
- ❑ Does the problem concern a particular topic of law through which West's digest system and headnotes could be used to narrow the scope of the cases retrieved to those most likely relevant to the problem at hand?
- ❑ Have the cases been validated using a citator such as KeyCite or Shepard's?
- ❑ Is the case relatively recent, and if so, is there a need to review the briefs or oral arguments to understand the issues at bar and how counsel argued them?
- ❑ Is the source of cases used the most cost efficient and still most likely to provide the most complete set of results?
- ❑ Is there a need to locate trial court documents? Does the researcher have access to one of the online services that provides them or will the clerk of the court for the matter need to be called?

# Chapter 7

# Updating Law with a Citator

## I. Introduction

One of the hallmarks of legal research is that the law changes. Cases, statutes, and regulations may all be amended by legal authorities which can result in changing their meaning or effect. Legal researchers are tasked to identify the current status of the law they use in their work product. They are required to faithfully represent to the court that the cases, statutes, and regulations the lawyer is relying upon for their legal arguments is in fact still valid law and accurately represents the current state of the law. Previous chapters have covered some methods for updating research. These have included consulting pocket parts, supplements and websites for updated statutory information, and the Colorado Secretary of State's website for updated regulatory information. This chapter covers a different tool for updating authority. It is the citator.

The earliest citator was produced by Frank B. Shepard in the latter half of the 19th century. It was published as *Shepard's Citations*, referred to as Shepard's. It solved the problem of ensuring that cases were still valid and had not been overturned or had the soundness of the decision questioned by later court. The earliest versions of Shepard's were little notes that attorneys pasted into the margins of their case reporters. The note would indicate the volume and page number of a later case that cited to the case they were reading, something the attorney would otherwise manually do by hand-written citation (See Figure 7-1). The notes were prepared by editors at Shepard's company and attorneys would subscribe to the service. In later years, Shepard's citations would be published in separate volumes, organized by court reporter volume and page number for each case being researched. In addition to indicating which later court cited to the current case, it would also indicate if that later case

**Figure 7-1. Shepard's Notes in a *Colorado Reports* Case**

248 GRIFFITH v. WRIGHT. [Dec. T.,

in its facts, and the court refused to disturb the verdict.

The judgment of the court below is affirmed with costs.

*Affirmed.*

---

DECEMBER TERM, 1882.

---

GRIFFITH v. WRIGHT.

| | |
|---|---|
| 6 | 248 |
| 8 | 350 |
| 9 | 24 |
| 11 | 407 |
| 11 | 410 |
| 6 | 248 |
| 13 | 570 |
| 6 | 248 |
| 14 | 510 |

20/402
22/172
10a30

The essential elements of estoppel by conduct are:

(*a*) There must have been a representation or concealment of material facts.

(*b*) The representations must have been made with *knowledge* of the facts, unless the party making them was bound to know the facts, or ignorance thereof was the result of gross negligence.

(*c*) The party to whom the representations were made must have been ignorant of the truth of the matter.

(*d*) They must have been made with the intention that they should act upon them; but gross and culpable negligence upon the part of the party sought to be estopped, the effect of which is to work a fraud on the party setting up the estoppel, supplies the place of intent.

(*e*) The other party must have been induced to act upon them. All the essential elements must be present.

*Error to District Court of Ouray County.*

THE facts are stated in the opinion.

Mr. WM. STORY and THOMAS GEORGE, for plaintiff in error.

Messrs. STALLCUP and LUTHE, for defendants in error.

BECK, J. The decree in this case enjoining the plaintiff in error from selling the lots mentioned in the trust deed, and decreeing the cancellation and release of the trust deed, must have been based on the ground of estoppel by conduct, although the proofs fail to show payment of the treated the current case negatively and even to what headnote in the current case was impacted by the latter case. The publication became so commonly used by attorneys that they refer to this process as "Shepardizing."

These features are found in the current online version of Shepard's which is produced by LexisNexis and found on Lexis Advance. Since 1996, West has produced its own citator, called KeyCite. It works the same way as Shepard's, though as this chapter will indicate, it uses different symbols to denote the status of a law. Fundamentally, current citators provide the same two valuable services as their ancestors. First, they provide the status or validity of a case, statute, or regulation. Second, they help the researcher locate additional authority.

Citators are classified as finding aids. They provide no discussion or commentary about the authority, save to indicate the editor's opinion about the status of the law. Other online services, including Bloomberg Law and Casemaker, provide some citator functions. This chapter will review the mechanics of citators and how researchers use them to locate relevant Colorado law.

## II. Nomenclature and Usage

Citators provide two functions. They indicate if the authority is still good law and they also help the researcher find additional, relevant authority. The starting point is always the authority being currently researched. This authority—case, statute, or regulation—can be referred to as the "cited authority" or "case in hand" or "cited case" or "Shepardized case" or even "KeyCited case."[1] While citators apply to statutes and regulations, they are mostly used to validate case law. This chapter will focus on using citators to validate and extend case law research and will use the term "*cited case*" to denote the case that is being researched. Alternatively, the case that cites the cited case is often referred to as the "*citing case*."

A case's validity can be challenged in two ways. It can be challenged by a later opinion issued by a court in its appellate line. For example, a Colorado Court of Appeals decision can be appealed to the Colorado Supreme Court which may issue a negative opinion on the Court of Appeals decision. This evolution of the case is termed its history or *direct history*.

A case's validity may also be challenged by a case outside of its direct history. For example, a Colorado Supreme Court decision may be questioned by the

1. While citators are used for cases, statutes, and regulations, they are primarily used for case law research.

**Table 7-1. Partial List of Treatment Indicators for Case Citators**

| Treatment | Direct History | Indirect History |
|---|---|---|
| Negative | Reversed, Affirmed in Part and Reversed in Part | Overruled, Abrogated, Superseded |
| Cautionary | Affirmed on Other Grounds; Modified, Superseded | Criticized, Distinguished, Questioned |
| Positive or Neutral | Affirmed, Certification Denied | Explained, Followed, Harmonized |

Kansas Supreme Court. While the Kansas court has no power to reverse or overrule the Colorado court, the Kansas court may challenge the soundness of the Colorado decision. Similarly, a later Colorado Supreme Court decision may overrule the earlier Colorado Supreme Court decision and the law from that prior case is no longer good law. In both situations, this evolution of the case is termed its *indirect history*.

Cited cases can receive three types of treatment by later courts—negative, cautionary, or positive. (See Table 7-1.) Treatment is assigned by legal editors at the publishing companies. If a case receives negative or cautionary analysis, researchers need to explore the basis for that designation. The case may still be valid for how the researcher intended to use the case.

Negative treatment indicates the case is no longer "good" law. The citing case has determined that the holding or rationale of the cited case is legally unsound. Negative analysis may be marked as "Reversed" or "Overruled." If the latter case is within the cited case's history, then the case will be reversed. If the latter case is outside of the cited case's history, then it would be overruled. If researchers are relying on a case that has been marked with negative treatment, researchers need to review the citing case to determine why it was so designated. If the cited case was reversed, the cited case is likely not usable because this designation would be assigned by a court higher in the direct history of the cited case. If it was overruled, only part of the case may no longer be good law. Researchers need to determine whether the particular point of law of the cited case is no longer good law or was not implicated by the citing case.

Cautionary treatment indicates the cited case's rationale is not applicable to the citing case's facts or challenged by the citing case. Cautionary analysis may be marked as "Affirmed on Other Grounds," "Criticized," "Distinguished," or "Questioned." As with negative treatment, researchers need to explore the citing case to determine what part of the cited case is being challenged.

Finally, positive or neutral analysis indicates the citing case agrees with the holding and rationale of the cited case, or is simply noting the cited case as support for its own rationale and holding. Positive or neutral analysis may be marked as "Affirmed," "Explained," "Followed," or "Harmonized."

## III. Implementing Citator Analysis in Citator Services

Each citator implements this analysis function in similar but different ways (See Table 7-2). All services mark the case with a treatment symbol and provide links to the citing cases in its direct and indirect history. Citators are not particularly difficult to use, and offer a great deal of assistance to researchers. The following examples show how the various citators indicate status and implement direct and indirect history.

### A. Lexis Advance's Shepard's Citator Service

Lexis Advance's citator service is Shepard's. Figure 7-2 shows the initial case display of the *Martin* case. The Shepard's signal is seen in the Figure 7-2 Box A. In this case, the symbol is a red stop sign and indicates the case has received negative treatment. Researchers can glean an initial indication of the reason for the negative analysis by referring to Box B in Figure 7-2 and can retrieve a full Shepard's report by following the links denoted in the figure.

In this instance, the Shepard's brief report indicates that subsequent appellate history treated this cited case negatively.

At this point, researchers should retrieve a full Shepard's report for this case, which is displayed in Figure 7-3. On the figure, in Box A, researchers are presented with the different types of information provided by the citator, including Appellate History, Citing Decisions, and Other Citing Sources. The default view is Citing Decisions, which is another term for Indirect History. In Box B, researchers are notified that the Direct History includes negative analysis. The list of citing cases follows, and this list is initially sorted by court hierarchy, which can be changed, as noted in Box C. The cited case is highlighted in yellow in the citing references. Researchers can further narrow this list of cases by choosing options in Box D including narrowing by type of analysis and court. Finally, re-

**Table 7-2. Citator Symbols and Their Meaning**

| Treatment | Indicator | Case/Agency Decision | Statute/Regulation |
|---|---|---|---|
| **Negative** | | | |
| Shepard's | Red Stop Sign | strong negative history or treatment of your case (for example, overruled by or reversed) | NA |
| | Red Exclamation Point (!) in neutral circle | NA | strong negative treatment of the statutory section (for example, the section may have been found to be unconstitutional or void) |
| KeyCite | Red Flag | no longer good for at least one point of law | amended, repealed, superseded, or held unconstitutional or preempted in whole or in part. |
| BCite | White Negative Sign (-) in red square;<br>White Circle in Red Background | Negative treatment | NA |
| Casemaker | Red "thumbs down" | Case reversed, overruled in whole or in part, superseded, questioned, vacated, withdrawn or criticized. | NA |
| **Cautionary** | | | |
| Shepard's | White 'Q' in Yellow Background | treatment that questions the continuing validity or precedential value of your case because of intervening circumstances, including judicial or legislative overruling. | NA |
| | Yellow Triangle | history or treatment that may have a significant negative impact on your case (for example, limited or criticized by). | NA |

**Table 7-2. Citator Symbols and Their Meaning, *continued***

| Treatment | Indicator | Case/Agency Decision | Statute/Regulation |
|---|---|---|---|
| **Cautionary** | | | |
| KeyCite | Yellow Flag | the case or administrative decision has some negative treatment, but not reversed or overruled. | proposed legislation or rule available, court decision has questioned validity, or prior version received negative treatment from a court. |
| BCite | White Forward Slash (/) in Blue Square;<br>White Triangle in yellow square | Cautionary Analysis. | NA |
| Casemaker | NA | NA | NA |
| **Positive or Neutral** | | | |
| Shepard's | White Plus Sign (+) in Green Diamond | history or treatment that has a positive impact on your case (for example, affirmed or followed by). | NA |
| | White 'A' in blue octagon | treatment of your case that is neither positive nor negative (for example, explained). | NA |
| | White 'I' in blue octagon | citing references are available for your case, but the references do not have history or treatment analysis (for example, the references are law review citations). | NA |
| KeyCite | Blue-Stripped Flag | A blue-striped flag indicates a document has been appealed to the U.S. Courts of Appeals or the U.S. Supreme Court (excluding appeals originating from agencies). | |
| BCite | White Plus Sign (+) in Green Square | Positive treatment. | NA |
| Casemaker | Green "thumbs up" | Case is good law. | NA |

**Figure 7-2 Shepard's Indicators for a Case on Lexis Advance**

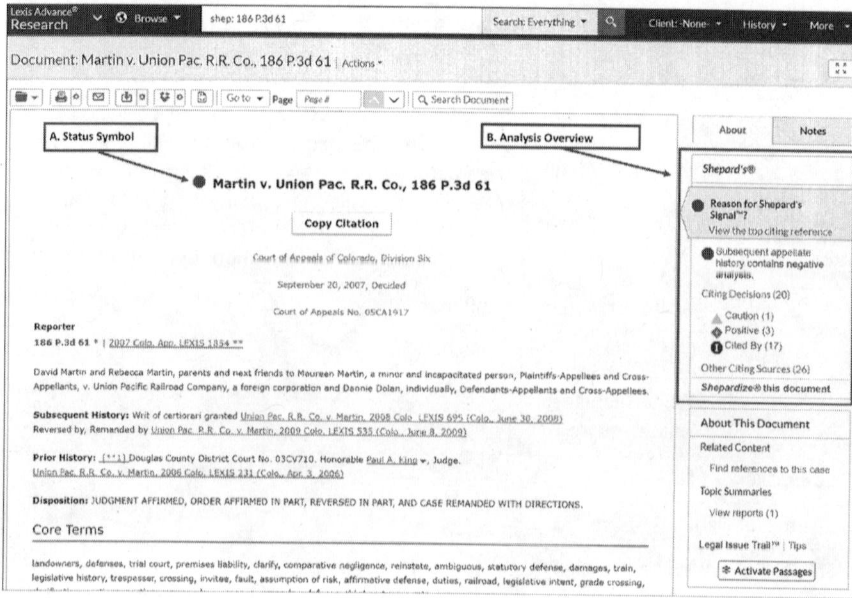


Reprinted with the permission of LexisNexis.

searchers should note the Shepard's symbols attached to the citing cases, as noted by Box E. Initially, these are confusing. They indicate how the citing case is itself treated by their citing cases. In Figure 7-3, the first case has received neutral treatment while the second case has received negative treatment.

Most importantly, researchers will want to read the negative citing cases. They can locate these cases by clicking through the Appellate History link, as shown in Figure 7-4. In this figure, Box A is the cited case. In Shepard's this cited case is called the "Shepardized" case. Box B provides the citation of the case that reversed the cited case. In this example, the Colorado Supreme Court reversed a decision of the Colorado Court of Appeals. Researchers can click on the case name to read the full opinion of the citing case.

## B. Westlaw's KeyCite Service

KeyCite provides the same functionality as Shepard's but does so with a different presentation of the information. Figure 7-5 shows the *Martin* case on Westlaw. In Box A, researchers should note the red flag indicating the case has received negative treatment. In Box B, the KeyCite service provides the type of negative treatment and citing case that negatively affected the cited case.

**Figure 7-3. Citing References in Shepard's**

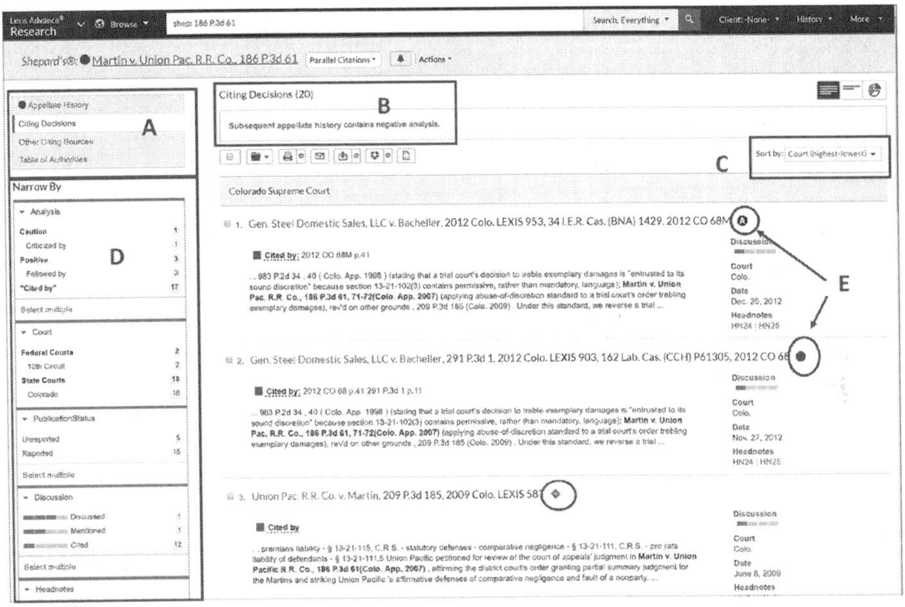


Reprinted with the permission of LexisNexis.

Researchers should also note the six tabs under the case name in Box A. These tabs contain the KeyCite analysis providing access to direct and indirect history as well as secondary authority and other documents that cite to the cited case.

Researchers can jump directly to the negative citing case, as noted, or click on the "Negative Treatment" tab to view all negative citing cases, as shown in Figure 7-6.

The History tab provides a complete case history, as shown in Figure 7-7. Notably, KeyCite defaults to a graphical display of the case history, showing which cases occurred in the trial and appellate courts. Researchers can open to any of the cases in the display. A similar feature is offered in Shepard's on Lexis Advance.

Finally, researchers can locate citing cases in the indirect history. In Westlaw, indirect history is called "Citing References" and can be found under that named tab, as shown in Figure 7-8. This history includes appellate court cases, trial court cases, and secondary authority. Figure 7-8 is showing the appellate court case listing, as indicated by Box B. Researchers can narrow results using the post-search filters in Box C. These filters limit the cases by court and treatment, among other options.

## Figure 7-4. Direct History in Shepard's

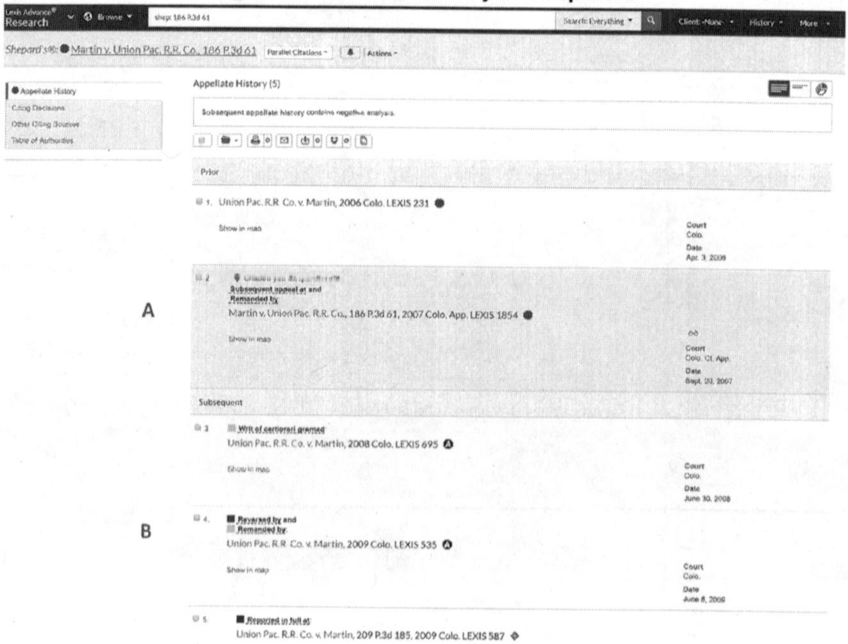


Reprinted with the permission of LexisNexis.

## Figure 7-5. KeyCite Signals in a Westlaw Case

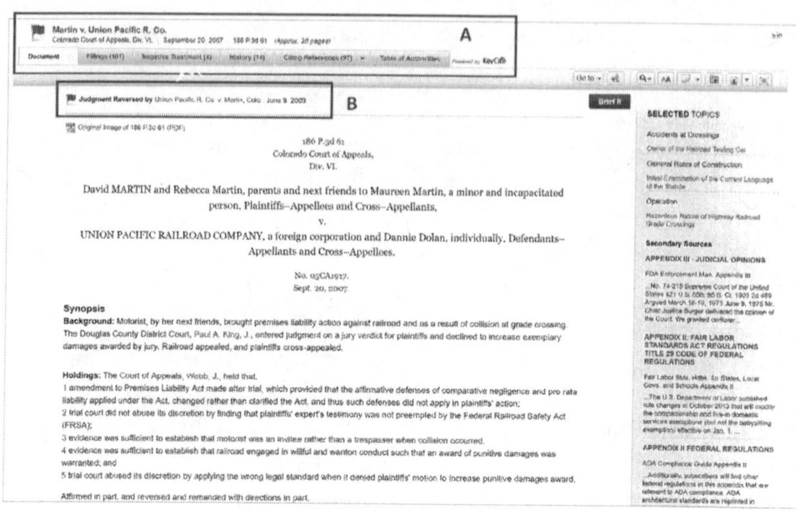


Reprinted from Westlaw with permission of Thomson Reuters.

**Figure 7-6. Negative Direct History in a KeyCite Report**

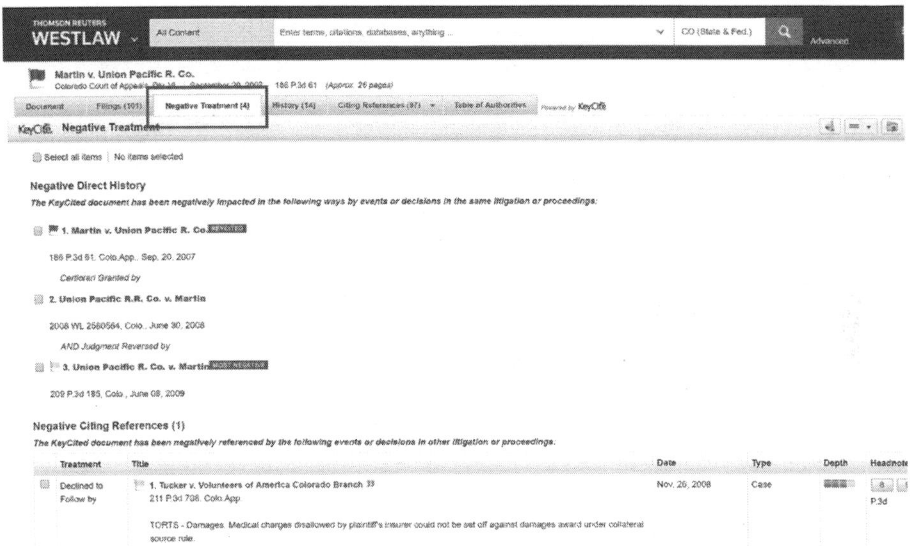


Reprinted from Westlaw with permission of Thomson Reuters.

## C. BloombergLaw's BCite Service

Bloomberg's citation service, like BloombergLaw itself, is a relative newcomer to the legal research platform market. The service is called BCite and while somewhat more limited than Shepard's and KeyCite, it does offer basic citator service providing both a direct and indirect history of a case. BCite provides indirect history citing cases under the "Case Analysis" tab which can be filtered by court and treatment, among other things.

## Figure 7-7. Graphical Display of Direct History in a KeyCite Report

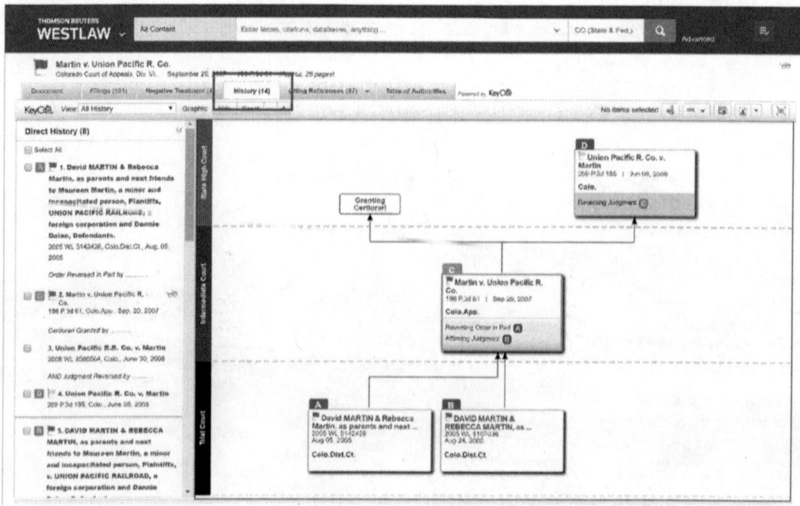


Reprinted from Westlaw with permission of Thomson Reuters.

## Figure 7-8. Citing References Report in KeyCite

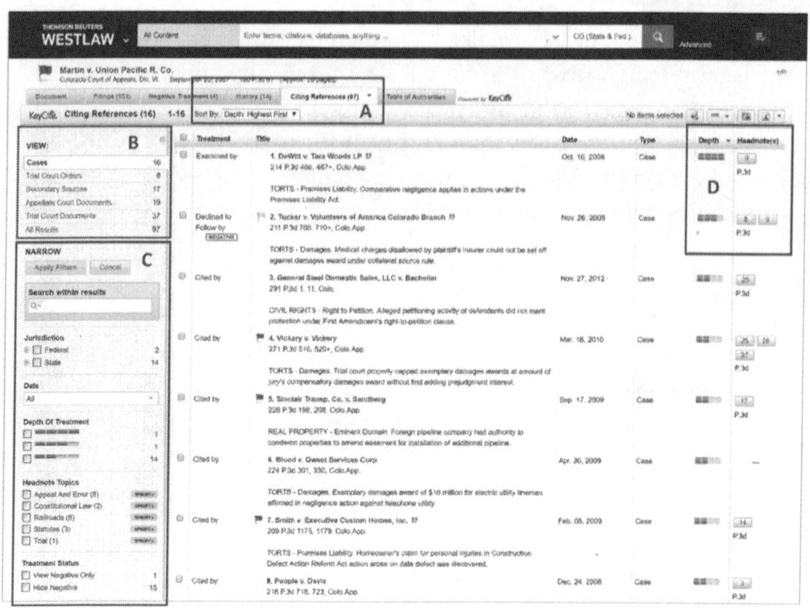


Reprinted from Westlaw with permission of Thomson Reuters.

## D. Casemaker

The Casemaker research platform offers a simplified citator. Treatment of a case is indicated above the case name and citation, as shown in Figure 7-9. In this instance, the negative treatment of this case is given a red "thumbs down" symbol. Researchers will need to click on the symbol to retrieve a full citator report.

**Figure 7-9. Citator Signals in Casemaker**

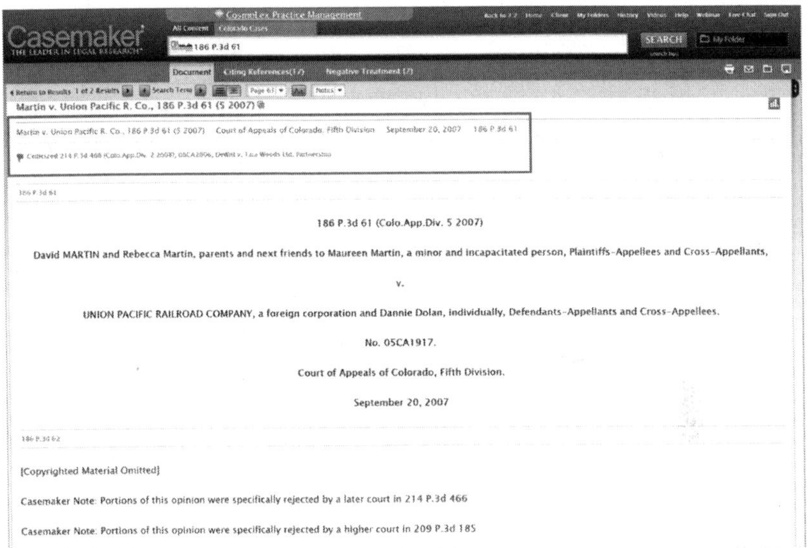




Researchers can review the full citator report. It includes Negative Treatment (Figure 7-10) and Citing Materials (Figure 7-11). The latter is the equivalent of Indirect History.

## Figure 7-10. Negative Treatment in Casemaker

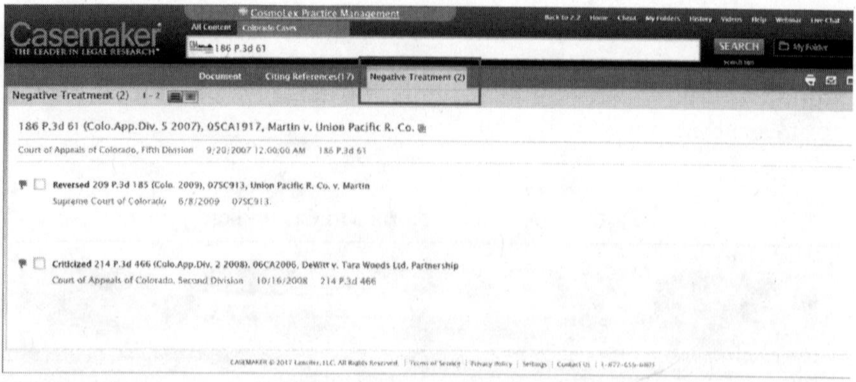

Reprinted with permission of Casemaker.

## Figure 7-11. Citing References in Casemaker

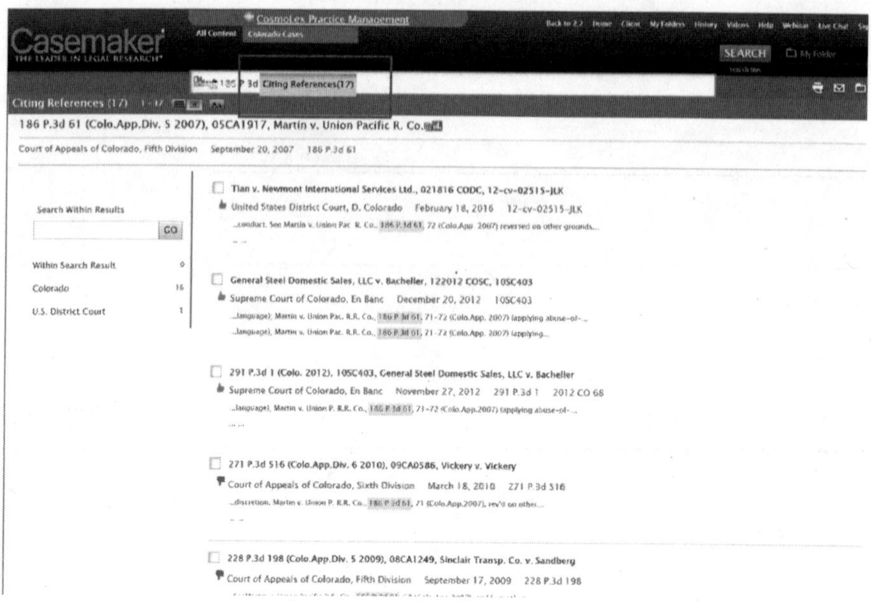

Reprinted with permission of Casemaker.

All of these preceding examples have shown the citator report for the same Colorado case, Martin v. Union Pacific R. Co., 186 P.3d 61 (2007). Readers may note that some of the citators provided different numbers of citing cases. For some cited cases, the citators may even report their status differently. Again, each publishing company may use different methods to determine the status of a case, leading to potential different citator report outcomes. Researchers need to explore the underlying authority supporting or undermining a particular cited case. If available, they may also want to use two or more services to ensure they are receiving a complete understanding of the status of the cited case.

## IV. Other Features of Citators

### A. Finding Cases with Citing References

In addition to validating law, citators also help researchers to find additional, relevant case law. This capability is offered through the indirect history, which may be termed in citator services as "citing references," "citing decisions," or "citing documents." These cases are ones that have cited the cited case for the holding or some proposition of law stated within the case. These citing cases are deemed relevant because if they are citing the cited case, they must have some relevant relationship to the cited case.

Researchers use these references to expand their case law research. At this point, researchers should note the difference between case finding in a digest and a citator. The citator looks forward in time from the publication of the cited case. While the citing cases may cite the cited case for a point of law, the citing cases will only be those cases doing so after the cited case was published. Furthermore, the list of citing cases may not be comprehensive for any particular point of law from the cited case. In contrast, the digest is a comprehensive collection of cases citing a particular point of law. It is comprehensive in time and in coverage. Digests will include all cases, whenever published, not just those cases published after our cited case. Plus, it includes all cases from all jurisdictions whether or not they have cited the citing case. Therefore, while researchers should use citing reference to expand their case law research, they should continue to use a digest for comprehensive topical case law research.

Figures 7-4, 7-8 and 7-11 all show citing references for the *Martin* case from Shepard's, KeyCite, and Casemaker. All three displays are relatively similar. They all include a list of cases with citation and brief description. They all include post-search filters in the left-hand column of the page. They all provide a means to narrow the list of cases by jurisdiction and level of court. They all provide "depth of treatment" indicators which are an estimate of how much the citing case discussed the cited case. Finally, Shepard's and KeyCite indicate the headnote from the cited case that is referenced by the citing case. The next two sections will address headnotes and depth of treatment indicators.

## B. Headnotes

Headnotes are the summaries of the points of law discussed in cases. As noted in Chapter 6, West provides the most comprehensive and long-standing collection of headnotes. Headnotes are useful because they enable researchers to find all cases citing a particular topic or point of law. LexisNexis also provides headnote analysis for cases published on its Lexis Advance service. Citators from West and LexisNexis identify which headnotes from the cited case are noted by the citing cases. Researchers should also recall that West and LexisNexis use a different system of headnotes, and these are not interchangeable. These headnote identifiers appear in the list of citing references or citing decisions. For example, in Figure 7-8, Box D highlights that the *DeWitt* case referenced headnote 9 from the *Martin* case. Likewise, the *Tucker* case referenced headnotes 8 and 9 from the *Martin* case. This means that the *DeWitt* court found *Martin* relevant only for headnote 8 while the *Tucker* court only found *Martin* relevant for headnotes 8 and 9. Researchers can use this information in two ways. First, researchers relying upon a case for a particular headnote can narrow the list of citing references to only those cases citing the cited case for that particular headnote. This narrowing is done through the post-search filters on the left-hand column of the page. Second, researchers can still use a case that receives cautionary or even negative treatment if that treatment does not apply to the headnote in question. The case may still have other defects, and researchers need to fully explore such cases. But the main value is that this feature saves time and increases research efficiency and effectiveness.

Shepard's has a long but varied history with headnotes. Shepard's will also indicate which headnotes have been tagged by the citing case. Online, those headnotes point to the Lexis case headnotes, not the West case headnotes. In print, Shepard's included headnotes until 2006. Notably, those headnotes referenced West's headnotes from their reporter system.

Neither BloombergLaw's BCite nor Casemaker offer this feature.

### C. Depth of Treatment Indicators

Online citators provide another useful feature for research—depth of treatment or discussion indicators. These indicators, often displayed as a row of boxes which are partially to fully completed, are estimates of how much the citing case discussed the cited case. While inexact, a case that is marked with all of the boxes completed has discussed the cited case a great deal. Whereas, a case that is marked as one or two boxes completed has only discussed the cited case a little bit. For example, in Figure 7-8, Box D, the *DeWitt* case shows a completely filled out depth of treatment indicator for its discussion of the *Martin* case. This suggests that *DeWitt* spoke at length about *Martin*. The next case in the list, *Tucker*, has three of the four boxes complete, suggesting that the *Tucker* court discussed *Martin* a little less than the *Dewitt* court. Similarly, in Figure 7-3, the *General Steel* court only briefly discussed *Martin* as indicated by the one box of four that is filled in. These indicators are guides and can help researchers focus on cases that might prove more useful for research.

## V. Using Citators for Colorado Legal Research

With the various features offered by citators, how can researchers of Colorado law benefit from their use? First, Colorado legal researchers need to validate their case, statutory, and regulatory law as all legal researchers must. Second, Colorado legal researchers can use the services to find additional, and more recent, case law citing the cited case for its holding or for any point of law identified in its headnotes. It is in this application that Colorado legal researchers can use the post-search filters to narrow the list of cases to those from Colorado and related federal courts. Finally, Colorado legal researchers can find relevant secondary authority and other forms of primary authority. The citations to secondary authority, also typically found in the citing references tab, can lead researchers to the broader understanding and additional citations of the authority, as noted in Chapters 9 and 10.

## VI. Summary

Updating law is an important step in the legal research process. Citators help researchers update their case, statutory and regulatory law research by identifying later authority that cites to and may undermine the credibility of earlier authority. Citators are most particularly used for case law research. The case being researched is called the cited case while the later case is called the citing case. Citators also help deepen case law research by including citations to all cases that have cited the case being researched. Some citators allow researchers to narrow cases by headnotes, or points of law, referenced in the cited case. The oldest citator is Shepard's Citations, which is now part of Lexis Nexis and available in both print and online formats. West produces its own citator, KeyCite, which is part of Westlaw. BloombergLaw's citator is BCite and Casemaker also offers citator features. Researchers should use citator analysis as an indication of the status of a case but need to probe into the underlying cases to determine why and to what extent a later case undermines an earlier case. Researchers can use two more citators to ensure accurate coverage.

**Citator Checklist**

- ❑ Is the authority being researched included by a citator? Is it a case, statute or regulation?
- ❑ For the citator service you are using, how does it indicate the status of the authority? What do the symbols mean?
- ❑ For cases that receive negative treatment, did you determine why? Was it a case in the cited cases direct or indirect history? Is the case from a binding jurisdiction?
- ❑ For cases receiving negative treatment, does the citing case reverse the cited case, overturn it completely, or undermine one or more points of law from the cited case? Are you using the cited case for one of those points of law?
- ❑ For all cases, did you check the citing references to find additional relevant cases? Did you narrow by headnote to focus on those cases most relevant to your research problem? Did you use the depth of treatment indicators to help identify the most helpful cases?

# Chapter 8

# Researching Colorado Court Rules

## I. Introduction

Court rules provide for the orderly operation of courts and assist in the disposition of litigation before the courts. Article VI, Section 21 of the Colorado Constitution grants to the Colorado Supreme Court the authority to "promulgate rules governing all courts," including "practice and procedure in civil and criminal cases."[1] The Colorado Supreme Court has promulgated court rules for civil procedure, criminal procedure, evidence, appellate procedure, and other matters falling within the court's jurisdiction (See Table 8-1 for a complete list of Colorado court rules). Courts may issue their own local rules, however, those rules must not be inconsistent with the Colorado Rules of Civil Procedure and must be approved by the Colorado Supreme Court.[2] Legal researchers need to identify which rules apply to their particular matter and how to interpret those rules.

This chapter will address finding both the rules that govern litigation in Colorado and the forms litigants can use related to those rules, as well as updating those rules.

## II. Rules Publications

### A. Print

Most jurisdictions, including Colorado, publish court rules in their set of state statutes. Court rules have been included in Colorado statutory editions since 1908. In the CRS, the entire collection of court rules is published in two

1. Colo. Const. art. VI, §21.
2. Colo. R. Civ. P. 121(b).

**Table 8-1. Listing of Colorado Court Rules**

- ❑ Colorado Rules of Civil Procedure
- ❑ Rules Governing Admission to the Bar
- ❑ Unauthorized Practice of Law Rules
- ❑ Colorado Rules of Procedure Regarding Attorney Discipline and Disability Proceedings, Colorado Attorneys' Fund for Client Protection and Mandatory Continuing Legal Education and Judicial Education
- ❑ Code of Professional Responsibility (Former Appendix to Chapters 18 to 20)
- ❑ Colorado Rules of Professional Conduct (Appendix to Chapters 18 to 20)
- ❑ Library
- ❑ Professional Service Companies
- ❑ Rules Governing Contingent Fees
- ❑ Rules of Procedure for Judicial Bypass of Parental Notification Requirements
- ❑ Rules of Judicial Discipline
- ❑ Rules of County Court Civil Procedure
- ❑ Rules of Procedure for Small Claims Courts
- ❑ Rules of Probate Procedure
- ❑ Rules of Juvenile Procedure
- ❑ Rules of Criminal Procedure
- ❑ Rules Governing the Creation, Appointment, Terms, and Procedure for the Public Defender Commission
- ❑ Rules for County Court Violations Bureaus
- ❑ Rules for Traffic Infractions
- ❑ Municipal Court Rules of Procedure
- ❑ Rules of Jury Selection and Service
- ❑ Appellate Rules
- ❑ Rules of Evidence
- ❑ Rules for Reapportionment Commission Proceedings
- ❑ Rules for Magistrates
- ❑ Uniform Local Rules for All State Water Court Divisions
- ❑ Rules Governing the Commissions on Judicial Performance
- ❑ Public Access to Records and Information
- ❑ Local Court Rules

volumes entitled "Court Rules." The researcher will need to consult the table of contents for each of the two volumes to determine which volume publishes which set of rules. In addition to the rule text, the publications also include case annotations, research cross-references, and forms in the various appendices to the rule collections.

In the CRSA, most of the court rules are published in a separate set of volumes. Rules published in these volumes include the rules of civil procedure, county court and small claims court procedure, and appellate court procedure, among others. However, West has published other sets of rules following the code sections they pertain to. For example, the Colorado Rules of Probate Procedure are printed after the end of Title 15—"Probate, Trusts, and Fiduciaries."

Colorado court rules are printed in other publications as well. West publishes all of the Colorado court rules in a single volume called *Colorado Court Rules*.[3] Designed for practitioners needing access to the rules' text, this softbound volume is compact and complete, including forms, but unannotated. It is published annually and updated with a semi-annual pocket part incorporating any rules changes since publication of the softbound volume. The researcher should consult the preface of both the softbound volume and pocket part supplement to determine currentness. This volume is one of two volumes in a Colorado court rules set. The companion volume contains federal court rules for the federal courts in Colorado.

West also publishes the Colorado Rules of Civil Procedure as part of its *Colorado Practice Series*.[4] This helpful publication reprints the rules and includes extensive commentary and annotations. The series also includes civil procedure forms with commentary.[5]

Additionally, publishers may also reprint some selection of court rule sets as separate publications. These are designed to be handy references for practitioners. For example, the Colorado Bar Association publishes the rules of evidence in a separate volume to aid litigator, student, and researcher alike.[6] While a researcher is currently best advised to search the judiciary's website for local court rules, some print publications compile the local rules from district and county courts.[7]

## B. Online

A digital version of the CRS is available through the General Assembly's website as well as on LexisNexis. Likewise, the CRSA is found on Westlaw. Researchers can also access court rules as separate collections on both services. On LexisNexis, court rules are found in the collection titled Colorado Local, State & Federal Court Rules.[8] This collection includes many of the court rules

3. *Colorado Court Rules* (Thomson-West 2016).

4. Sheila K. Hyatt & Stephen A. Hess, *Colorado Civil Rules Annotated* (4th ed., Thomson-West 2005).

5. Debra Knapp, *Colorado Civil Procedure Forms and Commentary* (2d ed., Thomson-West 2005).

6. Ellen Buckley, *Colorado Rules of Evidence Annotated* (2009–2010 ed., Continuing Legal Education in Colorado, Inc. 2009).

7. *Colorado Local Court Rules* (Robert L. Tonsing & Ethan A. Jacobson eds., Colorado Legal Publishing Co., Inc. 2002).

8. This collection is the CORULE file.

found in the CRS but also includes the local rules for the First Judicial District and the County Court for the City and County of Denver, and rules regulating practice before the federal district court and bankruptcy courts in Colorado.[9] On Westlaw, the Colorado rules are found within the Colorado Court Rules Annotated database. This database contains court rules governing practice in Colorado state courts and as with LexisNexis includes the local court rules for the First Judicial District court encompassing Jefferson and Gilpin counties.

The Colorado court rules are also available without charge from LexisNexis through the General Assembly's website. They are part of the online CRS collection as a separate listing entitled "Colorado Court Rules." The contents and presentation of the rules are exactly as published in the print edition of the CRS.

For local court rules, researchers can consult the judiciary's website at www.courts.state.co.us. Each district and county court has a page on the judiciary's website. In addition to information about the court, this page may include a link to their local rules, if adopted. Of course, researchers can also call any court's clerk to determine if it has adopted local rules.

Similarly, Colorado's water courts have adopted their own set of local rules. These rules are available on the water courts' page on the judicial branch's website.[10]

# III. Research Method

## A. Determining Which Rules to Use

To use these court rules, the researcher must first determine which court will hear the action and the subject matter of the action. Is this a civil or criminal case? Is the case before an appellate court or a trial court? If it is before a trial court, is it a district court, county court, or municipal court? Is the case proceeding in small claims court or, alternatively, in water court? Is the subject of the case controlled by special rules crafted for that subject? For example, does the case concern attorney or judicial discipline or admission to the bar?

---

9. Researchers can find this collection of court rules in a number of different ways including navigating through the State tab to the Colorado collection or typing "Colorado Rules" or CORULE while browsing for sources. Of course, researchers can also enter in a citation directly or search by keyword in the search bar.

10. Water Courts, Colorado State Judicial Branch, https://www.courts.state.co.us/Courts/Water/Rules.cfm.

Although a researcher should be able to answer these questions with relative ease, inexperienced researchers may find it helpful to ask these questions when approaching a court rules research question.

Once the appropriate court and subject matter are determined, the researcher can locate the appropriate rules in the CRS or other Colorado court rules publication. If the researcher is in doubt as to whether these rules apply to the matter, she should read the "scope" or "scope and purpose" rule for that particular set of rules. Generally located as one of the first few rules, this helpful rule states which matters this set of rules applies to.

## B. Finding Rules

As with statutory research, in rules research it is most helpful to use an annotated set of court rules. Both the CRS and CRSA contain annotated court rules, as do their digital counterparts on the General Assembly's website, LexisNexis, and Westlaw.

In the CRS, while the rules are indexed in the statute's general index volumes, most sets of rules also contain their own index. If provided, this index will immediately follow the rules themselves. Researchers should note that the index to the Rules of Civil Procedure is located after the Colorado Code of Judicial Conduct, Chapter 24 of the CRCP.

In the CRSA, the rules are indexed in the multivolume general index. Additionally, the rules are indexed in the index that follows each title where rules appear.

## C. Reading Rules

Structurally, court rules are similar to statutes, and researchers should read them like they read statutory language. After reading the rule and checking cross-references to other rules, the researcher should review the editorially provided annotations and the case summaries in particular.

If the researchers avail themselves of one of the Colorado rules practice treatises, they can use this publication to find and interpret the rules. As with other legal topics, secondary authority is often the best starting point for research.

## D. Finding Forms

The Colorado Supreme Court has included approved forms for use with the rules. These forms provide approved pleadings that litigants can use for their own actions. These forms are published in appendices following the rule sets. The CRS, CRSA, and other collections of Colorado court rules will include those forms. The Colorado Supreme Court has also posted these forms on their website.[11]

## E. Updating Rules Research

From time to time, court rules need to be revised and created. As court rules are a creature of the Colorado Supreme Court, the Court has established standing committees to review, amend, and author court rules.[12] With approval from the Supreme Court, these new and amended rules are eventually integrated into the print and online collections. Until such publication, researchers have a few resources to check for new or amended rules.

### 1. Print Resources

Researchers have few options when using print resources to update their court rules research. West publishes a Legislative Service update as part of its CRSA set. This publication includes an appendix of court rule changes. West compiles those amended rules based on orders it receives from the Colorado courts. These publications include changes to both rule language and approved forms. West publishes a cumulative table of court rules changes toward the back of each Legislative Services issue. When using the CRSA set, researchers should also check the appropriate pocket part and Interim Update Service for rules changes.

Other print resources for rules changes include bar journal articles and continuing legal education (CLE) program materials. As with legislative history research, *The Colorado Lawyer*, a publication of the Colorado Bar Association, can be an excellent source for articles discussing court rule changes. For example, the June 2009 issue included an article authored by two Colorado water law practitioners on changes to the Uniform Local Rules for All State Water Court Divisions.[13] Likewise, the Colorado Bar Association may sponsor a "rules update" CLE in which a practitioner discusses changes to court rules.[14] Researchers may obtain a copy of the program materials from a local law library or by contacting the program's sponsor.

11. List of Forms and Instructions by Category, Colorado State Judicial Branch, available at www.courts.state.co.us/Forms/Index.cfm.

12. *Civil Rules Committee and the Rules of Criminal Procedure Committee*, The Legal Research Corner, 33 Col. Law. 75 (Aug. 2004).

13. James S. Witwer & P. Andrew Jones, *Statutory and Rule Changes to Water Court Practice*, 38 Colo. Law. 53 (June 2009).

14. See e.g., *New C.R.C.P. Changes* (Colorado Bar Association CLE, Inc. 2005).

### 2. Judiciary's Website

As the print tools are limited, a researcher must check the Colorado State Judiciary's website for any information regarding new rules. The Supreme Court's page includes a link to adopted and proposed rule changes.[15] This page lists rule changes back to 1997. It also includes information on currently proposed rule changes, complete with hearing dates to discuss the changes and public comments submitted by interested parties.

The Supreme Court's website also contains a listing of the Chief Justice Directives issued by the Chief Justice of the Colorado Supreme Court since January 1, 1985.[16] These directives assist the Chief Justice in implementing the policies and procedures of the court. A directive may issue a court rule in a new matter. Searching the directives is somewhat imprecise. Researchers can use the provided search interface to search for a topic by keyword or directive number.

### 3. Other Online Resources

Westlaw produces a database containing court orders, opinions, and notices that update both Colorado state and federal court rules. The database is called the Colorado Rules Updates Orders. It is the online counterpart to the CRSA Legislative Service. LexisNexis updates its court rules file directly with any new or amended rules that it receives from the Colorado courts.

## IV. Summary

Researching Colorado court rules is a relatively straightforward process. Rule collections are published in the annotated codes, online databases, and in secondary publications. Researchers need only be aware of the types of rules that have been issued by the court and determine if any apply to the matter at hand in the court in which the action is taking place or for the subject matter of the issue. Researchers should consult the Colorado Supreme Court's website for pending or recently adopted rules or use one of the commercial publications for this purpose.

15. Adopted and Proposed Rule Changes, Supreme Court, Colorado State Judicial Branch, www.courts.state.co.us/Courts/Supreme_Court/Rule_Changes.cfm.

16. Chief Justice Directives, Colorado State Judicial Branch, https://www.courts.state.co.us/Courts/Supreme_Court/Directives/Index.cfm.

### Court Rules Research Checklist

- ❑ In what court will the action be litigated?
- ❑ Does this court have a special set of rules that apply to it? For example, is this a county court or small claims court?
- ❑ Is the subject matter of the action controlled by a special collection of rules? For example, does this matter have to do with attorney regulation or judicial conduct?
- ❑ Have I located a comprehensive collection of court rules such as one that exists in the CRS?
- ❑ Did I peruse the table of contents to get an overall awareness of the available rules?
- ❑ Do I need to consult the case annotations to interpret the rule?
- ❑ Should I consult one of the secondary authorities published for this collection of rules to both locate and understand how the rules apply?
- ❑ Has this rule been updated? Did I check the Colorado Supreme Court's website or another source to be sure the rule has not been changed since the publication of the rule I am using?

# Chapter 9

# Learning the Law Using Secondary Authority

## I. Introduction

When a researcher confronts a new area of law, one of the challenges is to learn the parameters of that area of law. What legal concepts are involved? What are the key issues? What language does a court use to describe them? What are the leading cases and relevant statutes? Secondary authority helps the researcher answer these questions.

Secondary authority includes a variety of resources. These range from broad, descriptive resources such as legal encyclopedia entries to dense legal commentary that one finds in law journal articles. Secondary authority also includes scholarly treatises and manuals to guide attorneys in their practices. Regardless, all secondary authority helps the researcher understand the law and provides citations to other secondary authority and, more importantly, primary authority. Ultimately, the researcher wants to locate primary authority—cases, statutes, and regulations—that can be used to persuade a court.

Colorado legal researchers can turn to secondary authority written about Colorado law or consult the secondary authority whose coverage is national in scope. This chapter will discuss secondary authority resources and research methods. The next chapter will examine resources specifically written for the Colorado practitioner.

## II. Legal Encyclopedias

Legal encyclopedia entries provide a broad, descriptive overview of an area of law. They also provide citations to additional secondary and primary authority. Legal encyclopedias are easy to use. Sets include an index in which a researcher uses key words to look for articles. The index will then direct the researcher either to a specific volume and section or to another entry in the index. Updating encyclopedia research is also easy. Hardbound volumes will be updated with pocket parts or softbound supplements. Both pocket parts and supplements will be organized like the hardbound volume, requiring researchers to open only to the same topic and section in the update.

For Colorado law, there was an encyclopedia entitled *Colorado Law Annotated* (CLA).[1] Published by West and written by a member of the Colorado Bar, this two-volume set provided a general overview of a variety of topics. The topics are arranged alphabetically into chapters and include citations to Colorado law and West's topic and key number system. The set also includes an index, a Table of Cases, and a Table of Laws and Rules. These tables enable a researcher to identify quickly any coverage in the CLA pertaining to a particular case, law, or rule the researcher has on hand. The set was updated by pocket parts. However, West has discontinued this publication and it is no longer available. While it is becoming more outdated, this encyclopedia is still useful to researchers to provide a general introduction to Colorado legal topics.

The two national encyclopedias are published by West. They are *American Jurisprudence* (AmJur) and *Corpus Juris Secundum* (CJS). Both encyclopedias are currently in their second series. As West publications, their entries are tied into West's American Digest System, directing researchers to appropriate topics and key numbers to conduct additional case law research.

Both Westlaw and LexisNexis contain encyclopedia databases. Both AmJur and CJS are available on Westlaw. LexisNexis provides AmJur located under the "Secondary Legal" group on the "Legal" tab.

## III. American Law Reports

*American Law Reports* (ALR) can be an extremely useful research tool. It is somewhat similar to a legal encyclopedia as both provide a descriptive overview of an area of law. However, unlike an encyclopedia that comprehensively covers all legal topics, ALR articles, called annotations, address very specific legal issues. Editors select each narrow legal issue by identifying a leading case addressing the issue. That case and the issue it raises are then exhaustively researched, and an annotation analyzing and citing all of the related primary

1. Bruce D. Pringle, *Colorado Law Annotated* (2d. ed., Thomson/West 2006).

authority is written. For the legal researcher, the great advantage of ALR is that if an annotation exists on the researcher's legal issue much of the research is already compiled.

ALRs exist for both state and federal issues. Initially printed together, federal issues were published in their own ALR series starting in 1969. State issues continue to be published in the numbered ALR series, which is currently in the sixth series. All sets share a multivolume index. West currently publishes ALR and therefore it's tied into the American Digest System and the West family of publications. In fact, ALR includes a separate digest of annotations, which uses the American Digest System topics and key numbers. Updating of ALR series varies. The first and second series are kept current by separately bound volumes containing case updates. All other series are updated with pocket parts. Occasionally, an older annotation is superseded by a newer annotation. A researcher can consult a citator of ALR annotations to identify newer annotations on the same topic. ALR can also be found on both Westlaw and LexisNexis.

For the Colorado legal researcher, there is no equivalent Colorado law publication. However, an ALR annotation will cite Colorado case law, if applicable, and the researcher can then utilize the American Digest System to locate additional Colorado case law. Of course, the annotation will also help the researcher understand the parameters of the issue and how courts have dealt with it.

# IV. Legal Periodicals

A periodical is any publication that is published on a regular schedule. Law journals, law reviews, bar journals, and legal newspapers are an important source for descriptive and critical analysis of legal issues, practical information, and news updates about the law and legal profession.

## A. Law Journals

Law journals contain articles written by legal experts addressing some relatively narrow area of the law. These experts may be law professors, judges, or practitioners. Typically, the article reviews the current state of the law and then prescribes how the law should develop. In addition to reviewing law or proposing reform, law journal articles contain numerous citations to cases, statutes, and other research resources. Law journals may be general, publishing articles on a variety of topics, or may publish articles on a particular subject, such as environmental law. Law journals are either peer-reviewed or student-edited. In peer-reviewed journals, articles are selected and edited by other professionals with expertise in law.

Every law school produces its own law journal, often called a law review. Law school students are responsible for editing their law school's journals. These students, drawn from the top of their class, review and edit articles and book reviews submitted for publication and may also contribute shorter pieces in the form of case notes or comments.

Colorado is home to two law schools: the University of Colorado at Boulder (CU) and the University of Denver (DU). In addition to the flagship law review, the *University of Colorado Law Review*, CU students also produce two subject-specific law reviews, the *Colorado Natural Resources, Energy, and Environmental Law Review* and the *Colorado Technology Law Journal*.[2] DU law students produce five journals including the flagship law review, the *Denver University Law Review*. The school's other journals include the *Denver Journal of International Law and Policy, Sports and Entertainment Law Journal, Transportation Law Journal*, and *University of Denver Water Law Review*.

The Colorado Bar Association (CBA) also produces a law journal, *The Colorado Lawyer*. As the official journal of the CBA, it publishes substantive articles on Colorado law and practice written by Colorado attorneys, judges, law professors, and librarians. Furthermore, this publication informs CBA members of news and events of the Colorado Bar. It provides Colorado Supreme Court Chief Justice Directives, summaries of decisions handed down by appellate courts in Colorado, and summaries of disciplinary actions. It is published monthly.

## B. Legal Newspapers

Legal newspapers publish news articles about developments in the law and legal profession. Colorado practitioners can turn to *Law Week Colorado* for their weekly dose of Colorado legal news.[3] In addition to news articles, this newspaper is also a source for legal notices.

---

2. The two subject journals have each undergone a name change since the first edition of this text was published. Researchers can learn more about these journals at www.colorado.edu/law/research/journals.

3. *Law Week Colorado* is published by Circuit Media, LLC. The newspaper's website is www.lawweekonline.com.

## C. Finding Journal Articles

### 1. Article Citations

Researchers have a few sources to search for relevant law journal articles. One source for citations are references from other authority. As noted, secondary authority will cite not only primary but also additional secondary authority. Researchers will come across journal citations in encyclopedia entries, annotations, treatises, and other sources. Likewise, annotated codes include references to journal articles that are relevant to a code section or statutory article. All journal article citations will include a journal volume number followed by the name of the journal and the first page of the article. The researcher can use this citation to find the article in print or online.

The primary source for citations to journal articles, however, is the periodical index. This type of publication collects citations for articles published within a particular set of journals, and indexes those articles by subject and author. If the publisher is producing a periodical index in print, the index entries for a particular volume are further limited to articles published within a certain time frame. The two major print indexes are the *Index to Legal Periodicals and Books* (ILPB) and the *Current Law Index* (CLI). ILPB is older, with indexing of articles dating back to 1908. CLI indexes articles dating back to 1980. Both indexes work the same way. A researcher locates the volume covering the desired time span to be researched, and then looks up entries by subject or author. The entries give the title of the article and the citation to the journal in which it can be found. The researcher will then need to locate the journal and article.

Both ILPB and CLI are now online, available as subscription-based databases. In addition to providing bibliographic information, these publications may also provide links to the full text of the article. Both Westlaw and LexisNexis provide access to these periodical databases. ILPB is found both on Westlaw and LexisNexis. CLI is available on both Westlaw and LexisNexis; however, its online counterpart is called the Legal Resource Index. Consequently, researchers will find the CLI on Westlaw as the LRI database and on LexisNexis under the Legal Resource Index.

### 2. Articles

Law journal articles are published in law journals, of course. To locate the article, the researcher needs to locate either the print journal or its online counterpart. Print journal collections are becoming increasingly rare. Generally, academic law libraries still subscribe to some print journals, although a researcher should call the library or check its online catalog to be certain the title and particular journal volume are available. To locate an article, the researcher should find the journal title in the library and then locate the appropriately numbered volume. The researcher will find the article at the page number indicated in the citation.

As print journal collections diminish, researchers are finding journal articles in digital collections. Certainly, Westlaw and LexisNexis include numerous journals in their databases. In either service, researchers can generally locate journals under a secondary authority collection or by searching for the individual journal title. Researchers should note, however, that these subscription services include articles published only since 1980. Furthermore, full-text coverage for many journals does not begin until 1994. Additionally, when these two services provide the full text of the articles, they rarely will include any graphs, images, or other illustrations.

The W.S. Hein Company, Inc. provides a better source for many law journal articles. Through its database, HeinOnline, Hein has reproduced copies of the actual printed journal articles' portable document format (PDF) documents. Hein has digitized all issues of these journals, starting with the first issue. Researchers can locate articles in this database with an article citation, or can search by subject, author, or keyword. A HeinOnline subscription is available for an annual fee. Academic law libraries and other libraries are likely to subscribe to this database.

Google Scholar is another excellent source for locating journal articles.[4] Google indexed the HeinOnline holdings. Researchers can search Hein's collection and the many other academic journals that are available through Hein using the familiar Google search interface. Access to the articles, however, may be restricted and researchers will need a subscription to the datasource for access. This subscription may be provided through a subscribing library, such as the University of Colorado Law Library. Researchers should check with their local law library to determine what access is available.

Other digital sources for law journal articles may include the publisher's or law school's journal website. Digital versions of professional, peer-reviewed journals may only be available through the publisher's website. Likewise, some law schools may make recent issues of their law journals available through the law school's website.

*The Colorado Lawyer* is available online through the CBA's website, but access is restricted to CBA members. Recent issues of the DU and CU law jour-

---

4. *See* http://scholar.google.com.

nals, however, are available on the school's website. These journals are also available on Westlaw, LexisNexis, and HeinOnline.

## V. Treatises

Treatises are scholarly publications on the law. They may be quite broad in scope. For example, a treatise may cover the entire scope of criminal procedure. However, they may also be quite narrow to examine a particular aspect of a larger area. For example, a treatise may focus only on search and seizure law. Regardless of coverage, researchers use treatises to understand an area of law, to locate citations to primary and additional secondary authority, and often to help with their legal practice. Some treatises include practice pointers and forms. Treatises are written by legal experts, who may be law professors, practitioners, or judges. They may treat their subject in a single volume or in many volumes.

Due to this varying nature of treatises, researchers may have a difficult time identifying a treatise. Rarely will the title include the word "treatise" in it. Certain treatises have acquired a reputation as classics. Examples include *Prosser on Torts*, *Corbin on Contracts*, *Couch on Insurance*, and *Collier on Bankruptcy*, to name a few. In each of these cases, the original author—Prosser, Corbin, Couch, or Collier—likely wrote the scholarly treatise many years ago. Since each treatise's initial publication, another author or team of authors working through the publisher has updated and expanded the treatise, as the original author is no longer able to do so. Nonetheless, the publisher retains the name of the original author in the title. Not all treatises, however, need to be so weighty. The more commonplace hornbooks and nutshells also qualify as treatises.[5] Depending on a researcher's familiarity with a subject and research need, a researcher is likely to find a helpful treatise in a law library, on Westlaw and LexisNexis, or even available for purchase through Amazon.com.

There are some treatises written on Colorado law. These tend more toward the practical than scholarly, and hence will be covered in the next chapter on Colorado Practice Materials. Nonetheless, as with the other secondary authorities with national coverage, Colorado legal researchers can still consult these treatises to locate Colorado primary law as well as to understand the subject area.

---

5. Hornbooks and nutshells (a series of introductory texts published by West) are treatises used by law students and others to learn an area of law.

# VI. Restatements and Uniform Laws

## A. Restatements of the Law

During the early part of the 20th century, the legal profession witnessed a growth in case law publication. This growth resulted in the need for practitioners and courts to consult a larger number of decisions in order to discern legal precedent. To aid in this task, the American Law Institute (ALI) developed the restatements of the law. For common law subject areas (e.g., torts, contracts, property), ALI reporters[6] identified the predominant rules of law from the various cases on that subject published across jurisdictions. These rules were then published as restatements of the law. Each restatement includes the rule of law and case citations. ALI has issued newer editions of the restatements since their initial publication in the 1920s and has included additional subjects.

Researchers employ a two-step process when researching a restatement in print. The first step is to locate the restatement volume citing the rule of law. This part of the set will also include the reporter's comments or notes. The second step is to locate case law annotations. References to case law are published either in separate "appendix" volumes or in pocket part or softbound supplements. These updating volumes are organized by section number, corresponding to the restatement text. Each appendix volume covers cases from a particular time period. To locate all relevant judicial opinions, the researcher will need to consult each appendix volume from the date of the publication of the restatement until the current date. Restatements are available on both Westlaw and LexisNexis.

While there is no restatement of Colorado law, researchers can still use the restatement to locate Colorado case law, as it could contain citations to Colorado cases.

## B. Uniform Laws and Model Acts

Uniform laws are similar to restatements. Both attempt to state or establish a model rule or law. Furthermore, while both appear to be primary authority, they are still both secondary authorities. They differ in that, while restatements glean a rule from existing case law, uniform and model acts are drafted to serve as ideal templates for legislation. Legislatures have the option of adopting the uniform or model act in total, in part, or not at all. Perhaps the most well-known uniform law is the Uniform Commercial Code (UCC). Drafted by the

6. An ALI reporter is an individual expert in the law.

National Conference of Commissioners, this comprehensive legislative scheme addresses virtually all aspects of commercial law. All states, including Colorado,[7] have adopted part or all of the UCC.

Uniform laws and model acts exist on numerous other topics as well. Researchers can consult the *Uniform Laws Annotated*.[8] This multivolume set contains laws approved by the National Conference of Commissioners on Uniform State Laws and is published by West. For each uniform law, the set indicates which states have adopted the uniform law, case annotations interpreting or applying the law, and references to legal encyclopedia articles and the American Digest System. The set is updated by annual pocket parts.

Uniform laws can also be found online. They are included on Westlaw and Lexis Advance. The Uniform Law Commission also publishes these uniform laws on their website. In addition to containing the text of the law, they also provide commentary about the legislation and advocacy information for legislators and others to use to help adoption of the uniform law in state legislatures.[9]

The annotations are the value of this set to the Colorado legal researcher. If Colorado has adopted one of these uniform laws but has not litigated in Colorado courts some aspect of that uniform law, a researcher can turn to this set to locate cases from other jurisdictions that have addressed the section in question.

## VII. Summary

Secondary authority is an excellent method for researchers to familiarize themselves with an area of law by learning the key controlling primary authority as well as the language of the area of law. Researchers have a plethora of secondary authority to choose from including legal encyclopedias, law journal articles, *American Law Report* annotations, treatises, restatements of the law and uniform law collections. The initial challenge is for researchers to identify what type of secondary authority they should find to help them with their research problem. To this end, researchers can categorize these individual types of secondary authority by jurisdiction, depth of coverage, type of coverage, and application. Researchers are advised to start their legal research in secondary authority when researching an area of law new to them.

7. The UCC is codified in Title 4 of the *Colorado Revised Statutes*.
8. *Uniform Laws Annotated* (Thomson-West 2004).
9. Uniform Law Commission website, http://www.uniformlaws.org/Default.aspx.

### Secondary Authority Research Checklist

- ☐ Is this a new area of law to you? Are you familiar with the key authority and language of this area of law?
- ☐ Have you developed a list of concepts and keywords to use as search terms? Do you have a statutory or case citation to use?
- ☐ What type of secondary authority do you need? Are you looking for a broad, general overview of an area of law, or do you need a comprehensive understanding of a narrow issue of law?
- ☐ Do you need secondary authority to help identify new or novel legal arguments? Are you exploring a developing area of law?
- ☐ Are you a practitioner and need an overview of law accompanied by practice tips, pointers, checklists and forms?
- ☐ Have you established context for your research by using a table of contents or by locating the section within the larger work?
- ☐ Are you doing a fifty-state survey? Are you searching for general principles of common law?

# Chapter 10

# Learning Colorado Law Using Colorado Practice Materials

## I. Introduction

While secondary authorities provide scholarly analysis of law, they also provide help for the practitioner. For instance, secondary authorities include sample forms and practice pointers to help attorneys navigate a particular area of the law. Other secondary authorities may take the form of a looseleaf service—a publication containing commentary, cases, statutes, and regulations in a particular area of law. Colorado practice treatises are found online and are even available through Casemaker.

Practicing attorneys may also learn directly from other practitioners. Attorneys are required to obtain credits through continuing legal education (CLE) course offerings. These courses are usually given by other practitioners and give varying amounts of helpful information about the subject area of the CLE. These lecture materials are often published and can serve as a reference for attorneys tackling a problem in that subject area.

Finally, attorneys can learn about the law from jury instructions. The Colorado Supreme Court has written a number of civil and criminal jury instructions. Practitioners consult these instructions in part for the sake of the jury but also for a brief summary of the elements of an offense.

In the previous chapter, the researcher was introduced to the variety of secondary authority and their value to learning about the law. In this chapter, the researcher will be introduced to specific resources that discuss Colorado law. These resources include practice treatises, continuing legal education course materials, jury instructions and legal periodicals.

## II. Practice Treatises

The practice treatise combines scholarly analysis of law with the practical view of the attorney. Generally written by practitioners or former practitioners, these treatises can be a valuable source of insightful tips into the covered areas of law. For a complete list of Colorado practice treatises, the reader should consult the *Colorado State Documents Bibliography* published by the William S. Hein Company in conjunction with the American Association of Law Libraries.[1]

### A. Colorado Practice Series

Perhaps the best series of practice treatises for the Colorado practitioner is published by West. Titled the *Colorado Practice Series*, this multi-volume set combine's encyclopedic-like coverage with practical experience. The principal treatise in the set is the *Colorado Methods of Practice*, which provides an overview of numerous areas of law. Other treatises cover some of these same topics in greater detail, along with new topics (See Table 10-1 for a list of titles). The set contains two indexes. There is a single, separate volume for material in the *Methods of Practice* and a single, separate volume indexing the entire series. Each treatise title also includes its own index, as well as, other finding aids such as a table of cases or statutes. The books are hardbound, updated with an annual pocket part or softbound supplement. The *Colorado Practice Series* is also on Westlaw.

For the practitioner, this series provides a working knowledge of each area of law. The text cites Colorado cases, statutes, and key secondary authority through which researchers can broaden their research. As a West publication, the series is also keyed to the American Digest System of topics and key numbers. Finally, these volumes contain numerous sample forms and commentary that the practitioner can modify to fit a particular situation. For Colorado legal researchers, the *Colorado Practice Series* is an excellent starting point for research.

### B. Colorado Practice Treatises from Other Publishers

The other major publisher of Colorado practice treatises is the Colorado Bar Association through its publishing outlet, the CBA-CLE.[2] The CBA-CLE

1. Robert M. Linz, "Colorado Legal Resources: An Annotated Bibliography," State Documents Bibliography, William S. Hein, Company, Inc., 2015.

2. Until 2015, Bradford Publishing was the third major publisher of Colorado practice materials. However, in 2015 they were purchased by the CLE-CBA. For a complete catalog of resources, see the Colorado Bar Association, CBA-CLE Bookstore, www.cobar.org/cle/pubs.cfm?ID=20166.

**Table 10-1. Colorado Practice Series Titles**

| Colorado Practice Series Titles |
|---|
| *Colorado Appellate Law and Practice* |
| *Colorado Business Corporation Act and Article 90 Deskbook* |
| *Colorado Civil Procedure Forms and Commentary* |
| *Colorado Civil Rules Annotated* |
| *Colorado Civil Trial Practice* |
| *Colorado Creditor's Remedies — Debtor's Relief* |
| *Colorado Criminal Practice and Procedure* |
| *Colorado Elder Law* |
| *Colorado Employment Law and Practice* |
| *Colorado Employment Law and Practice Handbook* |
| *Colorado Evidence Law* |
| *Colorado Family Law and Practice* |
| *Colorado Family Law and Practice Handbook* |
| *Colorado Handbook on Civil Litigation* |
| *Colorado Handbook on Evidence* |
| *Colorado Methods of Practice* |
| *Colorado Worker's Compensation Practice and Procedure* |

identifies practitioners who are both experienced in an area of law and also good writers. The resulting treatises emphasize the practical over the scholarly, avoiding lengthy discussions of the law for straightforward discussion of the issues practitioners are likely to encounter in this area of law. Some of the treatises are written to provide even simpler review of an area of law, suitable for lay persons attempting to understand the law and either self-represent or avoid later legal difficulties.

The treatises may be hardbound or softbound or bound in three-ring binders to allow for easy updating and use. In addition to forms, these treatises generally contain organization contact information, checklists, and reprints of selected portions of the *Colorado Revised Statutes* or the *Code of Colorado Regulations*. Increasingly, these treatises also include a CD-ROM or DVD-ROM of text and forms from the treatise or provide access to a website for updates and forms. The treatises include an index, but researchers can usually locate relevant text by browsing the table of contents. Researchers should consult the local law library's catalog or the publisher's website to determine if a treatise is published in their practice area.

## III. Looseleaf Services

A looseleaf service is a form of a treatise that publishes commentary and analysis along with the primary law for a particular subject area. It gathers together and publishes the cases, statutes, and regulations that impact a particular practice area. Generally, looseleaf services exist for practice areas that are driven by statute or are heavily regulated. For example, looseleaf services exist for labor and employment law, tax law, and environmental law.

At first blush, looseleaf sets are daunting. They often encompass dozens of volumes composed of various parts for the primary law and commentary. But looseleafs do include several finding aids including an index, a table of contents, and various other tables. They also include instructions on how to use them.

Publishers of these services send frequent updates with new content as well as news and developments in the applicable practice area. Publishers send the new pages with instructions on how to interfile the new pages with the existing pages, and which older pages to remove. Each looseleaf service has an online version, which simplifies updating and provides some search advantages.

For attorneys practicing in an area of law covered by a looseleaf service, this publication may be their primary research tool. Though expensive, the looseleaf provides to the practitioner a comprehensive set of law, commentary, and news.

Researchers look to a few different publishers to find looseleaf services. These publishers include Commerce Clearing House (CCH), the Bureau of National Affairs (BNA), Matthew Bender, LexisNexis, and West. Researchers can also find looseleaf titles by searching the online catalogs of their local law libraries or speaking with a law librarian.

## IV. Form Books

Throughout this chapter and in others, researchers have already discovered sources for forms. These sources include the forms accompanying the court rules in the *Colorado Revised Statutes*, the court forms provided through the judiciary's website, the sample forms and commentary located in the *Colorado*

*Practice Series* and other practice treatises, and forms provided to practitioners as part of a looseleaf service.

In addition to these sources, publishers produce books consisting entirely of forms. These form books may include only litigation or transactional forms, or may offer a mixed collection. Form books may be drafted for a particular jurisdiction or be national in their coverage. Regardless, all form books provide a model contract, agreement, or pleading based upon existing law that guides the practitioner in the creation of his own form to address his particular situation. Many form books include commentary to aid the practitioner in understanding the form's application. Some publications include cross-references to cases, statutes, and other relevant authority. Form books may be hardbound, softbound, or looseleaf.

For the Colorado practitioner, form books are published by both West and LexisNexis. West publishes a two-volume set of corporate forms[3] and a three-volume set of litigation forms.[4] LexisNexis's publications are somewhat more extensive. It publishes forms for domestic relations,[5] business organizations,[6] real property,[7] and estate planning.[8] Colorado forms are also available on Westlaw and LexisNexis. In addition to these national publishers, researchers should consult the catalogs of the Continuing Legal Education in Colorado and Bradford Publishing. These local publishers sell individual forms or collections of forms tailored to Colorado law.

West and LexisNexis also produce forms books for the broader, national audience. West's titles include *West's Legal Forms*,[9] *American Jurisprudence Legal Forms*,[10] and *Nichols Cyclopedia of Legal Forms Annotated*.[11] LexisNexis

3. David L. Erikson, *Colorado Corporate Forms* (2d ed., Thomson Reuters/West 2009).

4. Richard W Laugesen, *Colorado Litigation Forms and Analysis* (Thomson Reuters/West 2009).

5. Robert T. Hinds, Jr. & Albert M. Bonin, *Colorado Domestic Relations Forms* (LexisNexis 1999).

6. John E. Moye, *Colorado Business Organization Forms* (LexisNexis 1999).

7. Beverly J. Quail, *Colorado Real Estate Forms* (LexisNexis 1999).

8. C. Jean Stewart, *Colorado Estate Planning, Will Drafting and Estate Administration Forms* (LexisNexis 2007).

9. *West's Legal Forms* (Thomson-West 2008).

10. *American Jurisprudence Legal Forms* (Lyle N. Warren ed., 2d ed., Thomson-West 2009).

11. Clark A. Nichols, *Nichols Cyclopedia of Legal Forms Annotated* (Thomson-West 2009).

publishes *Current Legal Forms*.[12] The West titles are hardbound sets updated with pocket parts. The LexisNexis title is in looseleaf format. Colorado legal researchers can turn to these sets to identify appropriate language for their own state forms. Not surprisingly, both publishers provide these forms on their online research platforms.

## V. Continuing Legal Education Materials

State bars require that their members maintain a current knowledge of the law by taking continuing legal education courses (CLE).[13] State bar associations and other competent organizations host continuing legal education seminars for practitioners. The CLE instructors are typically attorneys, judges, or law faculty who hold some special expertise in the subject area of the CLE. The presentations tend to focus on practical aspects of the law, either serving as practice updates or practice pointers sessions. As part of the presentation, the instructor will usually prepare handouts or presentation slides. These materials are often published, and law libraries and others may collect them.

For the legal researcher, the value of CLE publications lies in the practical information provided. To the extent the printed materials capture the instructor's live presentation, researchers can learn about an area of law from an insider's experience. This same strength, however, can also be a weakness, as the depth and quality of coverage is also limited by the instructor's capabilities. Nevertheless, these materials broaden a researcher's scope of knowledge and may add some useful practice pointers.

A number of companies produce CLE materials, including LexisNexis and West. For Colorado law, the Colorado Bar Association is an excellent source for these materials. Through its Continuing Legal Education unit, it publishes CLE materials.[14]

---

12. Jacob Rabkin & Mark H. Johnson, *Current Legal Forms with Tax Analysis* (LexisNexis 2009).

13. This requirement helps to assure members of the public that the attorney hired to represent them is knowledgeable and engaged in the practice of law. To fulfill this requirement, an attorney must earn a certain number of credit hours during a particular reporting period. The state bar may even specify that a certain number of hours must be earned in a particular area, such as in ethics. The seminars typically last from a few hours to two days. Upon completion, the practitioner submits a certificate of attendance to his or her state bar, which issues the credit.

14. Colorado Bar Association, Continuing Legal Education, Inc., www.cobar.org/index.cfm/ID/20023.

## VI. Jury Instructions

Jury instructions are directions that judges give before juries deliberate. These instructions outline the law, providing the elements necessary to establish liability or guilt. There are instructions for both civil and criminal trials. The Colorado Supreme Court has formed two standing committees—one for civil jury instructions[15] and the other for criminal jury instructions[16]—which periodically review and update jury instructions.

In addition to outlining the law, each instruction includes usage notes and source notes, containing case and statute citations. These citations provide authority for the creation and use of the instruction. Researchers can consult these notes to identify authority directly relevant to the instruction and to further their research. The instructions are updated as determined by the committees. The most updated version of the criminal jury instructions is available through the Criminal Jury Instructions Committee website, illustrated in Figure 10-1.[17]

Colorado jury instructions are published by CLE in Colorado and West. CLE publishes only the civil jury instructions,[18] while West publishes both the civil and criminal jury instructions in separate volumes. Both volumes provide cross-references to other West publications and the American Digest System of topics and key numbers. These instructions are also available on Westlaw.

## VII. Current Awareness Resources

An important part of practicing law is keeping current of changes in the law. In fact, failure to do so may be considered malpractice. This chapter has already identified tools to help researchers stay current including looseleaf subscription newsletters, and CLE seminars and publications. Throughout the book, researchers are directed to pocket parts and softbound supplements, and to citator services to update their legal research.

---

15. Pattern Civil Jury Instructions Committee, www.courts.state.co.us/Courts/Supreme_Court/Committees/Committee.cfm/Committee_ID/18.

16. Criminal Jury Instructions Committee, www.courts.state.co.us/Courts/Supreme_Court/Committees/Committee.cfm/Committee_ID/9.

17. Criminal Jury Instructions Committee, www.courts.state.co.us/Courts/Supreme_Court/Committees/Committee.cfm/Committee_ID/9. As of November 2009, the jury instructions were last updated in December 2008.

18. Colorado Jury Instructions for Civil Trials, www.cobar.org/cle/item.cfm?productid=LIPCJI09.

**Figure 10-1. Colorado Criminal Jury Instructions**

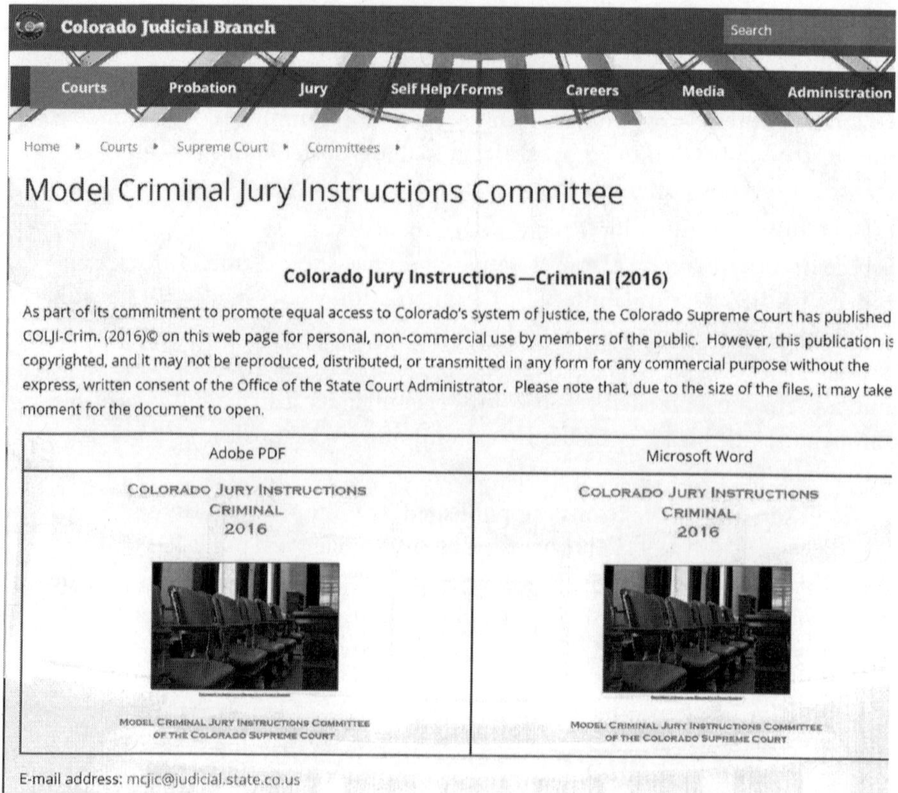


Source: www.courts.state.co.us/Courts/Supreme_Court/Committees/Committee.cfm/Committee_ID/9.

There are other resources as well. CLE Colorado publishes the *Annual Survey of Colorado Law*. For each area of law, Colorado practitioners identify the cases and statutory developments that shaped the area of law over the past year. Similarly, *The Colorado Lawyer* writes an annual legislative update, generally published in its August issue. Its purpose is to alert practitioners to legislation of general interest to attorneys.

As technology develops, practitioners can turn to other updating sources. These include law blogs, social media platforms, listservs, and publishers' email updates. Both Westlaw and LexisNexis have offered alert services for many years so that practitioners can follow changes to an existing case, be notified of cases from a particular court, or be informed of new developments in their practice area.

## VIII. Summary

Practice materials are a subset of secondary authority written by practitioners to aid other practitioners in quickly understanding and navigating an area of law. In Colorado, the major practice materials are published by Thomson Reuters and the Colorado Bar Association CLE, Inc. Between these two publishers, attorneys can find a practice treatise for most subject areas. All of these treatises combine descriptive analysis and commentary of the subject area and many also provide practice pointers and forms. Researchers should identify which treatises are available in their practice area by consulting the legal publishers' catalogs or speaking with someone familiar with these titles.

**Practice Treatises Research Checklist**

- ❑ Is there a practice treatise available for your practice area? Is it available through your current online service, or can you purchase it through one of the legal publishers?
- ❑ Did you develop a list of concepts and keywords to use to search the index, table of laws, rules or cases, or table of contents to locate relevant material?
- ❑ Does the practice treatise contain the forms and guidance you are seeking?
- ❑ Have you used the citations provided by the treatise to expand and update your research?
- ❑ Did you check the authorship and publication date of the treatise?
- ❑ Have you checked for updates to the treatise, whether provided in a supplement, online or on a DVD?

# Chapter 11

# Researching Local Government Law

## I. Introduction

Even though all citizens are impacted daily by the actions of local government, researching local government law can be quite a daunting challenge. While relying on familiar research resources and techniques, researchers also need to use new resources to find the primary sources of local government law.

Local governments include municipalities, counties, and special districts. As with the state and federal government, local governments may be composed of legislative, executive, and judicial branches. At the local level, however, these branches may be less distinct than at the state and federal level. Local governments exercise authority pursuant to their plenary powers to regulate the health, safety, and morals of the citizens and generally to provide for their common welfare. Thus, local governments create law on a broad range of topics, though within the limits set by the Colorado and United States constitutions and on topics not preempted by state or federal government. These laws can take the form of ordinances, resolutions, codes, orders, or court decisions. Home rule cities and counties will also have a charter that serves as the local government's constitution. Table 11-1 lists the types of Colorado local governments and the sources for their authority.

Researchers may need to locate local government law for many reasons. Researchers could look to the building code, land use plan, service plan, budget, or other similar types of documents necessary for the provision of government services. Home purchasers or property developers may want to consult the property records of a potential property. Businesses and concerned citizens alike may be interested in regulations concerning the sale of tobacco, alcohol, or marijuana. Of course, sometimes researchers may simply need to locate the names of the officials or determine when meetings will be convened.

**Table 11-1. Types of Colorado Local Governments and Their Authority**

| Type | Constitution | Statute |
|---|---|---|
| County | Art. XIV | Title 30 |
| Home Rule County | Art. XIV, Sec. 16 | Title 30, Art. 35 |
| Municipality | | Title 31 |
| Home Rule Municipality | Art. XX | |
| City and County of Denver | Art. XX, Sec. 1 | |
| City and County of Broomfield | Art. XX, Sec. 10 | |
| Special Districts | | Title 32 |

This chapter introduces the researcher to the forms of Colorado local government, the authority that denotes their powers, and the sources that contain that law. Furthermore, the chapter discusses the type of law generated by local governments, how it is published and where researchers can find it. Finally, researchers will be introduced to the various secondary authority available when researching local government and Colorado-specific resources.

## II. Local Government Organization in Colorado

Given the nation's tendency to favor local rule over national government, local governance is regulated by the states.[1] Local governments are unable to act without an explicit or implied grant of authority from the state. In the Colorado Constitution and in Titles 29 through 32 of the Colorado Revised Statutes, the citizens of Colorado and the General Assembly define the scope of authority local governments can exercise in such matters as budget and taxation, zoning and land use planning, and appointment of officers, among many other areas.

In some instances, this restrictive approach interfered with local municipalities' ability to respond to local problems. In the late nineteenth century,

1. Indeed, the United States Constitution is designed to limit the power of the federal government and ensure that "the powers not delegated to the United States ... are reserved to the States respectively, or to the people." U.S. Const. amend. X.

municipal governments pushed for greater autonomy in the form of "home rule" government. In home rule governments, local citizens have far greater control over the governance of their city. In Colorado, both municipalities and counties can exercise home rule. For cities, this right of home rule is embodied in Article XX of the state constitution. Currently, eighty-nine of Colorado's cities are home rule municipalities.[2] The General Assembly also empowers counties to incorporate as home rule counties "in order to better meet and resolve the problems of growth and urbanization" and to realize other values.[3] Home rule counties have the authority granted to all county governments and also possess power to expend funds, incur indebtedness, build and maintain roads and parks, and establish hospitals and firehouses, among other activities.[4]

In addition to counties and municipalities, Colorado local government can also take the form of special districts. Title 32 enumerates these various special districts, which are governing districts for the provision of special services.[5] These include the more familiar school and library districts, but they also provide for football and baseball stadiums and regional transportation to the services for specific groups of citizens of the various metropolitan districts. Special districts can be formed by state action or citizen initiative. In either case, the proposed district must create a service plan detailing the services the district will provide and the how the services will be funded.[6] These services can include trash removal, the provision of parks and recreation, fire protection, street maintenance, and many other common services citizens enjoy. If a district provides two or more of these services, it is classified as a metropolitan district.[7] The Highlands Ranch Metropolitan District in Douglas County is an example of such a district.

Denver and Broomfield are special cases. Under Section 1 of Article XX in the state constitution, Denver is to be governed as a combined city-county government. It largely operates as a home rule municipality, but certain county functions fall under the control of the state government. Broomfield is also a combined city-county government. The Colorado constitution was amended

2. Statistic located on the Colorado Department of Local Affairs website at www.dola.state.co.us/.

3. Colo. Rev. Stat. § 30-35-102 (LexisNexis 2017).

4. Colo. Rev. Stat. § 30-35-201 (LexisNexis 2017).

5. Colo. Rev. Stat. § 32-1-102(1) (LexisNexis 2017).

6. Colo. Rev. Stat. § 32-1-202(2)(a)-(b) (LexisNexis 2017).

7. Colo. Rev. Stat. § 32-1-103(10) (LexisNexis 2017).

in 1998 to transform Broomfield into its own city-county government because it occupied parts of four counties. It was organized in 2001 as the state's sixty-fourth county[8] under Section 10 of Article XX in the Colorado Constitution.

## III. Researching Primary Authority: Charter and Ordinances

Regardless of form, each local government generates law and is required to publish its laws.[9] Depending on the question, the researcher might want to find these primary authorities. In addition, the researcher may need to locate commentary about the scope and limitations of local government law. Researchers can locate this secondary authority in a variety of publications.

### A. Colorado Revised Statutes

The starting point for local government research is the Colorado Constitution and Titles 29 to 32 of the Colorado Revised Statutes. These documents delineate the scope of the authority granted to local governments by the legislature. They describe the range of activities and the types of powers local government may exercise as well as defining local government's creation, expansion, and contraction (See chapters 2and 3 for information on researching the Colorado Revise Statutes and the Colorado Constitution).

### B. Local Government Websites

The local government's website is the best place for information about the structure and organization of local government, including access to or links to its ordinances. The coverage on these websites varies somewhat. Almost all of them, however, provide information about the community, the structure and type of local government, and its leaders. For example, the website for the City of Golden informs the reader that the city is a home rule municipality and the county seat of Jefferson County.[10] The website also provides a history of the

---

8. See the City and County of Broomfield's website at http://www.broomfield.org/index.aspx?NID=27. Technically, Colorado has only 62 counties and two city-county governments.

9. Colo. Rev. Stat. § 30-15-405 (LexisNexis 2017).

10. See the Government link on the City of Golden's website, currently available at http://www.cityofgolden.net/government/ (last visited July 31, 2018).

**Figure 11-1. Colorado Department of Local Affairs Website**

Source: www.dola.state.co.us.

city, services provided, and helpful information for citizens and visitors. Local government websites may also provide minutes of council meetings and some even provide audio and video recordings of meetings.

In addition to this public service information, most local government websites publish or link to the government's charter and ordinances. These documents will likely be searchable online and may be provided as PDF documents. These websites may also contain a copy of the government's budget, land use codes, building codes, zoning codes, and land use development plans. The best of these sites are designed with an understanding of how to most effectively provide answers to citizen's information needs.

To use these websites, however, a researcher needs to find them. An easy and direct method to find local government websites is to search for them on Google using a few keywords. Alternatively, the Colorado Department of Local Affairs, Division of Local Government, maintains a list of active Colorado municipalities on its website with a link to the local governments' websites, where available.[11] The Department of Local Affairs is an excellent source for other local government information, as well. The website is shown in Figure 11-1.

### C. Commercial Information Providers

As noted, not all local government websites host the government's charter and codes. Many municipalities outsource this task to commercial information providers. The most comprehensive of these providers is the Municipal Code Corporation typically referred to as Municode.com.[12] Its website contains the ordinances, charters, and land use codes of more than 4,100 local governments. This figure includes a large number of Colorado local governments such as Denver, Boulder, Aurora, Englewood, and Wheat Ridge, and Larimer and Pueblo Counties. There is no fee to view the codes, but there are charges for premium services or to purchase the codes in print. LexisNexis republishes the Municipal Code Corporation's Colorado municipality's ordinances in the Colorado Municipal Codes library on Lexis Advance.

## IV. Researching Primary Authority: Judicial Decisions in Local Law

Local government case law research falls into one of two areas. First, researchers may be trying to find judicial decisions rendered by local government courts. These courts will be trial courts, whether they exist as county courts or municipal courts, the latter of which is charged with reviewing violations of municipal ordinances. Unfortunately, most state trial court documents are not available through an online database or website. For these types of documents, the researcher should check availability by calling the clerk of the county or municipality for the court's jurisdiction.

11. This information is contained within the Local Government Information System maintained on the Division of Local Government website at https://dola.colorado.gov/lgis/.

12. The Municipal Code Corporation's website is www.municode.com.

Second, researchers may need appellate court cases involving local government. To aid researchers, West publishes *Ordinance Law Annotations: A Comprehensive Digest of American Cases that Interpret or Apply City and County Ordinances* (See Figure 11-2). A digest is a subject-organized summary of case law. In thirteen volumes, this publication gathers case summaries on the broad range of subjects faced by local governments. In addition to the annotations, each topic includes an editorial comment and cross-references to *American Jurisprudence 2d* and *American Law Reports* annotations.

This publication also references West's Topic and Key Number System implemented in its digests, reporters, and other print and online publications. Researchers may find pertinent local government law issues in the West digest topics of Towns, Municipal Corporations, Counties, Schools, Zoning and Planning, and Elections. To identify Colorado cases on Westlaw, researchers can run a topic or headnote search on these topics, narrowed with appropriate keywords for their particular issues in the Colorado Cases database. Alternatively, researchers can consult the Descriptive-Word Index or topics volumes in the print Colorado or Pacific digests.

Although LexisNexis does not implement West's American Digest System, it utilizes its own system of headnotes. For local government topics, these headnotes are classified under the Governments—Local Governments topic. Local Government subtopics include Boundaries, Charters, Ordinances and Regulations, Elections, Police Power, and Libraries, among others.

## V. Researching Secondary Authority

### A. Colorado Municipal League Publications

The Colorado Municipal League (CML), whose members represent 97% of Colorado's 271 municipalities, publishes a number of local government law titles.[13] CML is a non-profit, non-partisan organization that advocates on behalf of its members and assists them in managing their local governments. To this end, CML has published numerous titles covering a broad range of issues. These titles include information on taxation, fees, and public financing; proper regulations of animals and nuisances; and guidance on conducting open meetings and making open records.

13. The Colorado Municipal League's web is www.cml.org/. County governments are represented by a similar organization, Colorado Counties, Inc., www.ccionline.org/.

## Figure 11-2. Ordinance Law Annotations, Excerpt

§ 7 ORDINANCE LAW ANNOTATIONS

### § 7 License requirements

**Research References**

West's Key Number Digest, Animals ⚷3, 66, 68; Municipal Corporations ⚷595, 597, 604, 604, 629, 631(3)
The Law of Municipal Corporations (3d ed.) (MUNICORP)
Municipal Legal Forms (MUNI-LF)
Municipal Ordinances (MUNIORD)
Am. Jur. 2d, Animals §§ 24, 107, 112
C.J.S., Animals §§ 12, 14, 16, 438
McQuillin, The Law of Municipal Corporations § 26.54 (3d ed.)
Matthews, Municipal Ordinances § 41:22
Municipal Legal Forms §§ 3A.05.50, 3A.06, 47.33.40

The law requiring any dog wearing a tax tag to be regarded as personalty and imposing liability on anyone injuring or destroying such a dog did not destroy property rights in an untagged dog. Scharfeld v. Richardson, 133 F.2d 340, 145 A.L.R. 980 (App. D.C. 1942).

The licensing of dogs and the regulation of the manner in which they shall be kept and controlled are within the legitimate sphere of the police power, and ordinances may provide for the impounding of dogs and for their destruction or other disposition. Simpson v. City of Los Angeles, 40 Cal. 2d 271, 253 P.2d 464 (1953).

A county ordinance requiring an owner to license his dog was not enforceable in Indian country because it was a local regulatory measure as well as a device to impose a tax on dog ownership. People v. Lowry, 29 Cal. App. 4th Supp. 6, 34 Cal. Rptr. 2d 382 (App. Dep't Super. Ct. 1994).

Although dogs are regarded as property, they stand on a different basis from other domestic animals, and have always been subject to regulation under the police power. Consequently, an ordinance taxing them for regulatory purposes is not a revenue measure within the constitutional provision that property taxes shall be uniform as to persons and property. City of Paxton v. Fitzsimmons, 253 Ill. 355, 97 N.E. 675 (1912).

A prohibition against keeping any unlicensed dog on the premises is not invalid for vagueness. The fact that the ordinance refers to "harbor" and "keep" is not vague and indefinite in relation to the ordinance. A city has the authority to prohibit the keeping of unlicensed animals under statutory grant. City of Choteau v. Joslyn, 208 Mont. 499, 678 P.2d 665 (1984).

An ordinance requiring licensing of dogs, and prohibiting any one person from keeping more than three dogs of licensing age is not unreasonable upon its face, and in absence of any evidence to the contrary, its validity will be sustained. State v. Beckert, 137 N.J.L. 562, 61 A.2d 213 (N.J. Sup. Ct. 1948).

Where the state commissioner of health has not issued an order requiring rabies certificates, a county may not make the production of a certificate mandatory before issuing dog licenses. Wickham v. Newkirk, 60 Misc. 2d 868, 303 N.Y.S.2d 919 (Sup 1969).

A city has power to enact an ordinance providing for the registration of, and imposing a license tax on, dogs kept or harbored within the city, and the power to require such registration and impose such tax is not restricted to dogs running at large. City of Dickinson v. Thress, 69 N.D. 748, 290 N.W. 653 (1940).

An ordinance making it unlawful for any person to keep, own, or harbor a

## B. Scholarly Treatises

Beyond the Colorado research tools, researchers may need to consult a scholarly treatise on local government law. Currently, there are two core treatises that address this area of the law.[14] They are *The Law of Municipal Corporations* by McQuillan and *Local Government Law* by Antieau.[15] Each of these multi-volume treatises comprehensively covers all aspects of local government law. Although these treatises are national in scope, the relevant Colorado law is cited in footnotes and tables.

Despite the weighty authority offered by these treatises, a researcher may need only an introduction to or general overview of this area of law. In that instance, a researcher should feel free to consult more general treatments, including the relevant articles from the legal encyclopedias *American Jurisprudence 2d* and *Corpus Juris Secundum*,[16] Chapter 54 of the *Colorado Practice Series*,[17] or treatises such as *Understanding Local Government Law*[18] or the *Local Government Law* hornbook.[19]

## C. Additional Research Tools

While all types of legal research can be aided by asking for help, local government research may be a prime candidate for telephone research. In searching

14. The first of the American treatises on the subject is John F. Dillon, *Treatise on the Law of Municipal Corporations* XV (1872). Over the course of the next forty years, a number of other treatises on the topic were written: Charles B. Elliott, *The Principles of the Law of Public Corporations* (1898); John W. Smith, *Commentaries on the Modern Law of Municipal Corporations* (1903); Howard S. Abbott, *A Treatise on the Law of Municipal Corporations* (1905); and *Eugene McQuillin, A Treatise on the Law of Municipal Corporations* (1911).

15. The current editions of these treatises are updated by each publishing company's editorial staff.

16. Both legal encyclopedias treat this subject under the topic of Municipal Corporations, which appears in volume 56 in *American Jurisprudence* and volumes 62 to 64A of *Corpus Juris Secundum.*

17. Kathleen K. Harrington, *Municipal Law and Practice*, ch. 54 in Cathy S. Krendl, *Methods of Practice* vol. 1C, (5th ed., Thomson-West 2006).

18. Sandra M. Stevenson, *Understanding Local Government Law* (LexisNexis 2003).

19. Osborne M. Reynolds, *Handbook of Local Government Law* (2d ed., Thomson-West 2001). For an even quicker and more general overview of the topic, researchers can also consult David J. McCarthy's & Laurie Reynolds, *Local Government Law in a Nutshell* (5th ed., Thomson-West 2003).

for some local government materials, a researcher may need to contact the county or city clerk to determine and obtain what is currently and historically available. Of course, researchers are always encouraged to contact their local library. Often, a local public library will collect a copy of the local government charter and ordinances. Likewise, academic and government law libraries may also contain these primary source materials as well as secondary authority and provide assistance in using them.

## VI. Current Awareness

Individuals who regularly research local government law will want to keep up with new developments. In addition to reading the local and legal newspapers, researchers should also read *The Colorado Lawyer* which contains a regular feature on government and administrative law (See Figure 11-3 for a sample article).

## VII. Summary

There are a variety of local government forms in Colorado, although the two major types are counties and municipalities. The powers and duties of local governments are governed by the Colorado Constitution and Titles 29 through 32 of the CRS. Counties and municipalities publish law as ordinances and these ordinances can be codified. For home rule entities, researchers will also need to locate their charter. When analyzing legal problems, researchers should consider if the subject matter of the problem would likely involve a local government ordinance and also determine which local government's law would apply. While researchers should consult the local government website for the charter and codes, these authorities are also likely to be found on the Municode.com website. Researchers should review the local government's website for other information such as government structure, meeting minutes, and contact information.

Attorneys practicing in this area contribute articles on various aspects of local government law. Practitioners should also consult the American Bar Association's Section on State and Local Government Law. This section publishes a newsletter addressing issues and news affecting this area of law. Finally, researchers should take advantage of existing technologies. Local governments will likely have a Facebook page and a Twitter account to keep abreast of news and other developments.

**Figure 11-3. An Article on Local Government Law, Excerpt from *The Colorado Lawyer***

**GOVERNMENT AND ADMINISTRATIVE LAW NEWS**

# Home Rule in Colorado: Evolution or Devolution

by John E. Hayes and Kristy M. Hartl

This column provides information to attorneys dealing with various state and federal administrative agencies, as well as attorneys representing public or private clients in the areas of municipal, county, and school or special district law.

**Column Editors:**

*Carolynne C. White of the Colorado Municipal League—(303) 831-6411, cwhite@cml.org; Brad Bailey, Assistant City Attorney, City of Littleton—(303) 795-3725, bbailey@littleton gov.org; Tiffanie Bleau, Denver, an attorney with Light, Harrington & Dawes, P.C.—(303) 298-1601, tbleau@lhdlaw.com*

**About The Authors:**

*This month's article was written by John E. Hayes, Denver, a partner with Hayes, Phillips, Hoffmann & Carberry, P.C.—(303) 825-6444, jehayes@hphclaw.com; and Kristy M. Hartl, Denver, an associate at Dufford & Brown PC—(303) 861-8013, khartl@duffordbrown.com. The firm of Hayes, Phillips, Hoffmann & Carberry, P.C. represented the City of Northglenn in* City of Northglenn v. Ibarra, *discussed in this article.*

**Judicial and legislative attitudes regarding home-rule powers appear to be changing, with less deference being afforded local enactments and a greater tendency to declare matters to be of state or mixed state and local concern. This article reviews Colorado case law and legislative trends regarding home rule.**

Article XX to the Colorado Constitution, which was enacted in 1902, specifies and delineates the powers possessed by home-rule cities and towns. For almost the first century of its existence, Article XX was regularly construed and applied in such a manner as to provide municipalities that had adopted home-rule charters plenary power to regulate within their boundaries matters of local concern. Those powers generally were protected by the courts and honored by the General Assembly.

Nonetheless, it appears that recent years have brought a significant change in attitude on the part of both the Colorado Supreme Court and the General Assembly relating to the extent and reach of municipal home rule. Although the judicial rules governing the interpretation of Article XX remain the same, those rules recently have been applied to uphold or determine regulations as matters of statewide concern or mixed state and local concern. Such interpretations negate or lessen the former reach and power of Article XX.

This article briefly reviews the history of home rule in Colorado,[1] placing particular emphasis on home-rule cases decided since 2000 and legislation adopted by the General Assembly in the last decade. The article also articulates changes in attitude on the part of the Colorado Supreme Court and the Colorado General Assembly toward municipal home rule and examines reasons for such changes.

## Overview of Colorado Home-Rule Doctrine

Article XX, entitled "Home Rule Cities and Towns," was added to the Colorado Constitution in 1902. In 1912, Colorado voters adopted § 6 as an amendment to Article XX (commonly known as the "Home Rule Amendment").[2] Article XX, § 6 granted home-rule powers to municipalities operating under its provisions and abrogated Dillon's Rule, which had provided:

> Municipal corporations owe their origin to, and derive their powers and rights wholly from, the legislature. It breathes into them the breath of life, without which they cannot exist. As it creates, so may it destroy. If it may destroy, it may abridge and control.[3]

### *Matters of Local, State, Or Mixed Concern*

The adoption of the home-rule provision of the Colorado Constitution altered the basic relationship between home-rule municipalities and the state by granting home-rule municipalities the same power over local affairs as that possessed by the legislature as to statewide matters.[4] With the advent of municipal home rule, three broad categories of regulatory matters developed. These include matters of: (1) local concern; (2) statewide concern; and (3) mixed state and local concern.

**Local Government Research Checklist**

- ❑ Is this a matter that of local concern and addressed by a local government ordinance?
- ❑ Is this local government home rule or statutory?
- ❑ Does an existing ordinance or code address this matter?
- ❑ Is the local government's ordinances located on Municode.Com or elsewhere? If on Municode.Com, did I check for updates to the ordinance?
- ❑ If not on a commercial website, do I need to call the local government to locate an ordinance?
- ❑ Does my research involve searching public records for property valuations or other real property related transaction? Have I checked the website of the county where the property is located for such records?
- ❑ Have I checked secondary authority for any guidance on my matter? Have I checked for articles in The Colorado Lawyer, a practice treatise or one of the publications from the Colorado Municipal League?

# Part II
# Research Methods

In Part I, we examined each of the content areas that make up legal research. We were concerned with resources and concepts and, to a lesser but visible extent, research methods. In Part II, we'll be providing step-by-step directions on how to research specific problems in each content area. Throughout these "how to" chapters, we'll see recurring themes and point out good research practices. We'll begin this exploration with a higher level examination of the principles or themes of legal research and how to plan and execute a research strategy.

# Chapter 12

# Research Analysis and Planning

## I. Introduction

In Part I, this text has covered the concepts, resources, and methods to research a particular legal authority. In Part II, this text will provide specific research steps for the authority discussed in Part I. However, before providing those details, this chapter will introduce the researcher to the process of legal research. This introduction will cover two broad concepts. The first concept is the idea of themes or patterns of publication that simplify the process of research. The second concept is the overall process of planning, recording, and sharing research.

## II. Legal Research Themes

As has been noted, law is published in various print publications, databases and websites. Also as has been noted, the goal of legal research is to locate all of the relevant authority to resolve the legal issue being researched. With this ultimate goal in view, legal publishers have developed methods to publish law to facilitate complete, thorough and updated research.

### A. Publication Patterns

The first recurring theme is how law is published. This theme is directly applicable to print publication but understanding it will help the researcher better use the online research systems. Publishers organize the law within each publication in either chronological order or topical order. For example, statutory law can be published either in the order in which it was enacted by the legislature (i.e., session laws) or by subject arrangement (i.e., codes). Likewise, regulations can be published in chronological order (i.e., the Colorado Register) or in topical order (i.e., Code of Colorado Regulations).

Both approaches have advantages and disadvantages that can aid researchers. Chronological publications tend to be published more quickly than topical ones. As law is enacted, promulgated, or decided, that authority can be quickly printed as there is little arranging to do to create the publication. However, it is difficult to use such publications to find all of the law on a particular topic. This is the advantage of the subject organization. For statutory and regulatory research, it may be easier to grasp how a law read at the time of publication using a chronological publication as it will print the law as it was enacted or promulgated. This sort of research can be done with a code, but the code may include other changes that were not part of the law enacted at that particular point in time.

Publication patterns are less relevant for online publications because a law can be integrated into a code or noted in a subject compilation more quickly than can be done in print. However, researchers should still understand the differences between the forms of these authority, and how they are produced and published, as it aids in doing tasks such as historical research.

## B. Contextual Research

Researchers should also establish the context of authority. For instance, a researcher doing online statutory or regulatory research could locate an authority but be unclear whether the law actually applies to the researcher's particular legal situation. This problem occurs because keyword searching codes may result in locating multiple code sections in which the keywords appear, but not all of those code sections have legal significance for the research problem. The solution to this problem is to situate the search results within the overall scheme of the code by referring to the surrounding code sections using the table of contents of the code, whether researching in print or online.

Researchers can also establish context by searching the table of contents directly or using some other structured index. For example, when searching case law, researchers can use a case law digest, which organizes law topically, and provides citations to cases which address the topic. This type of tool can be particularly useful for identifying related cases even if the fact patterns and vocabulary varies among the relevant cases.

To help overcome the confusion that may result from doing keyword searches in online databases, researchers should remember to look for contextual clues and use contextual tools.

## C. Resource Connectivity

Another theme is connectivity. The ultimate goal of legal research is to find all of the relevant authority applicable to the legal problem being researched. Legal publishers understand this goal, and have built into their print and online publications the ability to cross-reference other primary and secondary authority. For example, an annotated code prints the statute but also cases interpreting and applying that statute as well as secondary authority commenting on the statute. Researchers doing statutory research should take advantage of these cross-links to obtain a total understanding of the statute and to save time. Such cross-linking occurs in other publications and is especially well-developed in online research systems. For the researcher, the key is to find some starting point into the research system (i.e., keywords, citations) and then use the cross-linking to find all of the other relevant authority.

## D. Updating Research

Finally, it is critical that researchers use the most current version of law. There are a handful of techniques researchers need to know to update their legal research findings.

Print publications are updated either using pocket parts, separately-bound supplements, or updated looseleaf pages. If the book is hardbound, it is likely updated using a pocket part or a separately-bound supplement. The Colorado Practice Series is an example of a publication updated with a pocket part, as is West's Colorado Statutes Annotated. To use this type of publication, the researcher first checks the hardbound volume, and then checks the pocket part or supplement for updates. If the publication is bound in a three-ring or similar binder, it is likely updated with looseleaf pages. These pages are sent to the subscriber with updating instructions. The old pages are removed and the new pages inserted. To use this type of publication, the researcher simply notes the date the page of information was last updated, typically stamped at the bottom of the page or perhaps noted on the page of filing instructions located at the front of the volume, if retained.

In print publications the law may also be updated using a separate publication altogether. These separate publications can be used to update primary law and even some secondary law. For example, case law is updated using a citator. Traditionally, citators were published as separate publications, even by separate publishing companies. To use this type of tool, the researcher would consult the citator with the citation of the case she is updating, which would then indicate if the case was no longer good law or had been cited by other cases (See Chapter 7).

Citators are now integrated into the online systems. The most famous citator is Shepard's Citations, and it is now part of Lexis Advance. Westlaw uses KeyCite, and Bloomberg Law uses BCite. Each citator works in similar ways, and researchers need to remember to check the citator to see if the law is valid or has been challenged in some way.

When doing online research, researchers should also check the currency of the database being searched. It is not always true that an online database contains the most up-to-date information. Even online databases may be updated only periodically. Researchers can determine this currency by scanning the law or article for a currency date, or consulting the information page for the database itself. This information is usually linked through an "I" symbol or something similar next to the database name.

Updating is an important part of the research process, and failure to present the most updated law to a court can result in sanctions. Legal researchers always need to use these techniques when doing research.

## III. Research Analysis and Planning

Once the researcher develops a familiarity with the resources and methods of legal research, the question arises how best to navigate the resources to most effectively select the relevant ones. This task involves research analysis and planning. The researcher first uses legal analysis to fully understand the legal issues of the problem, and then uses research analysis to select appropriate resources and develop a strategy to use them appropriately.

### A. Developing a Research Plan

Researchers must begin researching by understanding the legal problem to be solved. This task is undertaken in the planning phase of legal research, and the end result of this phase is the creation of the research plan. With a properly prepared research plan, researchers will have confidence that they are checking the appropriate resources to find the legal authority to answer the right issue.

#### 1. Step 1 — Problem Analysis

There are two steps in developing a research plan. The first step is to engage in an analysis of the problem. In this step, the researcher thoroughly analyzes the problem to discover the issues, jurisdiction, area of law and key facts indicated by the problem. This involves legal analysis as well as research analysis.

- **Issue.** The legal issue or issues to be researched. While identifying the legal issues takes experience, researchers must identify the issue to determine which law addresses the client's problems.
- **Jurisdiction.** This is the jurisdiction in which the problem arises and controls the answer to the client's problems. Jurisdiction may be federal, state, or local. Or it may be a combination of jurisdictions and even involve foreign nations. Determining the correct jurisdiction allows the researcher to know which law is binding and which is persuasive, and which resources to select to find binding authority.
- **Area of Law.** This part of the plan is often less clear to novice researchers. In identifying the "area of law" a researcher is determining under which legal subject area(s) the problem arises. For example, is this a problem in Torts or Contracts, Property, Securities Regulation, or Bankruptcy? This is important because different types of law are predominant for different subject areas. Some subject areas are likely to be controlled by statutes, others by regulations, and still others by judicial decisions. Identifying the subject area prepares the researcher to be certain to check for that type of authority when doing the research. This identification can also help the researcher determine which resource to consult first to best use resource connectivity.
- **Key Facts.** Not all facts presented in a problem are legally significant in that they do not give rise to legal claims. The researcher's task is to determine which facts are important for resolving the problem and may serve as useful research terms.

In this first step, the researcher also develops a list of search terms to use in legal resources. There are the various shorthand methods researchers have created to develop this list of search terms. One method is called the Interrogative Pronoun Method. In this method, the researcher queries the facts of the problem and asks the "Who-What-When-Where-Why" of the problem.

- **Who.** Who are the individuals or entities involved in this problem? What are the relationships between these individuals or entities? Do the relationships give rise to any legal duties? For example, are the parties related as spouses, employer and employee, or agent and principal?

- **What.** What has happened? What is involved? What are the things or objects in the problem?
- **When.** When did the events take place, or are they to take place at an unknown future date? The answer to this question determines whether researchers need to find current law or historical law.
- **Where.** Where did the events take place? Is that location itself legally significant?
- **Why.** Why is this matter being brought to the attorney? What are the parties seeking? What is it about the problem or solution that is really important to them? Why is the matter being litigated or likely to be litigated? Asking this question helps the researcher understand the motivations of the parties and understand the problem broadly.

At the conclusion of this problem analysis, the researcher will have an understanding of the problem and a list of search terms to use. The search terms can be combined to formulate search phrases which can then be tailored to search for particular facts or legal concepts in the legal research resources. Online databases may allow the researcher to pose the search queries in plain language. This is typically how researchers enter terms into Google. But online databases also allow users to create more sophisticated and precise searches using Boolean operators. The researchers should check the database's online help to determine which method would work best and how to formulate those searches.

### 2. Step 2—Resource Strategy

In the second step of the research plan, the researcher develops a resource strategy to find the legal authority that addresses the issue(s) raised in the problem analysis step. A resource strategy is simply a listing of those resources—statutory codes, treatises, law reviews, practice guides, case law databases, regulatory codes, etc.—that will lead the researcher to find all of the relevant applicable authority for the legal problem. Ideally, the resource list should be as specific as possible. For example, if the problem might involve Colorado statutory law, a step in the resource strategy checklist should list "Check the Colorado Revised Statutes." Sometimes, it may only be possible to identify a type of resource to use. For example, a step in the resource strategy may be "Check for a jurisdictional practice treatise" instead of a specific title.

Additionally, the resource strategy should always include the search terms developed during the problem analysis. For each resource, the researcher should list the search terms or phrases that will likely succeed in finding relevant law in that particular resource. For a print publication, that might mean identifying terms to use in the index or table of contents. For an online publication, that might mean search phrases written using Boolean operators for use in the search field.

This list of resources should be put into the order that is most logical for the researcher to understand the law and to find the law. That is to say, the researcher is likely to start research by consulting secondary authority resources and then work towards primary authority resources. However, the resource strategy will vary from researcher to researcher. It will be based upon the researcher's experience in the subject area, as well as the search terms derived from the research problem. Whichever strategy is used, however, must include consulting those resources likely to contain the primary authority that could address the legal issue.

A few additional factors will impact the resource strategy. The first is the amount of money available to spend on the research project. A more limited budget might dictate that expensive subscription-based resources, such as Westlaw and Lexis Advance, are unusable for the project. Rather, the researcher may be forced to use a free resource. The second is the amount of time available for the project. An answer that is expected to be produced in a few hours or days may force the researcher to consult certain key resources instead of performing an exhaustive survey of all available resources. These two considerations may determine the selection of resources for the resources strategy.

## B. Questions and Assumptions

As the researcher considers the problem, she will have questions about the problem and need to make certain assumptions about the problem. The researchers should list those questions and assumptions in the research plan. If possible, the researcher should confer with the attorney or client to have those questions answered and assumptions confirmed. If not, as the researchers convey the research results to the client or assigning attorney, she should note the assumptions on which the research is based.

## C. The Research Plan Document

When joining the two steps in the research plan, the researcher should produce a written document to guide the research process. Figure 12-1 contains a sample template. Again, the template provides a suggested resource strategy. The actual resource strategy will vary from researcher to researcher and problem to problem. It may not always be necessary to produce a written research plan, especially for simpler problems. However, for more complicated research problems, or problems that will be researched over a long period of time, committing a research plan to paper can be quite helpful. Regardless of whether the plan is written, the researcher should always pause before beginning research and compose a thoughtful plan of action.

## D. Tracking Research in a Log

Once the research plan is complete, the researcher can begin working the plan, and putting the plan into action. The researcher can turn to the resource strategy and start with the first step listed, then proceed to the second step and so on. As research is conducted, however, the researcher may uncover new information—cases, search terms, or citations—that should be pursued. This too is part of the research process. It is a continuation of the analysis of the problem. Those new leads should also be followed. As the original and new plan evolve, it will become difficult to keep track of what resources have been researched, when they were researched and what was learned from them. To solve this problem, researchers use a research log.

The research log is simply a record of the research process. It should contain some basic elements including the resource searched, the terms used to search the resource, the date the resource was searched, the relevant findings from the resource, citations and leads derived from the resource, and the currency or validity of the resource or authority.

- Resource. The resource that was searched. This should be the particular title of the publication or the database. Examples include the "Colorado Practice Series, Vol 9" or "Colorado Cases on Westlaw."
- Search Terms. These are the actual search terms used in the resource. This entry should also include the number of results retrieved. This indicates how successful the search was and what other search terms to try.
- Date. This is the date when the resource was searched. This will be helpful for updating your research.
- Findings. These are the researcher's notes about what was found in that resource that was or was not helpful to understanding and solving the legal problem.

**Figure 12-1. Sample Research Plan**

**Part I: Problem Analysis**

- ❑ Factual Analysis
    - o What
    - o Who
    - o When
    - o Where
    - o Why
- ❑ Issue(s)
- ❑ Jurisdiction(s)
- ❑ Area(s) of Law
- ❑ Keywords
    - o Search Terms
    - o T&C or Natural Language Phrases
- ❑ Assumptions
- ❑ Questions

(If you have multiple issues, you may need to have a separate plan for each issue)

**Part II: Resource Strategy**

1. Practice Treatise (print)
    a. Search Term A in Index
2. AmJur (print)
    a. Search TermB and TermC in Index
3. CJS (online Westlaw — if AmJur isn't helpful)
    a. Search TermA /p TermB
4. Colorado Revised Statutes (Westlaw)
    a. CI(12 /s 101)
    b. OR Consult Article 12 in online Table of Contents
    c. Search for Term A
5. CRS — Case annotations in CRS
6. If no cases from CRS, check out Colorado Cases database
    a. Search DI(Term C)
    b. OR "Term A Term B Term C"

**Figure 12-2. Research Log Template**

| Step | Date | Resource/ Terms | Findings/ Value | Next Steps/ Citations Found | Status |
|---|---|---|---|---|---|
| 1 | | | | | |

- Citations and Leads. This records citations that should be pursued, or additional steps that should be taken. Some researchers may put such next steps in a different font color to draw their attention to the need to complete the step before finalizing the research.
- Validity and Currency. All legal authority needs to be checked to ensure that it is still valid. In this step, the researcher notes whether the cases, statutes and regulations are still the current statements of the law. For secondary authority, this information would include the last date the publication was updated.

While researchers should develop their own mechanism to capture this information, one approach is to record it in a spreadsheet. Figures 12-2 and 12-3 contain sample research log templates. Initially, the research log will be an annotated resource strategy. But the researcher may add steps to the initial plan or abandon steps from the initial plan. Either outcome is part of the research process. The key is to record the actual research so that researchers can ensure all appropriate resources were checked. A good rule of thumb to determine if a research log is well written is that it should contain sufficient detail so that another researcher could continue researching the problem using that log without having to re-research something because she could not determine if it had been done or done correctly.

**Figure 12-3. Research Log Template — Alternative Form**

| Searches | Results & Analysis |
|---|---|
| *Date:*<br>*Source:*<br>*Database / Title:*<br>*Currency / Validity:*<br>*Search (phrase or path):* | *What you found to help your research. Citations.*<br><br>*Application to your problem*<br><br>*New research steps based upon your research.* |

## E. Sharing Research in a Research Product

The final step in the research process is to share the results of the research. This sharing may occur in written form as a memo, brief, letter, or email. Or it may occur when the lawyer converses with other attorneys or clients about the legal matter. Either way, this research product is the goal of the research work. In sharing it the researcher shares what he has located and synthesizes the applicable law. If after researching the problem, the researcher is unable to produce the product, then perhaps more research is needed. This may indicate a lack of understanding of the law uncovered and the subsequent need to do more research.

## F. Signs When to Stop Researching

Typically, a researcher is done researching when the various primary and secondary authority all cite to the same authority. This circularity is an indication that the researcher has found the relevant authorities. Researchers should also consider their research complete if they consult a good secondary authority later in the process and discover they have found the authority cited in the secondary authority and understand the discussion. Finally, of course, research is not complete until all primary authorities have been updated using a citator or other appropriate tool, as noted earlier in the chapter.

# IV. Summary

Legal research requires analysis and planning in order to do well. There are three basic steps in the research process—developing a research plan, noting findings in a research log, and communicating what has been learned from research. The plan consists of two steps. The first is to analyze the legal problem and the second is to develop a resource strategy. In the first step, researchers identify the issues to be researched, jurisdiction of the problem, and any relevant facts. In the second step, researchers use their knowledge of legal resources to develop a strategy to navigate legal resources to find relevant legal authority to answer the legal issues. As researchers implement their resource strategy, they should note in their research log the authority they located and whether it helped their problem; any citations to pursue for further research; the dates the research was completed and when their research was updated. The final step is to distill what was learned to provide a legal opinion as written or oral advice. Researchers can greatly improve their research effectiveness if they learn the basic themes of legal research. These include chronological and topical publication patterns; taking advantage of contextual research techniques; identifying and following the connectivity of legal publications; and utilizing the various methods of updating legal authority. Through analysis, planning and understanding the design of the legal research system, researchers can research with confidence.

## Chapter 13

# Research Skills in the Online World

## I. Introduction

Online research and resources have certainly captured the mindshare of users. Researchers labor under the impression that "it's all online." They tend to dismiss print resources, fail to learn how to use them, and then dread the prospect of using one. Consequently, many researchers are unfamiliar with research using a print resource. However, print resources offer an advantage that is often lost in electronic resources, as they help researchers understand the context of legal research. As users abandon print for online resources, researchers should keep in mind useful features of print resources and return to print when online resources miss the mark. Often, researchers can quickly locate pertinent authority using a print resource—especially a print treatise—when online searching is confusing and fruitless.

This chapter introduces researchers to features of print resources. It also provides instruction in more effectively researching using online resources.

## II. Features of Print Resources

### A. Index

An *index* is a representation of the contents of a book or collection. More directly, it is an effort on part of the publisher or author to provide the reader with entry points to the topics contained within the publication. Indexers attempt to identify what search terms readers are likely to use and include them in the index. Legal materials utilize a sophisticated, technical vocabulary. As a researcher, it is best to understand the vocabulary and think broadly about search terms.

Indexes are usually published at the back of the book. Multivolume titles will likely have one or more separate index volumes for the entire set. Some titles may have both a set index and a volume index. Regardless of location, researchers turn to the index to discover where the topic is treated in the materials.

The challenge to using the index is to develop a broad list of keywords. For the main topic, the researchers should consider how else that topic is expressed in legal literature and should develop alternative keywords that are both more general and more specific. This step of the research process is typically completed when the researcher analyzes the research problem, identifying the key facts and legal issues arising from the problem.

## B. Table of Contents

Readers are very familiar with a table of contents. Practically every book contains a table of contents listing what topics are covered in the book and on what page the topic can be found. Readers turn to the table of contents for context. Legal resources also contain tables of contents. These tables may be located at the front of a book, or they may be located at the front of a topic. As is true for any table of contents, researchers should locate a table of contents to ascertain how the author has organized the topic, how broadly the topic has been treated, and what the presentation of the topics indicate about their relation to each other. The researcher will also discover the scope of the topic and perhaps related entries.

## C. Conversion and Translation Tables

Conversion and translation tables relate older citations to newer citations. More particularly, theses tables indicate where old sections of a statute or text are now located in a newer edition of the publication. For example, legislatures will reorganize and renumber their codes. Some of the older code sections may be repealed and some continue into the new code under a different section number. Researchers need a method to identify where in the new code the old code section now exists. Conversion and translation tables solve this problem.

## D. Tables of Cases, Statutes, and Regulations

Similar to the conversion table, legal resources will often include a table where legal authority is treated within the resource. For example, legal encyclopedias and treatises publish a table of laws and rules. The researcher uses this table to locate where in the legal encyclopedia or treatise that statute, regulation, or court rule is discussed.

### E. Table of Words and Phrases

The table of words and phrases list words and phrases that have been judicially or legislatively defined. The table directs the researcher to a case or statutory citation in which the word or phrase is used by a court or legislature. The researcher can then locate the case or statute to read the phrase's "official" definition. This tool is also available on the online research services.

## III. Online Researching

### A. Searching Concepts

#### 1. Terms and Connectors Searching

Novice researchers tend to search Westlaw or Lexis Advance as if they were searching Google. They enter a few keywords and then click on the search button. While that can work quite successfully, researchers may be able to improve their search results by using Terms and Connectors searching. The researcher's goal is to increase precision—the number of relevant documents retrieved in a search versus the total number of documents retrieved by that search. This is done, in part, by more carefully specifying the relationship of the search terms to one another.

Terms and Connectors searching is one way to increase precision. Terms and Connectors is also known as Boolean searching because it employs the Boolean operators of AND, OR, and NOT. With these connectors, researchers can specify the relationship of terms to one another. The AND connector narrows a search because it requires that the two terms both exist in the document or part of the document being searched. The OR connector broadens the search because only one or the other term needs to exist in the document or part of the document being searched. The NOT connector narrows the search as it eliminates documents containing the term following that connector.

In addition to using Boolean operators, researchers can also specify the proximity of one term to another. In Westlaw, these proximity operators are P, S, / and + symbols. In Lexis Advance, these operators are W/n, PRE/n, W/p, and W/s. These operators allow the researcher to specify whether the search terms appear together within a paragraph (P or W/p), sentence (S or W/s), within a number of terms of each other (/ or W/n), or with the first term pre-

**Table 13-1. Terms and Connector Searches in Westlaw**

(Search conducted in the Colorado State Cases database on September 8, 2017.)

| Search Query | Results |
|---|---|
| **premises OR liability OR grocery OR store**<br>*(any document containing any of the search terms)* | > 10,000 |
| **premises AND liability AND grocery store**<br>*(any document containing all of the search terms)* | 309 |
| **premises /S liability AND grocery store**<br>*(any document where "premises" and "liability" occur in the same sentence)* | 138 |
| **premises +1 liability AND grocery store**<br>*(any document where "liability" is the next term following "premises" expressing the legal concept of "premises liability")* | 103 |
| **premises +1 liability /P grocery store**<br>*(the same search as before but now either term "grocery" or "store" must occur within the same paragraph as "premises liability")* | 60 |
| **premises +1 liability /P grocery /3 store**<br>*(the same search as before but now the terms "grocery" and "store" must occur within three terms of each other)* | 9 |

ceding the second term by a number of terms (+ or PRE/n). Simply put, these specify that the terms must be within so many terms of each other.

Using Boolean operators and proximity connectors will greatly increase a researcher's chances of locating authority expressing the legal concepts or fact patterns. Table 13-1 shows the increasing precision of using Terms and Connectors in a search of the Colorado State Cases database on Westlaw.

## 2. Database Design and Field Searching

Understanding database design is another way to increase the precision of searching as researchers can search only particular parts of the document. These parts are called fields in Westlaw and segments in Lexis Advance. This searching is possible due to the way in which documents are digitized.

Westlaw and Lexis Advance are really database aggregators: these systems provide a common interface to numerous databases of documents. Databases are composed of tables, and tables are composed of rows and columns. The rows are records and the columns are fields in the records. In a contact database, for example, the columns would represent pieces of data such as last name,

**Table 13-2. Contact Database**

Fields in Columns

Records in Rows

| Last Name | First Name | Street Addr | City | State | Zip | Country |
|---|---|---|---|---|---|---|
| Smith | Bob | 12 Elm St. | Boulder | CO | 80309 | USA |
| Jones | Jane | 333 Maple St. | Arvada | CO | 80004 | USA |

first name, city, and zip code while the rows would be an individual contact entry in the database. (See Table 13-2.)

Likewise, cases (and other documents) are also put into a similar database structure, though a much more complicated database structure to be sure. Each case would be a record in the table. The columns represent the various parts of the case. For example, every case will have a title containing the names of the parties. Every case will have a citation. Every case will report the judge authoring the opinion. If the case is published in a West reporter or on Westlaw, it will also have headnotes containing the topics and key numbers discussed in the case.[1] Researchers can search for data in these fields by specifying that the search terms only search within that field.

If a researcher were searching for a case in which one of the party's name is "Sugar" the researcher could search for that term in the Title field, thus eliminating all cases that include "sugar" as a keyword. Likewise, if the researcher wanted to search for all cases that discuss a particular concept or focus on a particular subject, she could search for it in the Topic field. For example, the researcher could search for all cases dealing with the abandonment or waiver of homestead rights by searching under the topic Homestead in the Topic, Digest, or Headnote field. Overall, these techniques are unique to online searching. Given the linear nature of print, researchers simply could not query the print reporters or even the digests for specific fact patterns or search on particular fields within the case.

1. Cases, headnotes, topics, and key numbers are discussed in detail in Chapter 6.

## B. Online Searching Procedure

With the advent of the newest versions of Westlaw and Lexis Advance, the process of searching these research systems has been simplified. Previously, researchers would be required to select a database and enter search terms before running a search. Currently, researchers need only enter search terms and run the search. The systems default to retrieving results across the various content types (i.e., cases, statutes, regulations, secondary authority and others) and provide results matching the search terms. While this simplifies searching, it does not necessarily improve research or precision. The researcher is still required to parse the search results to determine relevant authority. But researchers can use some techniques to improve searching and researching in online systems.

First, use the analytical and planning process discussed in Chapter 12 to fully understand the problem to be researched. This analysis should include identifying the issue(s), likely resources that will help the researcher understand and answer the issues, and a robust set of keywords with which to search the resources.

Second, the researcher should consider the broad spectrum of resources, taking into account the financial and time constraints of resource selection. The best approach may be to use a free online resource for some parts of the project (i.e., reading cases from Google Scholar) but a subscription resource for others (i.e., using KeyCite or Headnotes on Westlaw).

Third, after selecting the online resource, determine which database or authority within that online resource is likely to contain the authority. Certainly, if the researcher has chosen to research the free online version of the Colorado Revised Statutes, the database and authority are known. However, if the researcher is using Westlaw, Lexis Advance, Bloomberg Law or Casemaker, the researcher should determine if they are looking for a particular kind of primary authority or secondary authority, and what particular databases contain it. Using this approach, the researcher can (1) check the currency and coverage of the database to ensure it will contain the required authority and (2) utilize the fields in the database to create more precise and effective searches.

The researcher can check currency and coverage of the database by finding the database information description. For Westlaw and Lexis Advance, this is usually found by following the link—typically an "i" symbol—located next to the database title (See Figure 13-1 for an example). The information may also be found by locating the online help for the database.

**Figure 13-1. Database Information Indicator on Westlaw**

Reprinted from Westlaw with permission of Thomson Reuters.

Often, the database will contain a template through which the researcher can enter search terms into the database's fields. This template may be found under an "advanced" search feature or on the online help (See Figure 13-2).

Next, the researcher should select that database and search in it directly using the search terms and phrases derived from the analysis and planning phase. On Westlaw, researchers can open directly to a database by entering the database's name into a database search box. Currently, this search box is located on the left-hand side of the Westlaw user interface, and is called "Search for a Database."[2] If researchers need help crafting terms and connectors searches, they may consult the online help for the connectors and sample searches.

## C. Parsing and Using the Search Results

Once the database is selected and the query entered, the service will return a list of documents containing the search terms. At this point, the researcher will need to scan through the document titles, and read those parts of the documents that contain the search terms. Both services allow researchers to run a search within these search results. If the search has returned unusable documents, the researcher can edit and rerun the search either in the same database

2. Users can also search for a database in this field without knowing the database identifier. The researcher enters a few keywords into this search box. Westlaw will return a list of possible databases to search.

**Figure 13-2. Search Template for Field Searching on Westlaw**

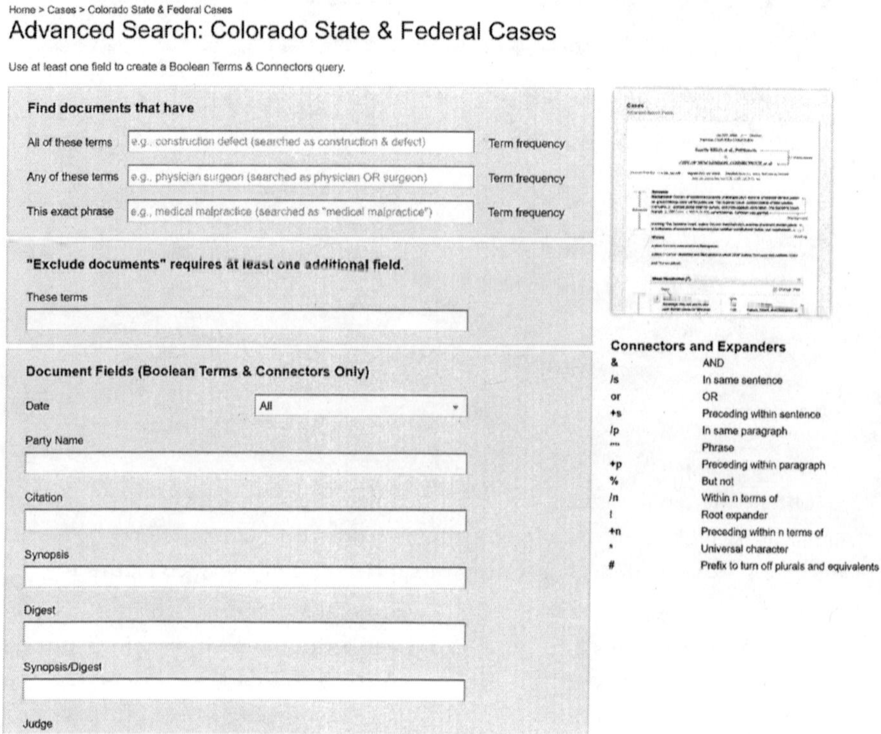

Reprinted from Westlaw with permission of Thomson Reuters.

or in different databases. Both services also allow the researcher to run a single search in multiple databases.

Both services provide methods to save, print, and download search results. One particularly useful feature is the "research trail" or history which captures each step in the search session. The researcher can then return to any step in that trail at a later time. Researchers can also save results in folders which can be shared with other users.

## D. Print Research Techniques in an Online World

Finally, the researcher should be aware of a few features to improve their ability to understand the context of the search results. These features include a table of contents, popular name table, and moving among search results using sections. These are features of print research. They help researchers establish context and simplify finding and understanding material. Researchers should look for these features while browsing online content. They typically appear in a top or side navigation bar. Each system will provide help on where to find them and how to use them.

## IV. Summary

Online research can be exhilarating due to the speed by which results can be located. However, it can also be overwhelming, leaving the researcher confused about the value and context of the search results. Using more traditional techniques for problem identification and resource selection along with online tools for contextual understanding of the search results will help lessen the feeling of being lost in search results and improve the efficiency and effectiveness of the search process.

## Chapter 14

# Researching Statutes[1]

## I. Introduction

Researchers will likely encounter the following tasks when researching statutes: (1) researching all the sections in an article of the Colorado Revised Statutes (CRS); (2) completing a "statutory history" that requires the researcher to see how a given statute was written many years ago, and possibly if there was similar statutory language before that statute was created; and (3) locating any pending legislation that may affect a statute. This chapter provides instructions and tips on completing these projects.

## II. Before Getting Started

The researcher should remember that statutory research often requires locating not just one statute, but rather, an entire article within the CRS. It is easy to miss important statutory sections so following the guidance in this chapter will help alleviate problems. Remember that a statute may be the subject of a law review article or discussed in a practice treatise and using those resources (discussed in chapter 9 and 10) will provide helpful explanations of statutory language.

1. This chapter was written by Peter Kersten, Intellectual Property, Environmental, and Water Law Librarian, and Adjunct Professor at the University of Denver Sturm College of Law in Denver, Colorado.

## III. Task One: Locating Statutes

Locating statutes is the simplest of these tasks; however, some discussion is warranted. If, for example, the researcher has been tasked with locating the Colorado statutes addressing trade secrets, the request may come as a request for a specific statute (i.e. locate CRS § 7-74-101), a request to locate the act in the code (i.e. Trade Secrets Act), or simply a collection of keywords. Use the steps below to locate statutes using any of these approaches.

### A. Before Getting Started

The researcher must be sure to locate all the relevant statutes for any research project. Unless the researcher is provided one specific citation, it is likely there are multiple relevant statutes to review, not just one. Think in terms of locating the relevant "article" rather than just one statute. Colorado statutes are divided up by title, article, and section (for example, C.R.S. § 7-74-102) and researchers should find the correct article, which may contain numerous relevant sections.

### B. Locating a Specific Statute with a Citation

The researcher may use print or online resources to locate a statute. If researching in print, be sure to use the most current version of the statutes. (The CRS is published every year; currency is crucial.) Online, the researcher can simply enter a search for the citation (example: C.R.S. § 7-74-102) to retrieve the statute. Practically speaking, even if given the simple task of locating a specific statute, be sure to review the surrounding statutes to see if others may be of value as well by using the table of contents, as discussed below.

### C. Locating a Statute without a Citation — Using the Index and Table of Contents

If the researcher does not know the specific statute number but instead knows the subject and/or some initial keywords, she should always start at the index and search for those topics and keywords to locate the relevant statute(s). If the researcher enters a basic keyword search, the results may lead the researcher off-course and he may miss some relevant statutory sections. After locating the statutes in the index and reviewing the statutory language, use

**Figure 14-1. CRS Article 74—Introductory Material**

TRADE SECRETS

ARTICLE 74

Uniform Trade Secrets Act

**Cross references:** For provisions concerning agreements not to compete, see § 8-2-113; for theft of a trade secret, see § 18-4-408.

**Law reviews:** For article, "Help for Colorado Trade Secret Owners", see 15 Colo. Law. 1993 (1986); for article, "An Introduction to the Law of Trade Secrets", see 23 Colo. Law. 2125 (1994); for article, "The Law of Trade Secrecy and Covenants Not to Compete in Colorado-Part I", see 30 Colo. Law. 7 (April 2001); for article, "The Inevitable Disclosure Doctrine: Safeguarding the Privacy of Trade Secrets", see 33 Colo. Law. 17 (October 2004); for article, "Four Strategies for Controlling Employee-Created IP", see 36 Colo. Law. 31 (April 2007); for article, "Trade Secrets, Duties of Confidentiality, and Misappropriation Claims Under the Colorado Trade Secrets Act", see 37 Colo. Law. 81 (August 2008); for article, "Keeping It Secret in Colorado", see 39 Colo. Law. 39 (November 2010).





the Table of Contents for that specific statutory article to review related sections. See Figures 14-1 and 14-2 for examples of print research and online research.

If researching in print, remember that each article contains a table of contents at the start and may have initial discussion about the article, and/or may refer to helpful secondary sources to help analyze the statute. See Figure 14-1 for an example.

If researching online, the table of contents will provide a "Refs & Annos" link listed before the statute sections and the researcher can quickly see all related statutory sections as well. See Figure 14-2 showing the layout of a statutory article online.

By starting with the index and table of contents, the researcher will better understand the structure of the code, and therefore the context. The researcher will also be alerted to important sections within the article, such as a definitions section, and may also see references to helpful secondary sources that explain the statute in detail, such as a bar journal or law review article.

**Figure 14-2. Colorado Revised Statutes, Article 74, as Found Online on Westlaw**

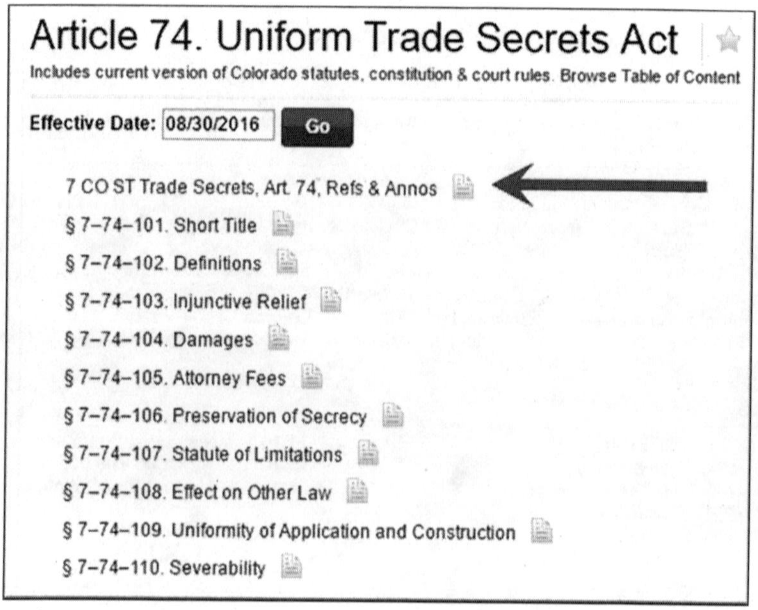


Reprinted from Westlaw with permission of Thomson Reuters.

## D. Locating a Statute by Act Name— Using the Popular Names Tables

If the researcher only has the name of an act, she should start at the Popular Names table to locate the statutory section(s). In the example above, the researcher would review the Popular Names Tables for "Trade Secrets Act" to find the corresponding citations. This table is available in print in the Index volumes of the CRS and CRSA and online in the CRSA (but not in the online CRS) (See Figure 14-3).

## E. Reading and Researching Statutes

After locating the relevant statute(s), the researcher should review the language and locate the definitions section and purpose section, if available. This preliminary step will alert the researcher to important information that may be highly relevant to their research project. In addition, the researcher must

**Figure 14-3. The Popular Names Table in the CRS on Westlaw**

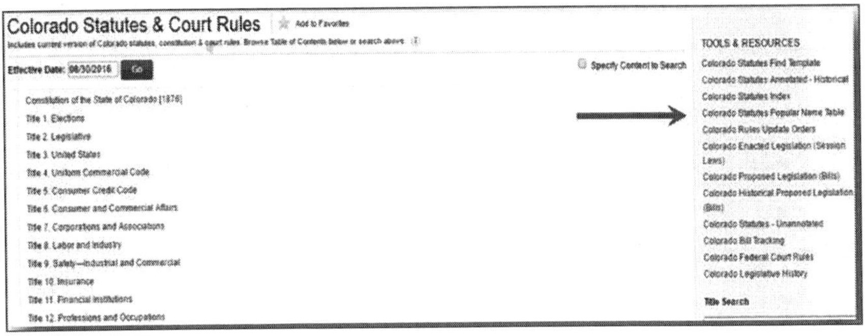


Reprinted from Westlaw with permission of Thomson Reuters.

also ensure the statutory language is current. This can be completed both online and in print.

### 1. Print

The print CRS provides the current version of the code; however, the researcher should ensure its accuracy by checking for any possible updates from the current legislative session since statutory language changes may be set to take effect (see Section V later in this chapter on "Updating Legislation"). In the print CRSA the researcher must review the pocket part to locate any changes along with the Legislative Service updates that come with the CRSA.

### 2. Online

When researching online, the researcher should remember that the statutory language is likely current, but should confirm this as changes made may take some time to be integrated online.

## IV. Task Two: Researching the History of a Statute

Researching the history of a statute requires investigation, often using older materials (possibly only available in print). For example, if the researcher is asked to research CRS § 21-1-103(3) to see if the first sentence was always part of the statute, working through historical statutes will be required. That statutory

**Figure 14-4. The Source Notes for a CRS Section on Lexis**

**HISTORY:** Source: L. 69: R&RE, p. 255, § 30. C.R.S. 1963: § 39-21-3.L. 81: (2) amended, p. 929, § 3, effective effective July 1 L. 90: IP(1) and (3) amended, p. 1038, § 1, effective July 1 L. 92: (2)(a) and (2)(b) amended, p. effective August 2.L. 2004: (3) amended, p. 725, § 1, effective August 4.L. 2013: IP(2) amended, (HB 13-1210),



section reads "[t]he determination of indigency shall be made by the public defender, subject to review by the court." What the researcher must determine is if this decision has always been made by the public defender, and before public defenders existed, if it was made by the attorney who took on the case, subject to review. To determine if this phrase always existed and figure out a similar statute existed before CRS § 21-1-103(3), the researcher should take the following steps to determine when this statute was enacted and amended, and review each relevant change either in the session laws or in historical versions of the code.

## A. Step One — Locate the Current Statute

First, locate the statute in the current version of the CRS. It is advisable to use the freely available official CRS (Lexis), discussed below. In this example, after locating the current CRS § 21-1-103, review its source note to determine when the statute was enacted and/or amended. (See Figure 14-4.)

### 1. Print

In the print CRS (Lexis), the researcher can locate all relevant history including what section(s) of this statute was amended in specific years, as shown in Figure 14-4 (showing the source notes to CRS § 21-1-103 which indicate subsections (1) and (3) were amended by the Laws of 1990). In the print CRSA (Westlaw), the source notes may not clearly show this information; however, relevant information can be located in the "Editor's and Revisor's Notes," shown after the statute.

### 2. Online

In the online CRS (Lexis) (also found on Casemaker and Bloomberg Law) and the online CRSA (Westlaw), the source note is found directly after the statute (although it is entitled "History" in the CRSA). In the official CRS, the source notes indicate what subsection(s) were affected by each amendment.

**Figure 14-5. Statutory History in CRS Source Note**

**HISTORY:** Source: L. 69: R&RE, p. 255, § 30. C.R.S. 1963: § 39-21-3L. 81: (2) amended, p. 929, § 3, effective July 1.L. 90: IP(1) and (3) amended, p. 1038, § 1, effective July 1.L. 92: (2)(a) and (2)(b) an effective August 2.L. 2004: (3) amended, p. 725, § 1, effective August 4.L. 2013: IP(2) amended, (HB



On Westlaw and also in the print CRSA, the source note may not contain the full history, which is located in the "Editor's and Revisor's Notes" under the "History" tab. Knowing which amendments can be disregarded will save the researcher time, so the researcher should use the official CRS for this research task if it is available.

## B. Step Two — Locate Past Versions of the Statute from the Source Notes

There are two ways to locate past versions of this statute. In the official CRS, the source notes list each session law citation (as shown in Figure 14-5), allowing the researcher to trace the language through the session laws. Importantly, the source notes list any previous statutory citation, which allows the researcher to trace the language through previous editions of the statutes (in the CRSA, in print and online, this information is found in the "Editor's and Revisor's Notes"). For this example, the source notes for CRS § 21-1-103 in the official CRS indicate that it was repealed and reenacted, (i.e. "R&RE") in 1969, and show the previous statutory citation (enacted under the prior 1963 code).

The researcher must then consult the 1963 version of the Colorado statutes, which is available only in print as a hardbound set with cumulative hardbound supplements. Therefore, a trip to the library will be required. (Note that older versions of the CRS are available on HeinOnline).

## C. Step Three — Check for Similar Statutes That Existed Previously

After locating the earliest version of the statute through the source notes, the researcher may be asked to see if a similar statute existed before the one researched. To do this, the researcher must search the index of the previous

**Figure 14-6. Searching for Pending Legislation on the Colorado General Assembly's Website**

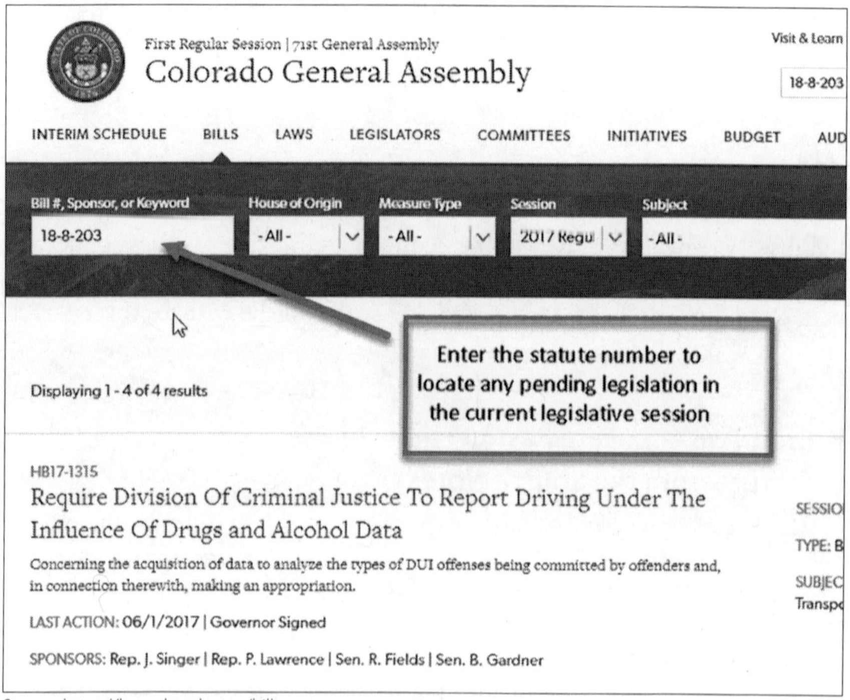


Source: https://leg.colorado.gov/bills

edition of the Colorado statutes (in this example, the researcher would review the index of the previous edition of the statutes (the 1953 version) to see if the subject of "indigency" was addressed). For this example, the subject of "indigency" was codified in the 1953 statutes in CRS 53 §§ 39-7-28 through 39-7-31. Note that the researcher may have to look at the source notes of these 1953 statutes and repeat this process to work back further, if requested.

## V. Task Three: Updating Legislation

Lastly, the researcher may be asked to check for pending legislation for a given statute. For this research scenario, if the researcher is asked to update CRS § 18-8-203, use the following method. The steps taken will depend on whether the Colorado General Assembly is in session (from January to May each year).

If completing this research during the legislative session, use the Colorado General Assembly's website to locate any pending legislation. As shown in

**Figure 14-7. The "Red Book" on the Colorado General Assembly's Website**

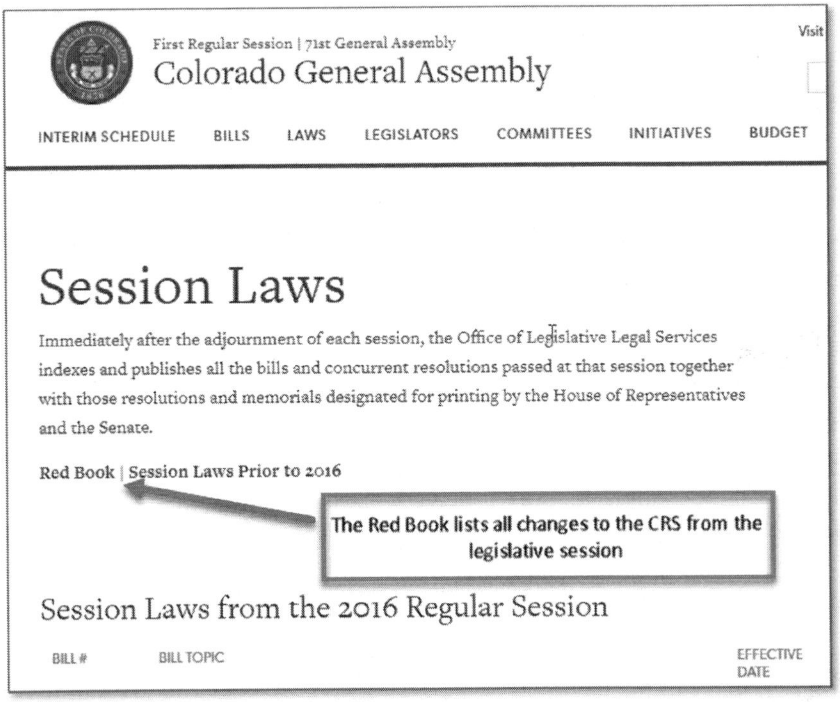


Source: https://leg.colorado.gov/session-laws

Figure 14-6, choose the current legislative session, and search by the specific statute number to search for pending legislation.

If the legislative session has ended for the year, the researcher should review the "Red Book," which reflects all changes made to the Colorado Revised Statutes during the legislative session that are set to take effect. To locate the red book, start at the "Session Laws" link on the Colorado General Assembly's website to locate the red book for each year. See Figure 14-7.

If completing this research in print during the legislative session, the researcher may use the pocket parts and the advanced legislative service pamphlets to locate any currently pending changes or can also use the General Assembly's website, as shown above. As a final reminder, if researching the statute online, the researcher should remember to check the currency of the database by check-

Figure 14-8. Locating the "Red Book" Online Shown Below

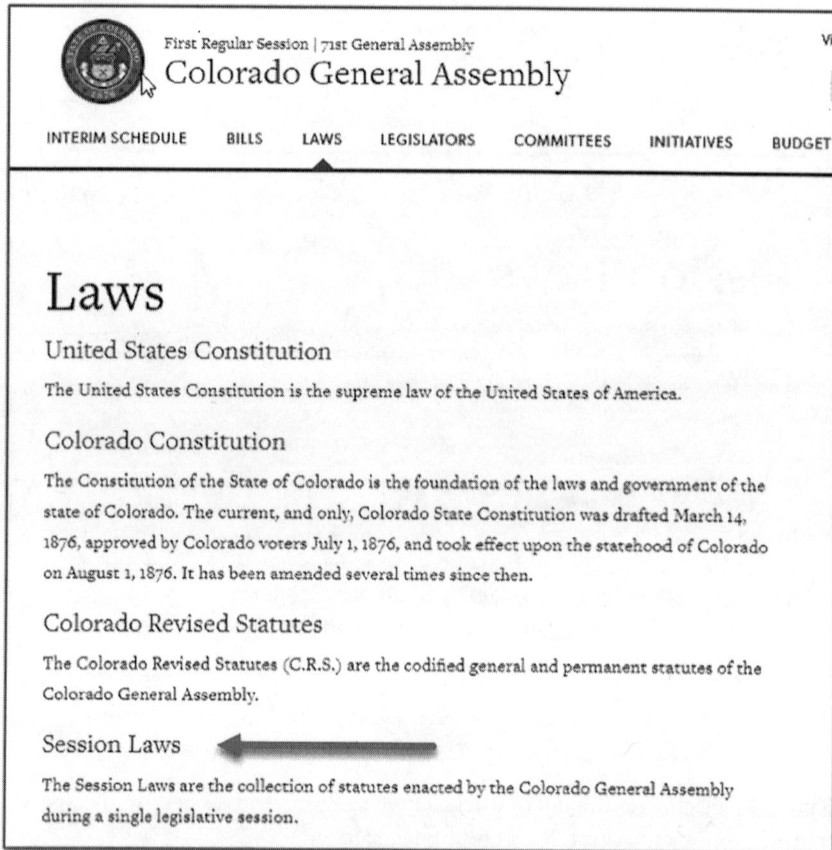


Source: https://leg.colorado.gov/session-laws

ing for a notation at the end of the code section indicating what date (or session law) through which the text is current (see Figure 14-8 for more information).

By following the steps provided above for each task, and taking time to ensure no statutory section or change is missed, the researcher will be able to complete these common statutory research projects with confidence and efficiency.

## Figure 14-9. Currentness of a Colorado Statute on Westlaw

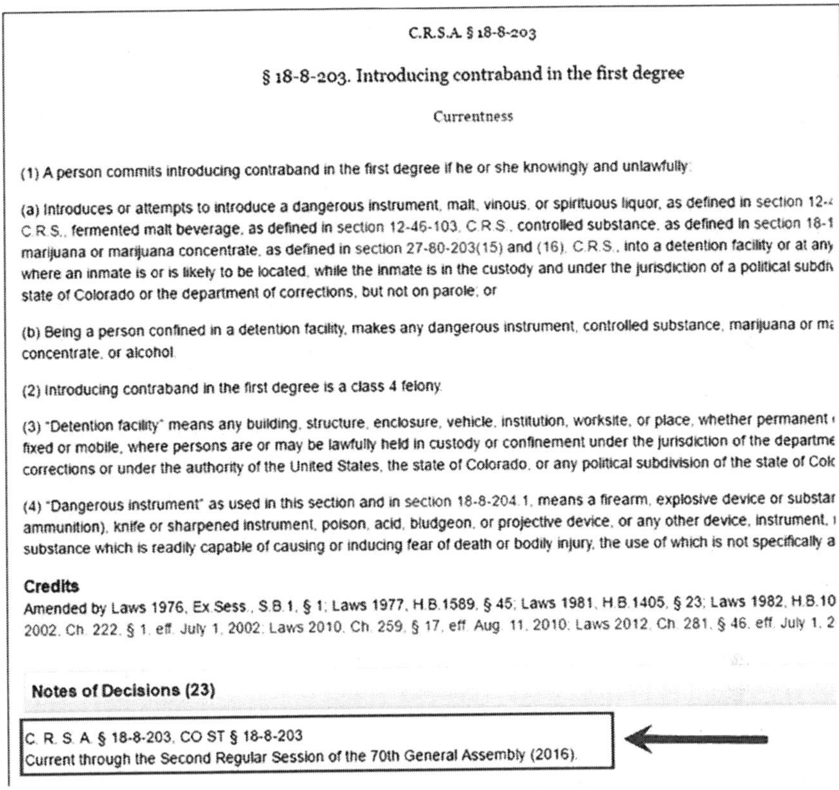

C.R.S.A. § 18-8-203

§ 18-8-203. Introducing contraband in the first degree

Currentness

(1) A person commits introducing contraband in the first degree if he or she knowingly and unlawfully:

(a) Introduces or attempts to introduce a dangerous instrument, malt, vinous, or spirituous liquor, as defined in section 12-4 C.R.S., fermented malt beverage, as defined in section 12-46-103, C.R.S., controlled substance, as defined in section 18-1 marijuana or marijuana concentrate, as defined in section 27-80-203(15) and (16), C.R.S., into a detention facility or at any where an inmate is or is likely to be located, while the inmate is in the custody and under the jurisdiction of a political subdiv state of Colorado or the department of corrections, but not on parole; or

(b) Being a person confined in a detention facility, makes any dangerous instrument, controlled substance, marijuana or ma concentrate, or alcohol.

(2) Introducing contraband in the first degree is a class 4 felony.

(3) "Detention facility" means any building, structure, enclosure, vehicle, institution, worksite, or place, whether permanent fixed or mobile, where persons are or may be lawfully held in custody or confinement under the jurisdiction of the departme corrections or under the authority of the United States, the state of Colorado, or any political subdivision of the state of Colo

(4) "Dangerous instrument" as used in this section and in section 18-8-204.1, means a firearm, explosive device or substar ammunition), knife or sharpened instrument, poison, acid, bludgeon, or projective device, or any other device, instrument, substance which is readily capable of causing or inducing fear of death or bodily injury, the use of which is not specifically a

**Credits**

Amended by Laws 1976, Ex.Sess., S.B.1, § 1; Laws 1977, H.B.1589, § 45; Laws 1981, H.B.1405, § 23; Laws 1982, H.B.10 2002, Ch. 222, § 1, eff. July 1, 2002; Laws 2010, Ch. 259, § 17, eff. Aug. 11, 2010; Laws 2012, Ch. 281, § 46, eff. July 1, 2

**Notes of Decisions (23)**

C. R. S. A. § 18-8-203, CO ST § 18-8-203
Current through the Second Regular Session of the 70th General Assembly (2016).

# Chapter 15

# Researching Regulations

## I. Introduction

Colorado regulatory research was introduced in Chapter 5. Regulations are created by executive branch agencies to implement legislation. Agencies and their regulations must operate under and within a grant of statutory authority. Regulations must comply with the State Administrative Procedures Act. Chapter 5 also covered the two Colorado regulatory publications: the Colorado Register (CR) and the Code of Colorado Regulations (CCR). This chapter will show researchers how to locate Colorado regulations using the CR and CCR published by the Colorado Secretary of State's office.

## II. Researching Current Rules by Citation, Keyword, or Browsing

Typically, the research process will start with either a regulatory citation or a need to locate regulations issued by an agency. Researchers can use either approach through the CCR provided through the Secretary of State's website (See Figure15-1).

To locate a regulation, the researcher needs a CCR citation. In this chapter, we will be locating regulation 1 CCR 204-13. Chapter 5 included a brief description of how to read the citation.

**Figure 15-1. CCR Search Box on Colorado Secretary of State's Website**

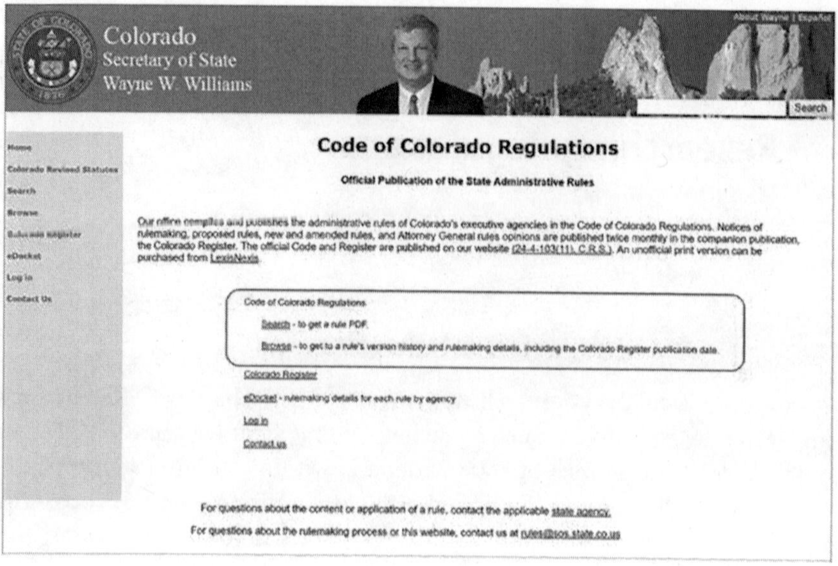


Source: www.sos.state.co.us/CCR/KeywordSearch.do.

## A. Online

The simplest method to find this regulation is to use the CCR website provided by the Colorado Secretary of State.[1] Using the "Search for Rules" search template, researchers can enter the CCR citation number to retrieve the current regulation. The document is provided in the .pdf format.

This search feature also allows researchers to search for regulations by keyword. The search will return a list of regulations in which the keyword(s) appears in the regulation text (See Figure 15-2).

Alternatively, researchers can use the Browse template and navigate through the hierarchy of departments to locate the regulation. This approach may prove more helpful to the researcher in getting a sense of the organization of the code (See Figure 15-3).

---

1. Researchers can also locate Colorado regulations on Westlaw, Lexis Advance, Bloomberg Law, and Casemaker.

**Figure 15-2. The CCR Can Be Searched by Word, Phrase, or CCR Number.**

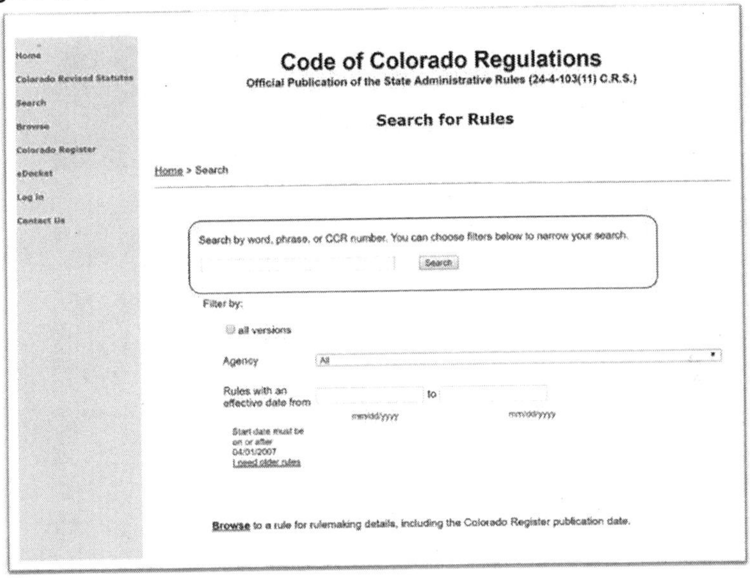


Source: https://www.sos.state.co.us/CCR/KeywordSearch.do

If a researcher has identified the specific agency and knows which department the agency belongs to, the researcher can expand the list of departments (See Figure 15-4).

## B. Print

To find this regulation in the print CCR, the researcher would locate volume 1 and then open to page 204-13. If researchers do not have a citation, they have two methods available to them to locate a regulation. First, they can turn to the set index. Located in its own volume, the researcher can use keywords to find the applicable code section. Alternatively, if they are searching for any regulations issued by a particular agency, they can do so by opening to the volume(s) of the CCR in which that agency's regulations are published. At this point, the researcher can scan the contents entries for pertinent regulations.

**Figure 15-3. The CCR Is Organized by Administrative Agency.**

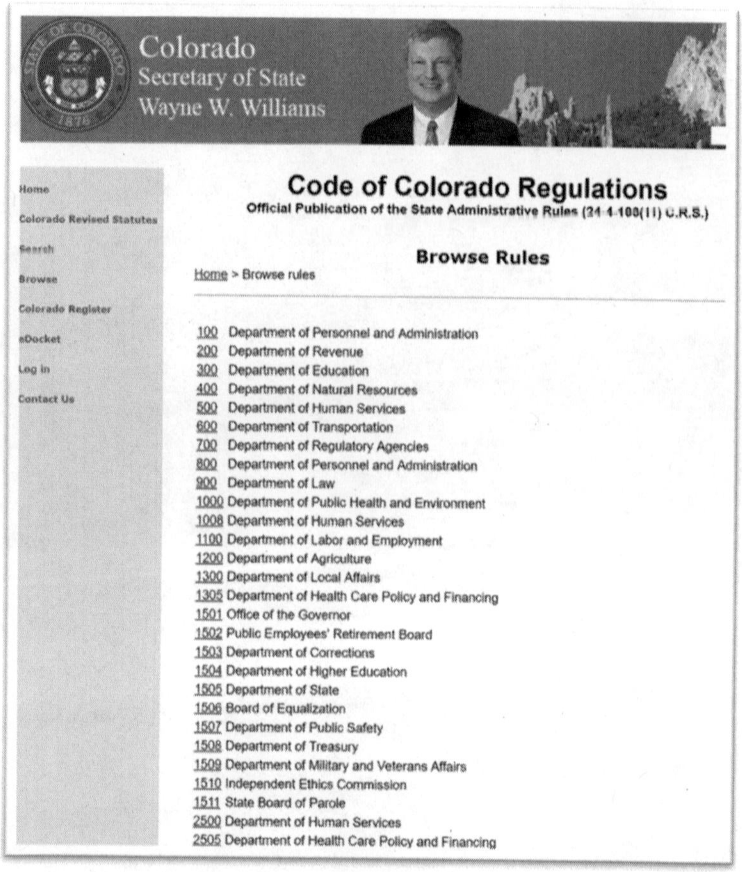


Source: https://www.sos.state.co.us/CCR/NumericalDeptList.do

## III. Researching Superseded Rules

Occasionally, a researcher needs to review the history and previous versions of a regulation to understand the intent of a rule or because a legal issue requires application of a previous version. Locating a historical rule can be challenging depending on when the rule was promulgated. Many times, researching superseded regulations requires researchers to use both the online and the print versions of the CR and CCR. The researcher needs to remember that the CR updates the CCR and that the researcher is looking for the CR citation for the regulation that updates the CCR section.

**Figure 15-4. The Organization of the CCR Reflects the Hierarchical Organization of the Executive Branch Departments. A Researcher Can Locate All of the Regulations for an Agency.**

| CCR# | Division name |
|---|---|
| 100 | Department of Personnel and Administration |
| | 101 Division of Finance and Procurement |
| | 102 State Buildings Division |
| | 103 Division of Central Services |
| | 104 Office of Administrative Courts |
| | 105 Division of Risk Management |
| | 106 Information Management Commission |
| | 107 State Capitol Buildings Group Grounds Permit Regulations (Rule recodified as 1 CCR 103-3) |
| | 108 State Use of Colorado Convention Center Display Space (Rule recodified as 1 CCR 103-4) |
| | 109 Executive Director of Department of Personnel and Administration |
| | 110 Telecommunications Services |
| | 111 Division of Information Technologies |
| | 801 State Personnel Board and State Personnel Director |
| 200 | Department of Revenue |
| | 201 Taxpayer Service Division - Tax Group |
| | 202 Division of Estate Tax |
| | 203 Division of Liquor Enforcement |
| | 204 Division of Motor Vehicles |
| | 205 Motor Vehicle Dealer Board |
| | 206 Lottery Commission |
| | 207 Division of Gaming - Rules promulgated by Gaming Commission |
| | 208 Colorado Racing Commission |
| | 209 Motor Carrier Services Division |
| | 210 Executive Director of the Department of Revenue |
| | 211 Hearings Division |
| | 212 Marijuana Enforcement Division |
| 300 | Department of Education |
| | 301 Colorado State Board of Education |
| | 302 Colorado State Charter School Institute |
| | 303 Division of Public School Capital Construction Assistance |
| | 304 Facility Schools Board |

Source: www.sos.state.co.us/CCR/NumericalDeptList.do.

## A. Online

The history of all regulations since 2007 and some from 2006 can be located in the online version of the CCR. Locating different versions of an existing regulation is quite easy. The researcher uses the same search template as when looking for current regulations. However, the researcher will check the box for "all versions" to retrieve versions of the regulation as they appeared in each edition of the CCR since 2007 (See Figure 15-5).

**Figure 15-5. CCR Search Page for Superseded Regulations**

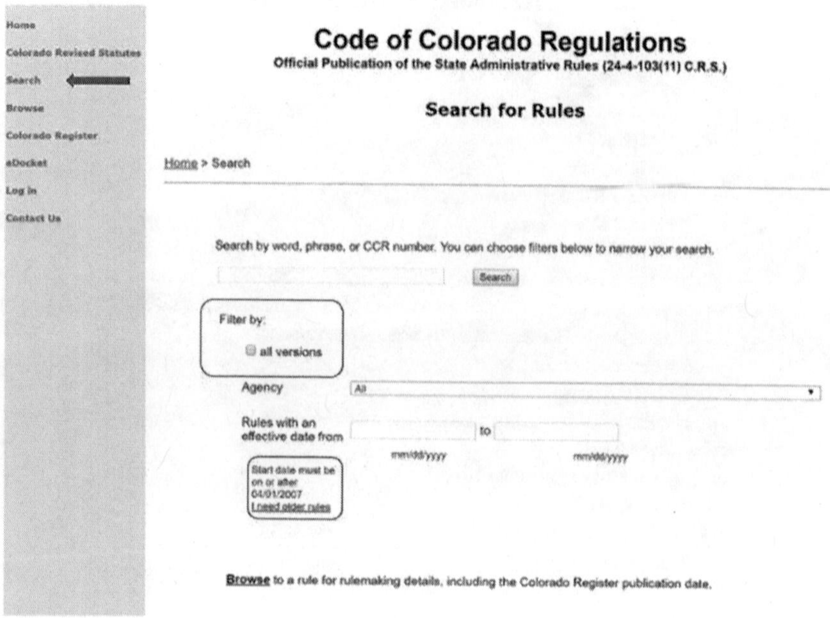


Source: https://www.sos.state.co.us/CCR/KeywordSearch.do

For regulations older than 2007, the researcher needs to take a few additional steps. First, the researcher will need to click on "I need older rules" when using the search interface (See Figure 15-5). Second, the researcher needs to consult the title page of the regulation. These title pages accompanying the print version of the CCR and for older editions of the CCR have been reproduced online. An example of a title page is reproduced in Figure 15-6.

To access the title page of the regulation online, the research clicks on the "rule history" link on the "Rules before 2007" webpage.[2] This launches the "Licensing Image View System" (See Figure 15-7).

The researcher enters the citation and selects "Rules Title Pages" from the Licensing Document Category/Type field.[3] The researcher can then retrieve a .pdf copy of the title page. Third, the researcher needs to review the "History

2. Rule History, http://www.sos.state.co.us/pubs/CCR/ruleHistory.html.
3. Instructions are provided on the website and should be consulted.

**Figure 15-6. Regulation Title Page in the CCR**

# DEPARTMENT OF REVENUE

DIVISION OF MOTOR VEHICLES

## PROOF OF IDENTITY, AGE, AND LAWFUL PRESENCE IN THE APPLICATION FOR DRIVER'S LICENSE OR IDENTIFICATION CARD

1 CCR 204-13

**EDITOR'S NOTES***

**Authority Cited:**
24-4-103, 24-72.1-103, 42-1-204, 42-2-107, and 42-2-302, C.R.S.

**History and Amendments:**
Adopted as emergency regulation 02/27/07, EFFECTIVE 02/27/07, **30 CR 4.** Adopted as emergency regulation 05/28/07, EFFECTIVE 05/28/07; adopted 05/31/07, EFFECTIVE 08/01/07, **30 CR 7.** Rule 2.3.1.1 adopted as emergency regulation 08/06/07, EFFECTIVE 08/06/07, **30 CR 9.** Rule 2.3.1.1 re-adopted as emergency regulation without changes (pages not reissued) 10/25/07, EFFECTIVE 10/25/07; Rule 2.3.1.1 adopted without changes (pages not reissued) 10/24/07, EFFECTIVE 12/30/07, **30 CR 12.** Rule 2.3.2.6 adopted as emergency regulation 03/14/08, EFFECTIVE 03/14/08, **31 CR 4.** Rule 2.3.2.6 adopted without changes (pages not reissued), 7.1 adopted 05/01/08, EFFECTIVE 06/30/08, **31 CR 6**. Rule replaced in its entirety, adopted as emergency regulation 11/07/08, EFFECTIVE 11/07/08, **31 CR 12.** Rule replaced in its entirety, adopted as emergency regulation 12/11/08, EFFECTIVE 12/11/08, **32 CR 1.** Entire rule adopted without changes (pages not reissued) 12/30/08, EFFECTIVE 03/02/09, **32 CR 2.**

**A.G. Opinions:**
30 AG Apr 204-13; 30 AG Jul 204-13 – 204-13a; 30 AG Sep 204-13; 30 AG Dec 204-13 – 204-13a; 31 AG Apr 204-13; 31 AG Jun 204-13; 31 AG Dec 204-13; 32 AG Jan 204-13; 32 AG Feb 204-13

**Annotations:**

*This Title Page does not constitute an official part of any regulation. Information contained on the Title Page is provided by the Publisher from sources deemed reliable and is solely for informational and historical purposes. See cautionary note in introductory Materials, How to Use the CCR.





and Amendments" section of the title page. This section contains a listing of all changes to the regulation. Each change is cited with a CR citation. Recall that final regulations are published in the CR and then filed into the CCR. With the CR citation, the researcher can view the regulation at the time it was promulgated and published. At this point, the researcher should note the citation(s) corresponding to the relevant time frame for the researcher's legal issue. In the listing, the citation follows the date the regulation was adopted and became effective (See Figure 15-6). The fourth and final step is to locate

**Figure 15-7. Researchers Use the Licensing Image View System to Find the Title Pages of Older Regulations Which in Turn Help Them Locate Superseded Regulations.**

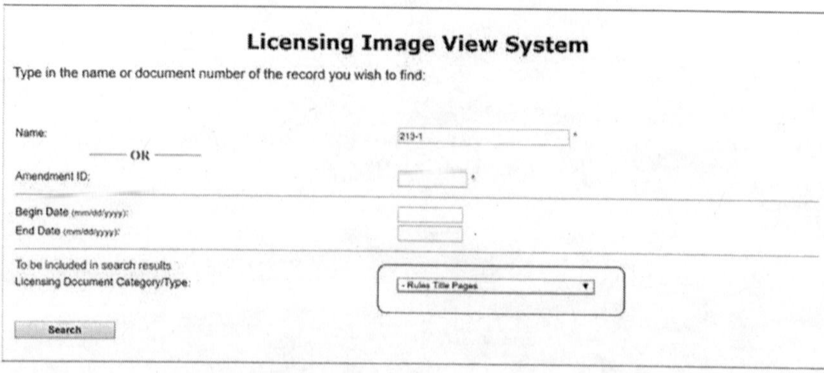


Source: http://www.sos.state.co.us/ImageView/

the CR issue in which the regulation was published. For this step, the researcher will need to consult the print issues of the CR as the CR is only available online from 2006 through the Colorado Secretary of State's website.

## B. Print

The process for finding superseded regulations in print is similar to the process for finding superseded regulations prior to 2007 online. Namely, the researcher needs to locate the title page for the regulation, note the CR citation of the regulation that was in effect for the relevant time period and then retrieve the issue of the CR (or more accurately, the pages from that issue containing the superseded regulation). In print, this title page is located at the front of the regulation itself. The researcher will consult the History and Amendments table located on the regulation's title page.[4] This table indicates when the regulation was amended and provides the CR citation in which the final rule was published. For example, the History and Amendments table for 1 CCR 204-13, reprinted in Figure 15-6, indicates the regulation was

4. The title page also contains citations to the statutory authority for the regulation, the attorney general advisory opinions regarding the regulation and related annotations.

adopted initially as an emergency regulation in 2007 and published in 30 CR 4, or the April issue of volume 30 of the CR. In August 2007, the regulation was amended by adding Rule 2.3.1.1, which was published in 30 CR 9, or the September issue of volume 30.

The researcher's next task is to locate a copy of that earlier regulation. This may be quite challenging, depending on how the subscribing library has maintained superseded CCR and CR pages. Currently, both the University of Colorado William A. Wise Law Library and the Colorado Supreme Court Library hold these superseded documents. The library may have organized the superseded CCR pages by CCR citation number and CR issue date, filing all the superseded CCR pages for a particular CR issue together in the same binder. Another library may have decided to keep all of the superseded versions of a regulation together in the same binder, likely compiling them in chronological order. Either way, the researcher will need to pull the superseded regulations volume and navigate to the cited CR page. The researcher should consult a librarian for guidance.

At this point, the researcher will have the original regulation and any prior editions, dating back to 1977 when the CR and CCR were first published. For earlier regulations, the researcher should contact the administrative agencies directly.

## IV. Researching Pending Rules

At the other end of the process is locating pending regulations. Researchers will want to know if an agency is considering changing an existing regulation or promulgating a new one. Researchers can consult the *Colorado Register* or use the e-Docket feature on the website.

### A. Using the *Colorado Register*

The *Colorado Register* is published twice per month. From the CR home, researchers can browse the recent issues to identify any proposed rules, read new rules that were adopted since the previous issue and review the "Notice of Rulemaking Hearings" and "Calendar of Hearings" to identify any proposed rules (See Figure 15-8). Online issues begin in 2006.

**Figure 15-8. The Colorado Register on the Colorado Secretary of State's Website**

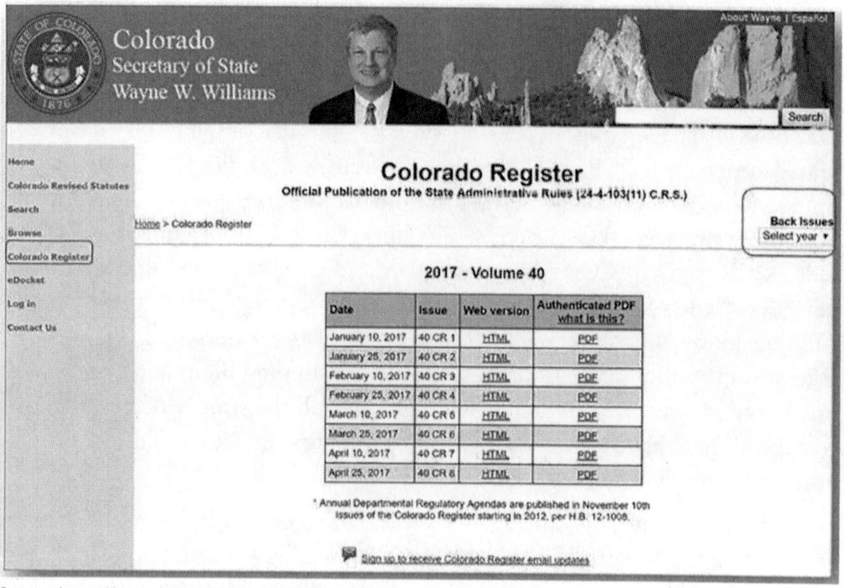


Source: https://www.sos.state.co.us/CCR/RegisterHome.do

## B. Using the e-Docket Service

Locating pending regulations is most easily accomplished online through the Secretary of State website using the eDocket feature (See Figure 15-9). The eDocket feature enables researchers to see at what point the proposed regulation is in the approval process and, if adopted, when it becomes effective and was inserted into the CR, and where it will appear in the CCR. Furthermore, the researcher can read and download the regulation (See Figure 15-10).

Researchers can search this system to locate pending regulations in two ways. First, they can search for a specific proposed regulation using the tracking number, if known. The tracking number is attached to the pending regulation. The researcher can enter this tracking number into the search template. Second, they can select an agency on the search template to track any pending regulations issued by that agency. Either way, they will also enter the starting and ending date of the search period to ascertain where that regulation is in the process.

**Figure 15-9. Docket for Pending Regulations**

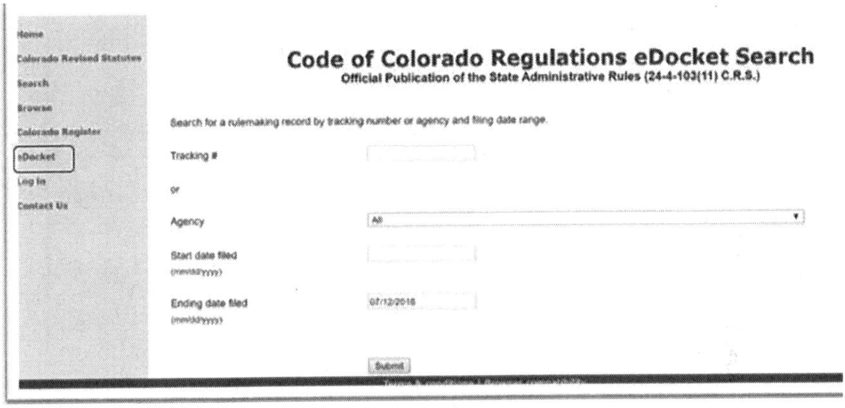


Source: https://www.sos.state.co.us/CCR/eDocketCriteria.do

The results will list any proposed rules that were filed within the indicated date range. If the rule has been adopted, the eDocket will also list the date the AG Opinion was issued, the date the permanent rule was filed with the Secretary of State, and the effective date. It will also indicate if the rule has been included in the CCR. Researchers can click on the tracking number to view more details about the new or proposed regulation.

**Figure 15-10. eDocket**

| Tracking Number | Agency | CCR Number | CCR Title | Type of Filing | Notice Filed with SOS | AGO Req/Emer AGO Req | AG Opinion Issued | Rules Filed with SOS/OLLS | Effective Date | Inserted into CCR |
|---|---|---|---|---|---|---|---|---|---|---|
| 2012-00919 | Division of Motor Vehicles, | 1 CCR 204-10 | TITLES AND REGISTRATIONS | Permanent | 10/10/2012 11:00:14 | 11/16/2012 11:04:43 | 12/03/2012 16:34:02 | 12/04/2012 08:21:56 | 01/14/2013 00:00:00 | 01/09/2013 12:34:37 |
| 2012-00920 | Division of Motor Vehicles, | 1 CCR 204-10 | TITLES AND REGISTRATIONS | Permanent | 10/10/2012 11:06:46 | 11/28/2012 13:42:42 | 12/03/2012 16:35:48 | 12/04/2012 08:23:40 | 01/14/2013 00:00:00 | 01/09/2013 00:00:00 |
| 2012-00954 | Division of Motor Vehicles, | 1 CCR 204-10 | TITLES AND REGISTRATIONS | Permanent | 10/30/2012 10:51:34 | 12/07/2012 07:42:00 | 12/21/2012 16:33:35 | 12/24/2012 06:29:32 | 01/30/2013 00:00:00 | 01/16/2013 10:03:43 |
| 2013-00198 | Division of Motor Vehicles, | 1 CCR 204-10 | TITLES AND REGISTRATIONS | Permanent | 02/22/2013 15:05:12 | 04/26/2013 08:16:27 | | | | |
| 2013-00199 | Division of Motor Vehicles, | 1 CCR 204-10 | TITLES AND REGISTRATIONS | Permanent | 02/22/2013 15:13:32 | 04/26/2013 08:20:25 | | | | |
| 2013-00200 | Division of Motor Vehicles, | 1 CCR 204-10 | TITLES AND REGISTRATIONS | Permanent | 02/22/2013 15:34:56 | 05/10/2013 13:08:38 | 05/14/2013 11:35:50 | 05/15/2013 13:17:50 | 06/30/2013 00:00:00 | |
| 2013-00201 | Division of Motor Vehicles, | 1 CCR 204-10 | TITLES AND REGISTRATIONS | Permanent | 02/22/2013 15:40:51 | 05/10/2013 13:11:35 | | | | |
| 2013-00202 | Division of Motor Vehicles, | 1 CCR 204-10 | TITLES AND REGISTRATIONS | Permanent | 02/22/2013 15:44:22 | 04/26/2013 08:29:21 | 05/10/2013 16:06:03 | 05/15/2013 13:20:20 | 06/30/2013 00:00:00 | |
| 2013-00203 | Division of Motor Vehicles, | 1 CCR 204-10 | TITLES AND REGISTRATIONS | Permanent | 02/22/2013 15:47:25 | 04/26/2013 08:32:55 | 05/10/2013 16:01:12 | 05/15/2013 13:21:57 | 06/30/2013 00:00:00 | |
| 2013-00204 | Division of Motor Vehicles, | 1 CCR 204-10 | TITLES AND REGISTRATIONS | Permanent | 02/22/2013 15:52:44 | 04/26/2013 08:39:57 | | | | |
| 2013-00341 | Division of Motor Vehicles, | 1 CCR 204-10 | TITLES AND REGISTRATIONS | Permanent | 04/23/2013 09:08:54 | | | | | |
| 2013-00342 | Division of Motor Vehicles, | 1 CCR 204-10 | TITLES AND REGISTRATIONS | Permanent | 04/23/2013 09:15:59 | | | | | |
| 2013-00343 | Division of Motor Vehicles, | 1 CCR 204-10 | TITLES AND REGISTRATIONS | Permanent | 04/23/2013 09:20:23 | | | | | |

Source: https://www.sos.state.co.us/CCR/eDocketCriteria.do

**Figure 15-11. eDocket Additional Information**

| | |
|---|---|
| Tracking Number | 2013-00341 |
| Type of Filing | Permanent Rule |
| Department | 200 Department of Revenue |
| Agency | 204 Division of Motor Vehicles |
| CCR Number | 1 CCR 204-10 |
| CCR Title | 1 CCR 204-10, Rule 26. Physical Inspection of Motor Vehicles, Titles and Registrations |
| Adopting Agency | |
| Hearing Date | 06/04/2013 |
| Hearing Time | 09:00 AM |
| Hearing Location | 1881 Pierce Street, Room 110 (Boards/Commissions Mtng Rm), Lakewood, CO 80214 |
| Proposed Rule | *ProposedRuleAttach2013-00341.DOC* |
| Description of Subjects/Issues | the purpose of this regulation is to establish criteria for the performance of physical inspections on motor vehicles. |
| Comments | Room 110 may be accessed through Entrance B. If special accommodations are necessary, please contact Dylan Ikenouye at (303) 205-5799 at least one day prior to the hearing date. |
| Public Name | Dylan Ikenouye |
| Public Title | Admin. Svc Mgr |
| Public Telephone | 303-205-5799 |
| Public Email | dylan.ikenouye@state.co.us |
| Submitted in response to issues raised by COLS/OLLS? | |
| Statutory Authority | 42-1-204, 42-3-105(1)(c)(I), and 42-6-107(1)(b), C.R.S. |
| Adopted Rules | |
| Redline | |
| Attorney General Opinion | |

Source: www.sos.state.co.us/CCR/eDocketDetails.do.

The additional details by the tracking number include the type of filing, the affected CCR Title, the Date and Time of the Rule Hearing, a link to the proposed rule and the statutory authority for the rule (See Figure 15-11).

If the rule has been adopted, this page will also include a link to the rules as adopted, a link to the AG Opinion, and the adoption and effective dates.

# Chapter 16

# Researching Cases and Related Judicial Documents

## I. Introduction

Chapter 6 covered the sources, publication and organization of Colorado case law. As with most other states, Colorado's court system contains both appellate courts and trial courts. It also contains a special court system to litigate water issues. Researchers will mainly be searching for appellate court opinions. However, researchers may also want to locate district court documents as well as briefs, oral arguments and other judicial branch documents. While the corpus of appellate court cases is rich and deep, finding other judicial branch documents is more challenging and draws from a shallower pool. As detailed guidance exists for using the subscription services for research, this chapter will focus on using the Colorado judiciary's website to locate these documents.

## II. Colorado Judicial Branch Website

The Colorado Judicial Branch website (https://www.courts.state.co.us/) is designed for citizens to learn about and interact with the Colorado court system. To meet these design goals, it provides information about the organization and functions of the various Colorado courts and workings of the judicial branch. Likewise, citizens can find information necessary to conduct business with the courts, including contact information, dockets, jury service, and probation. Within this framework, diligent legal researchers can locate

**Figure 16-1. The Colorado Judicial Branch Website**

Source: www.courts.state.co.us

judicial opinions including unpublished opinions, briefs, oral arguments and schedules, and chief justice directives (See Figure 16-1).

## A. Judicial Opinions

The judiciary's website contains a section on courts. Judicial opinions for the Supreme Court and Court of Appeals are located on their respective webpages. Coverage for both courts begins in 1998 though full text opinions are not available until 2000.

Researchers have two methods to locate published opinions once they arrive on the "Case Announcements" webpage for the respective court. The first method is to scan the list of past case announcements (See Figure 16-2). The researcher can use the drop-down menu to select a different year or a particular month. Once selected, the researcher will need to peruse each announcement for the case number or content of interest. Each case with an opinion is linked to an external .pdf document containing the opinion.

**Figure 16-2. Judicial Announcements on the Colorado Judicial Branch Website**

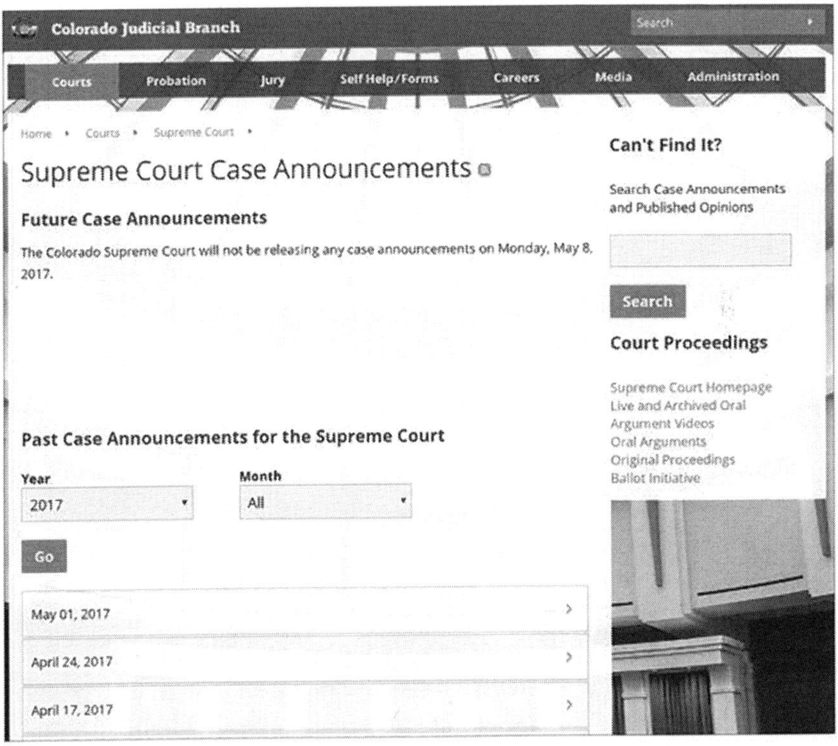


The second method is to use the search box located on the Case Announcements webpage. Researchers can enter any term or phrase into the search box; it will return documents in which that term or phrase appear. The court currently uses Google as the search engine and once the initial search is entered, researchers can then use the advanced Google search options which include phrase searching and a limited set of Boolean operators (See Figure 16-3).

## B. Unpublished Opinions

Under Colorado Appellate Rule 35(f), the Colorado Court of Appeals may mark certain opinions as unpublished. This decision is at the discretion of the Chief Judge and is likely to indicate the opinion is of little precedential value. Researchers can still obtain these unpublished opinions. To do so, the researcher will need to complete the Online Request form on the Court of Appeals "Case Announcements" webpage. Researchers will need to supply the case name,

**Figure 16-3. The Colorado Judicial Branch Website Uses Google as Its Search Engine.**

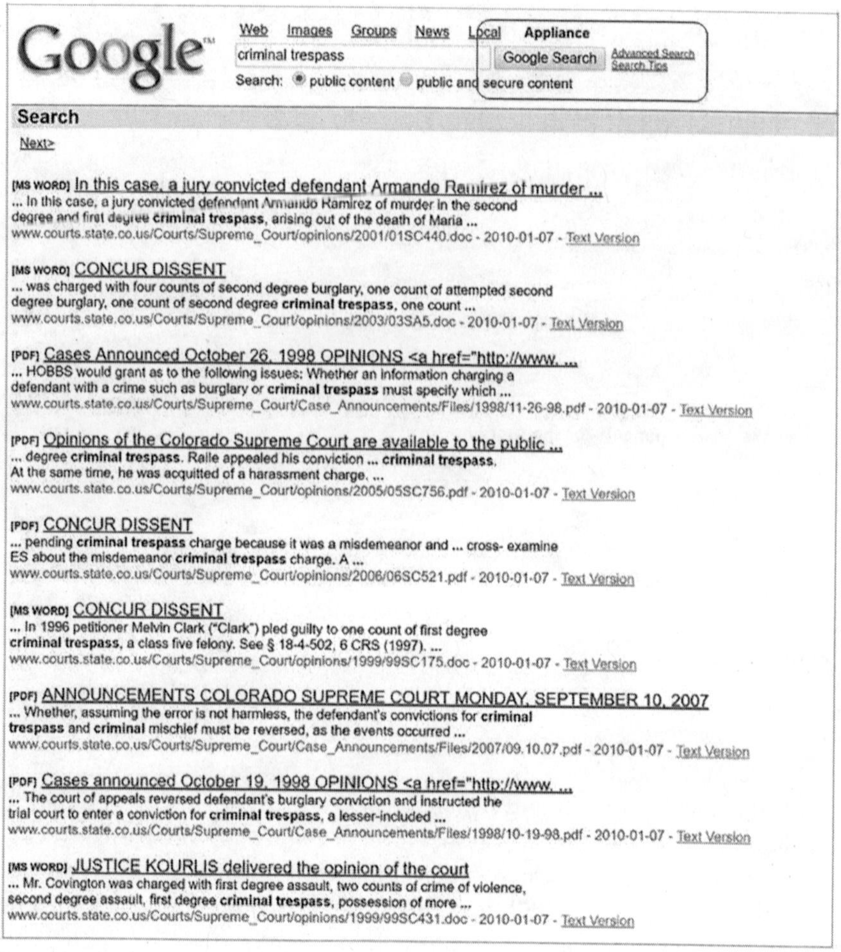


Source: searchweb.courts.state.co.us.

number, and announcement date, as well as their contact information. The request is sent to the Clerk of the Court, who will then email the opinion to the researcher. (See Figure 16-4.)

**Figure 16-4. Accessing Colorado Court of Appeals Unpublished Opinions**

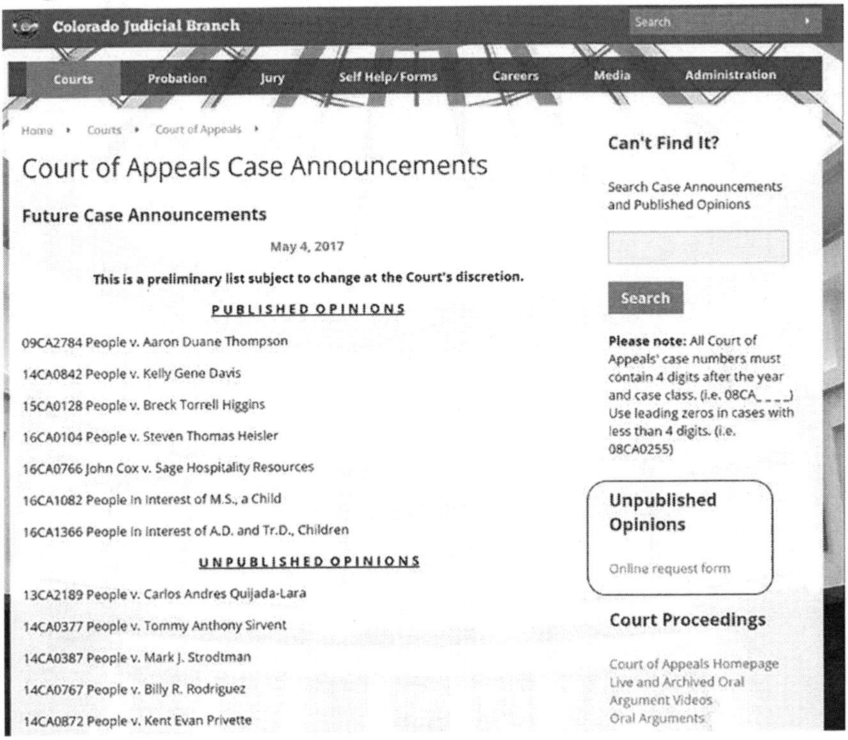


Source: www.courts.state.co.us/Courts/Court_of_Appeals/Case_Announcements

## C. Briefs and Oral Arguments

### 1. Briefs

The Colorado courts do not provide access to briefs through the court website. Researchers have a few options for obtaining briefs. First, they can contact the State Archives. Second, they can contact the University of Colorado law library which maintains an extensive collection of Supreme Court and Court of Appeals briefs dating to 1874.[1] Finally, Lexis and Westlaw subscribers have access to a limited selection of briefs on those services.

### 2. Oral Arguments

The courts' website does provide access to recent oral arguments held before those courts. These video recordings begin in 2005 and are accessible through the Appellate Courts Live Broadcast website. Researchers should locate the

1. The University of Colorado Law Library has digitized the Colorado Supreme Court Briefs as noted in Chapter 6, footnote 27.

**Figure 16-5. The Colorado Judicial Branch Provides a Limited Collection of Oral Arguments on Its Website.**

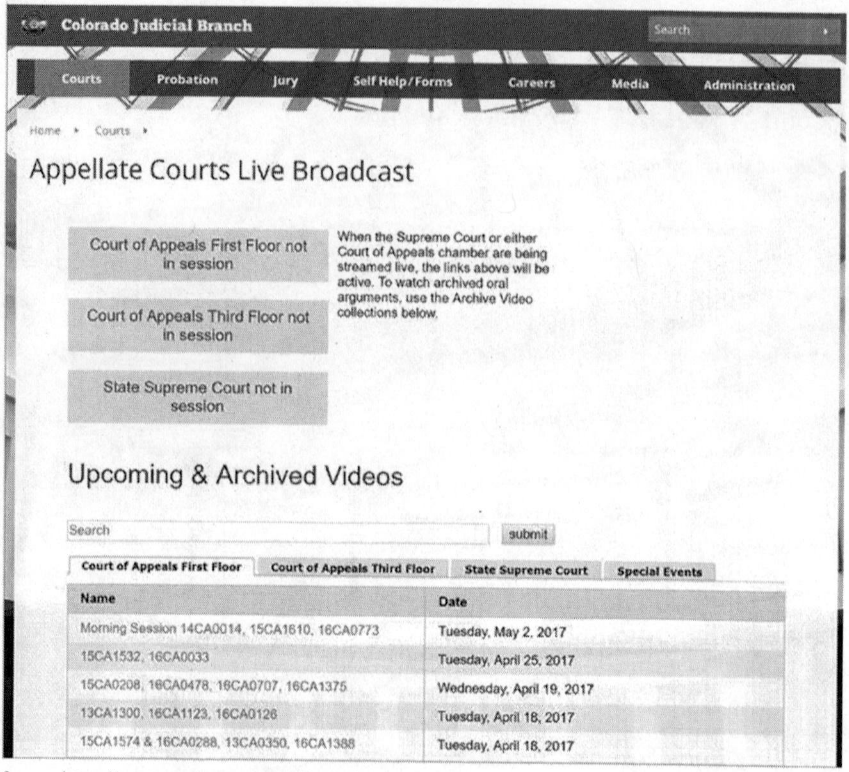


Source: https://www.courts.state.co.us/Courts/live/

oral arguments schedules on each court's webpage. Transcripts have been made of the arguments and the collection can be searched using terms and phrases.

At some point, perhaps, the court will develop a single, unified interface that provides access to the briefs, oral arguments, and court opinion on a single webpage.

## D. Chief Justice Directives

In addition to serving as a justice on the Colorado Supreme Court, the Chief Justice serves as the chief administrator for the Colorado court system. In this role, he or she ensures the smooth operation of the courts themselves.

**Figure 16-6. Researchers Can Locate Chief Justice Directives through This Search Interface.**

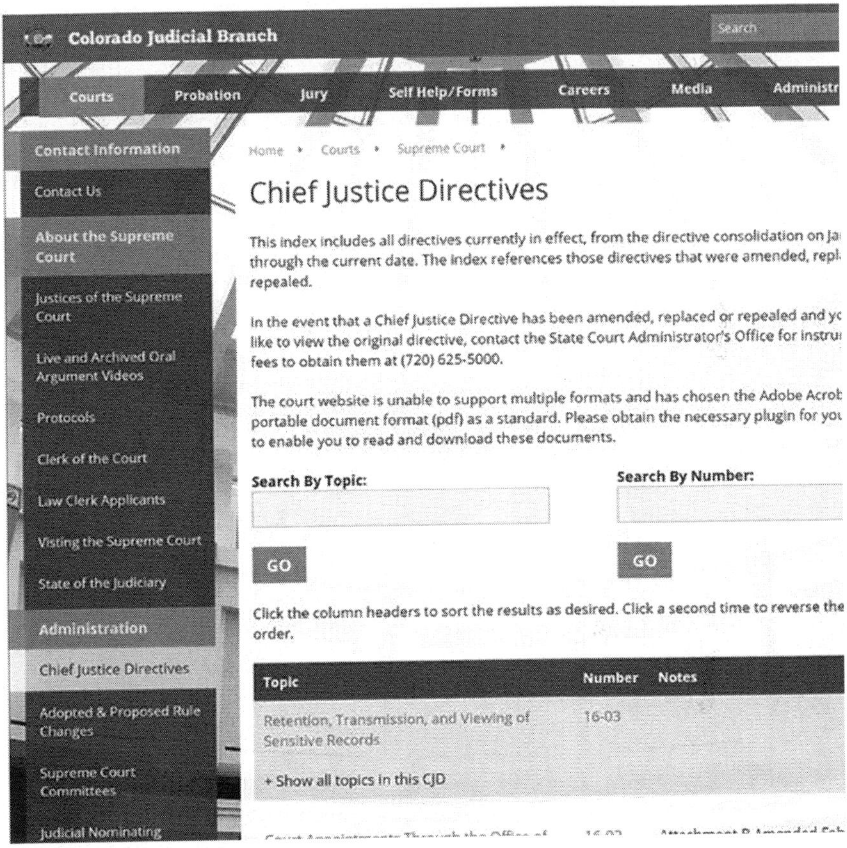


Source: www.courts.state.co.us/Courts/Supreme_Court/cjds/.

To this end, the Chief Justice can issue directives to aid the administration of the courts. These directives are available on the judiciary website at https://www.courts.state.co.us/Courts/Supreme_Court/cjds/.

While the collection is relatively small and can easily be browsed, researchers can search the collection by topic keyword or by directive number. The resulting list indicates if the directive is active or repealed (See Figure 16-6.)

# Chapter 17

# Researching Court Rules[1]

## I. Introduction

Researching court rules is similar to performing statutory research. The researcher will typically be asked to perform the projects discussed below, for example: 1) ensuring all court rules are accounted for in preparation for litigation; 2) delving into the interpretation of a court rule using case law and the rule's history in preparation for a hearing or other pre-trial matter; 3) updating a court rule and determining if any rule changes are pending and/or recently adopted. These projects can be handled efficiently and are discussed step-by-step below.

## II. Advice before Getting Started

As researchers approach court rules research, they should keep in a mind a few pointers. First, court rules are set up like statutes. The same types of information helpful in interpreting statutes are available to help interpret a court rule, although the depth can vary by rule. Second, along with state court rules, a given district, county, or municipal court may also have its own set of local rules an attorney has to consider. Finally, researchers should make use of free resources whenever possible, such as the Colorado Judicial Branch's website, at www.courts.state.co.us, for a wide variety of information.

1. This chapter was written by Peter Kersten, Intellectual Property, Environmental, and Water Law Librarian, and Adjunct Professor at the University of Denver Sturm College of Law in Denver, Colorado.

**Table 17-1. Local Court Rules Information in the CRS and CRSA**

| Resource | In Print | Online |
|---|---|---|
| Colorado Revised Statutes (official version published by Lexis) | CRS Court Rules Book 1 contains the local rules of the County Court of the City and County of Denver | CRS contains the local court rules of the 1st Judicial District for Gilpin and Jefferson counties and the local rules of the County Court of the City and County of Denver (both on Lexis and the free version online) |
| Colorado Revised Statutes Annotated (Westlaw) | CRSA Court Rules volumes contain the local rules of the 1st Judicial District for Gilpin and Jefferson counties | CRSA contains the local court rules for the 1st Judicial District for Gilpin and Jefferson counties |

## III. Task One: Locating Special Rules and Local Court Rules

Locating special and local rules is relatively simple, although it is incredibly important for the researcher not to overlook. To locate any special or local rules that may apply, the researcher can consult either the official Colorado Revised Statutes (published by Lexis) or the Colorado Revised Statutes Annotated (published by Westlaw). See Table 17-1 and the Figures 17-1 through 17-3 for more information. To ensure no local or specialty court rules are missed, the researcher should not hesitate to contact the Clerk of Court for the specific court if there is any doubt.

**Figure 17-1. Colorado Court Rules on Westlaw**

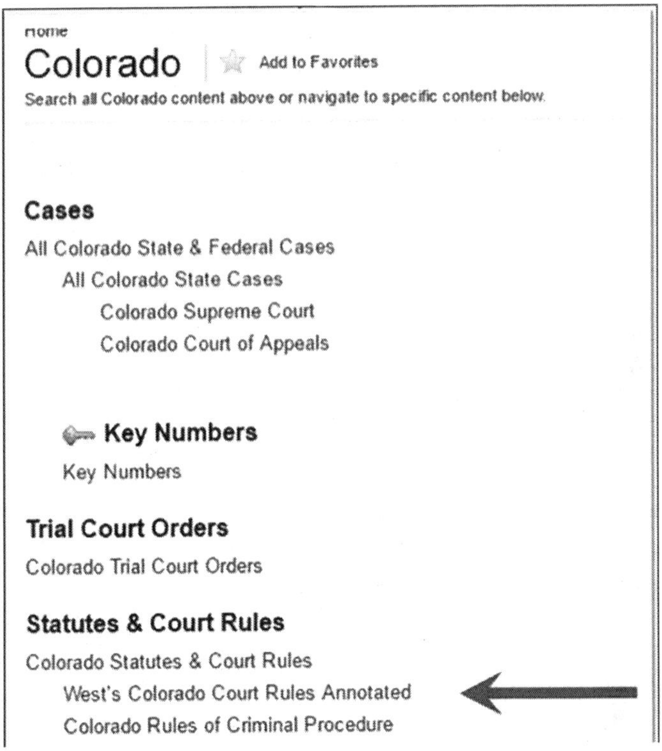


Reprinted from Westlaw with permission of Thomson Reuters.

**Figure 17-2. Colorado Court Rules on Lexis**

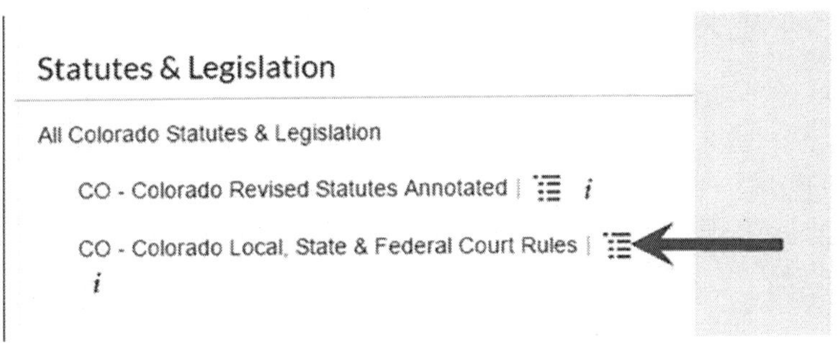


Reprinted with the permission of LexisNexis.

**Figure 17-3. Court Rules Are Created for the Broad Range of Courts and Subject Areas.**

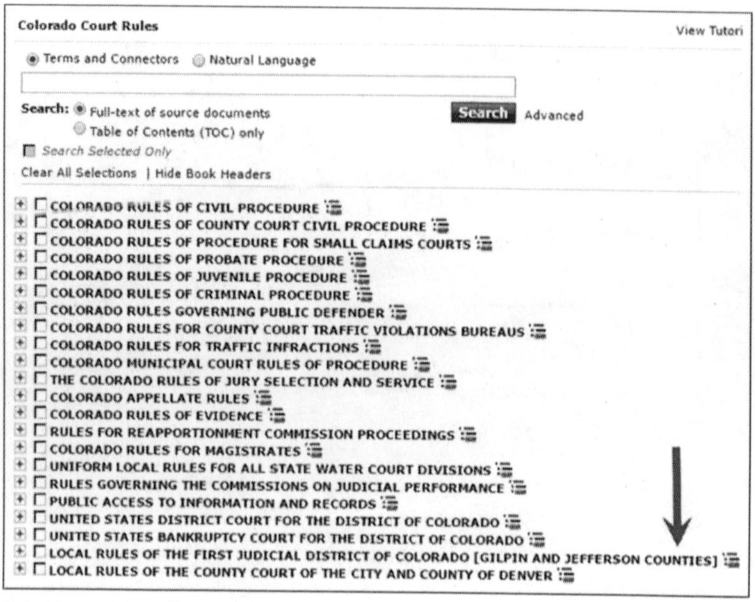


Reprinted with permission of LexisNexis.

## IV. Task Two: Reviewing the History of a Court Rule

As litigation progresses, there are often instances in which the researcher must provide authorities that support a certain interpretation of a court rule. This may be in preparation for a court hearing and, like statutory research, there is a method to finding these authorities.

If a researcher is tasked with providing authorities to support a motion to move for sanctions against another party for failure to answer discovery requests, delving into a court rule's history may be required. The following method provides accurate and complete research.

The researcher should first review the source note of the rule. Looking at this source note to Rule of Civil Procedure 37 for the example, the researcher

**Figure 17-4. Rule History Captured in Source Note**

**HISTORY: Source:** (a), (c), and (d) amended and adopted April 14, 1994, effective January 1, 1995 effective January 9, 1995; (a)(4) amended and adopted October 30, 1997, effective January 1, 1998 effective July 1, 2015, for cases filed on or after July 1, 2015.

Cross references: For general provisions governing discovery, see C.R.C.P. 26; for protective orders, questions, see C.R.C.P. 31; for depositions of public or private corporations, partnerships or associat 33; for production of documents and things and entry upon land for inspection and other purposes, s see C.R.C.P. 29; for civil contempt, see C.R.C.P. 107; for vacating a default judgment, see C.R.C.P. 6

COMMENTS 1990

[1] Subsection (b)(1) was modified to reflect that orders to deponents under subsection (a)(1), wher pending or from which the subpoena is issued pursuant to Section 13-90-111, C.R.S., and it is that c of the Colorado courts. For out-of-state depositions, any problems should be addressed by the court

1995

[2] Revised C.R.C.P. 37 is patterned substantially after Fed.R.Civ.P. 37 as amended in 1993 and has t discretionary rather than mandatory; and (2) there is no State Rule 37(e) [pertaining to sanctions fo C.R.C.P. 37 forms a part of a comprehensive case management system. See Committee Comments

2015

[3] The threat and, when required, application, of sanctions is necessary to convince litigants of the 37(a)(4) now authorizes, for motions to compel disclosures or discovery, imposition of sanctions aga award of expenses manifestly unjust." This change is intended to make it easier for judges to impos



will not only find a complete history of what sections have been amended, but also important commentary, as shown in Figure 17-4.

**TIP:** When completing this type of project, the researcher should first review the annotations to the court rule to see if any case law cited is relevant. After doing this, the researcher may be asked to delve into a court rule's history to see if other information, such as further evidence of intent behind the rule, can be gleaned.

If the researcher is tasked with locating more information than the commentary included after the court rule provides, the researcher can review relevant information on the Colorado Judicial Branch's website, www.courts.state.co.us. On this website, the researcher can review the "Adopted and Proposed Rule Changes" webpage, which provides links to all rules changes, dating back to 1997. See Figure 17-5.

If the researcher needs to review changes made prior to 1997, historical versions of mark-up documents and meeting minutes of the Supreme Court's rules committees are held with various entities in Colorado. The researcher can

**Figure 17-5. Court Rules on the Colorado Judicial Branch Website**

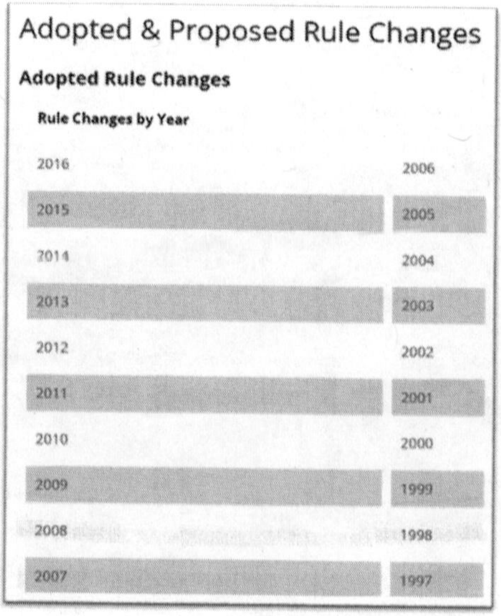


Source: www.courts.state.co.us/Courts/Supreme_Court/Rule_Changes.

contact the Office of the State Court Administrator for these documents (contact information at https://www.courts.state.co.us/Administration/Index.cfm).

**Figure 17-6. The Website of the Office of the State Court Administrator**

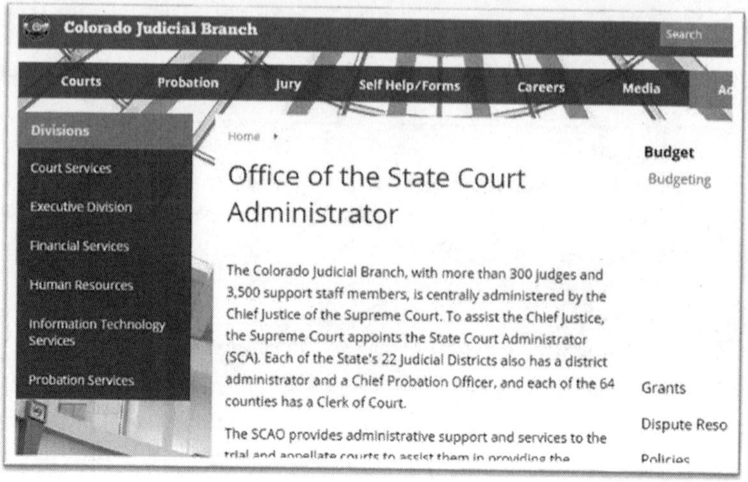


Source: www.courts.state.co.us/Administration/index.cfm.

**Figure 17-7. The Website for the Colorado Civil Rules Committee**

Source: www.courts.state.co.us/Courts/Supreme_Court/committees/committee.cfm?committe_ID=5.

If the researcher also needs to locate current meeting minutes and notes for any of the Supreme Court rules committees, this information is available at the Colorado Judicial Branch's website at https://www.courts.state.co.us/Courts/Supreme_Court/Committees/Index.cfm. In this research scenario, the "Civil Rules Committee," has meeting minutes and other documents available on its website for the researcher to review current and proposed changes, along with other information going back to 2012. See Figure 17-7.

In addition to reviewing the documents relating to past rules changes, the researcher can review the Chief Justice Directives, discussed in Chapter 16, to locate further information that contributed to a rule change. This information

**Figure 17-8. Consult the Chief Justice Directives for Rule Changes.**

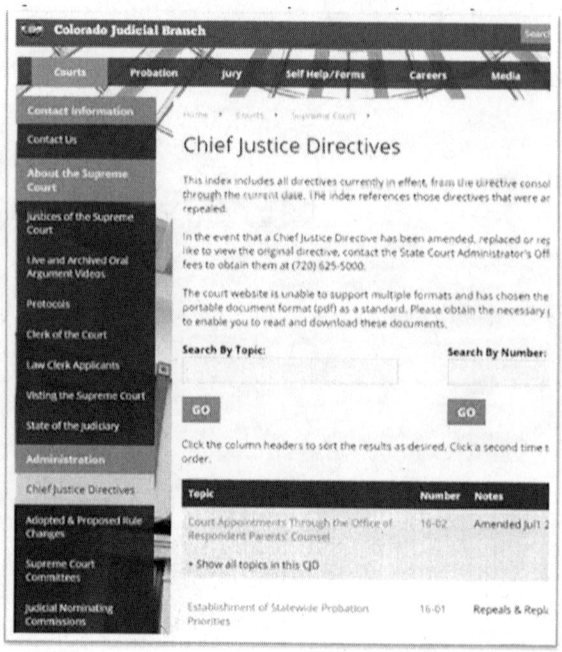


Source: www.courts.state.co.us/Courts/Supreme_Court/Directives/Index.cfm.

is available on the Court's website at https://www.courts.state.co.us/Courts/Supreme_Court/Directives/Index.cfm. (See Figure 17-8.)

In addition to reviewing case law relating to a court rule, the past amendments and related documentation discussed above, the researcher may also review relevant rules handbooks such as the Colorado Handbook on Civil Litigation, or the Colorado Civil Rules Annotated and Colorado Civil Procedure Forms and Commentary (both titles are part of the Colorado Practice Series).

## V. Task Three: Locating Pending or Recently Adopted Court Rules

In preparation for a court hearing on a matter, such as the example discussed in Task Two, the researcher may also have to determine whether there are any

**Figure 17-9. Court Rules Updates through Tools & Resources Side Panel on Westlaw.com**

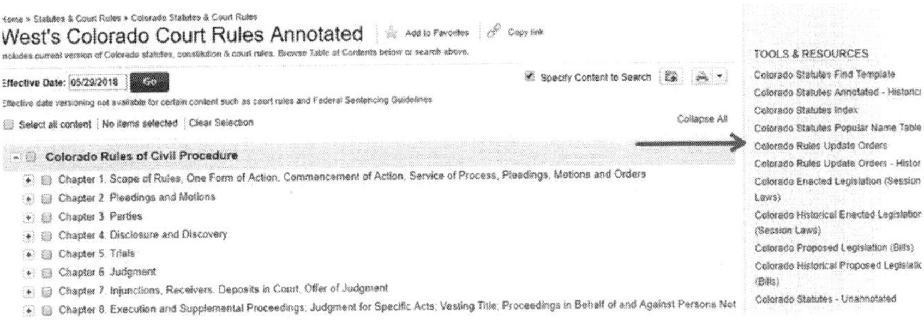


Reprinted from Westlaw with permission of Thomson Reuters.

pending or recently adopted changes to the court rule(s) involved. This process is uncomplicated but extremely important.

## A. Online

Both the CRS (Lexis) and the CRSA (Westlaw) incorporate recent changes into the court rules online. To see mark-up documents, conveniently showing specific changes, the researcher may also review the following:

- In the CRSA—"Colorado Rules Updates Orders," located on the court rules annotated page on Westlaw, shows recent changes from 2015 and 2016 to court rules. See Figures 17-9 and 17-10 for further information.
- Colorado Judicial Branch Website—the researcher can locate the mark-up documents on the "Adopted and Proposed Rule Changes" webpage for changes back to 1997, located at: https://www.courts.state.co.us/Courts/Supreme_Court/Rule_Changes.cfm.

## B. Print

The researcher may consult the CRS or CRSA in print as well. In the CRSA, the researcher may review any Legislative Service Update, any relevant pocket part(s), and the Interim Update Service. In the CRS, the researcher may review the "Colorado Court Rules Supplement," which is published every February, to see if any changes have been adopted.

**Figure 17-10. Sample of Colorado Court Orders Impacting Colorado Court Rules**

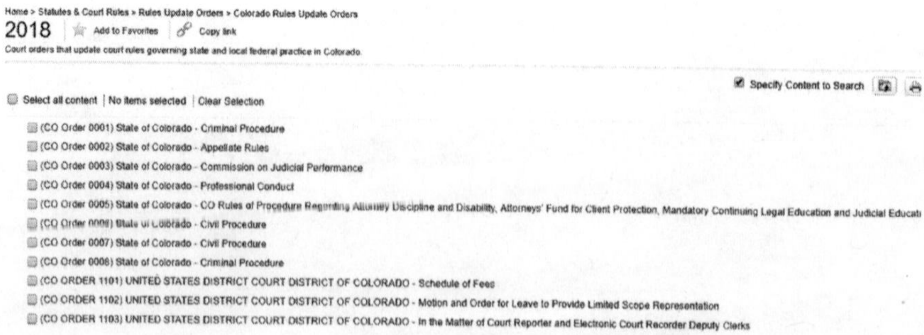
Home > Statutes & Court Rules > Rules Update Orders > Colorado Rules Update Orders

2018 Add to Favorites Copy link

Court orders that update court rules governing state and local federal practice in Colorado.

Specify Content to Search

Select all content | No items selected | Clear Selection

- (CO Order 0001) State of Colorado - Criminal Procedure
- (CO Order 0002) State of Colorado - Appellate Rules
- (CO Order 0003) State of Colorado - Commission on Judicial Performance
- (CO Order 0004) State of Colorado - Professional Conduct
- (CO Order 0005) State of Colorado - CO Rules of Procedure Regarding Attorney Discipline and Disability, Attorneys' Fund for Client Protection, Mandatory Continuing Legal Education and Judicial Educati
- (CO Order 0006) State of Colorado - Civil Procedure
- (CO Order 0007) State of Colorado - Civil Procedure
- (CO Order 0008) State of Colorado - Criminal Procedure
- (CO ORDER 1101) UNITED STATES DISTRICT COURT DISTRICT OF COLORADO - Schedule of Fees
- (CO ORDER 1102) UNITED STATES DISTRICT COURT DISTRICT OF COLORADO - Motion and Order for Leave to Provide Limited Scope Representation
- (CO ORDER 1103) UNITED STATES DISTRICT COURT DISTRICT OF COLORADO - In the Matter of Court Reporter and Electronic Court Recorder Deputy Clerks

Reprinted from Westlaw with permission of Thomson Reuters.

Other sources of information to see the most recent rule changes adopted and/or proposed include the Colorado Practice Series (in the *Colorado Civil Rules Annotated* and *Colorado Civil Rules Procedure Forms and Commentary* mentioned above) as well as the *Colorado Lawyer* (in the "Court Business" section). Recent issues are available online at http://www.cobar.org/-em-The-Colorado-Lawyer-em). Finally, there may be a relevant Continuing Legal Education (CLE) publication on recent rule changes (located at: www.cle.cobar.org).

# Chapter 18

# Researching Local Government Ordinances and Records

## I. Introduction

Chapter 11 included an overview of the types of local governments and resources in which researchers can find local law and other information. This chapter will show how to research the Municode.com website, the major source for local government ordinances, and how to find certain other types of information including property records, demographic information and budgets.

## II. Researching Local Government Ordinances

Researching local government ordinances is similar in form to researching state statutes. They follow a similar publication pattern in that the local law is first published as an ordinance and then inserted into a subject-organized code. Researchers may start their search for the charter, ordinances, and codes on the local government website but for many Colorado municipalities researchers will find these on the Municipal Code Corporation's website located at Municode.com.

### A. Locating Codes

If the address for the local government website is not known, then the researcher should start with Google to locate the address. Once on the local government website, the charter, ordinances and code may be in any number of locations. Typically, the researcher will have to scan through the site looking for it. On the City of Arvada website, these are located under a menu titled "City Hall." (See Figure 18-1.)

**Figure 18-1. The City of Arvada, Colorado, Website**

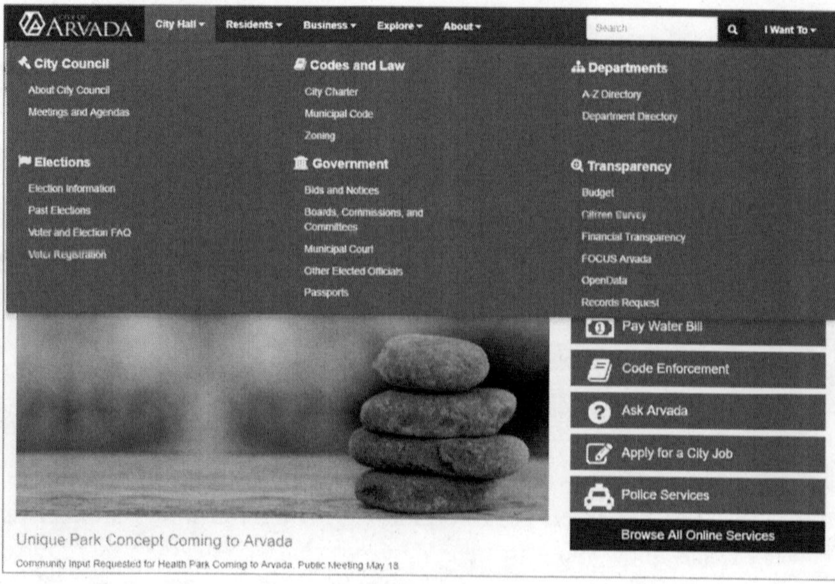


Source: www.arvada.org.

While the local government website may self-publish these documents, it may also redirect users to the Municode.com website, as is the case with the City of Arvada. (See Figure 18-2.)

Researchers can also take the direct route and search on Municode.com for the local government code. On this website, researchers should search the library of codes and select the state of Colorado. The researcher will then need to browse for the link to the local government code. (See Figure 18-3.) Again, researchers may want to use Google to jump directly to the local government code on the Municode.com website utilizing the "site" field in Google to create a search such as the following: arvada site:municode.com. This search restricts Google to only retrieving results from the Municode.com website.

## B. Using Municode.com to Research a Local Government Code

Municode.com provides researchers with an informative and user-friendly website. It contains several features which enable the researcher to perform current and historical code research. Referring to Figure 18-4, these features include a (A) table of contents of the chapters of the code, including (B) the

**Figure 18-2. The City of Arvada Municipal Code on Municode.com**

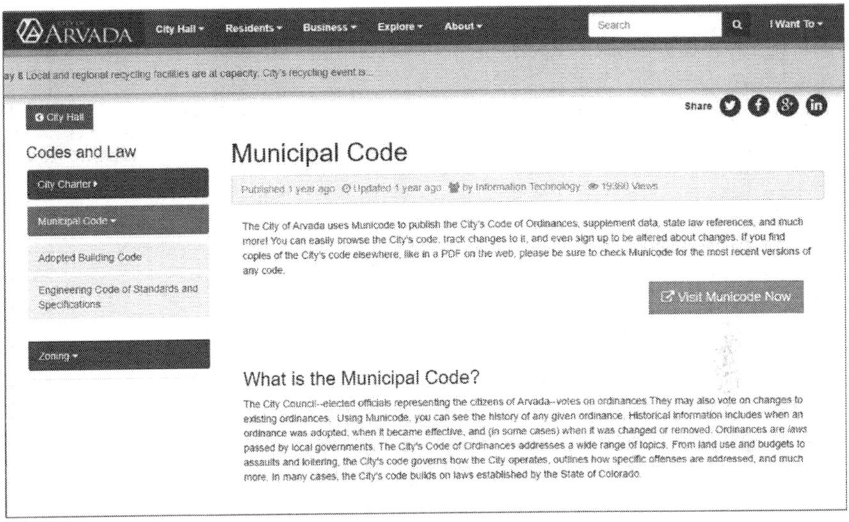


Source: www.arvada.org/city-hall/city-code/municipal-code.

charter, if a home rule municipality; (C) the date of the current version of the code which the user can change to an older version using the drop-down arrow next to the date; (D) a supplement history table so that a user can track changes to the code; (E) the date the code was last updated; (F) the last ordinance the code contains and the date that ordinance was adopted; (G) the ability to see how the code has changed; and (H) a list of ordinances adopted but not yet incorporated into the code. These features are clear and instill confidence in the researcher that the code is maintained and accurate.

Researchers can either browse the chapters for relevant content or use the search box at the top of the page for keyword searching. Advanced search options are available, giving researchers the ability to (a) search by phrase; (b) use Boolean operators and wildcard characters; and (c) use term proximity searching.

Finally, and importantly, researchers can sign up to receive email notifications when the code is updated.

After a code section is retrieved, Municode provides additional features to help research. Referring to Figure 18-5, these include (A) the statutory derivation for the code section including the ordinance(s) that created and modified it and where this section was located in a previous edition of the code; (B) a reference to applicable state law; and (C) methods to print and share the code section.

**Figure 18-3. Municode.com Hosts the Municipal Codes for Many Colorado Municipalities and a Few Counties**

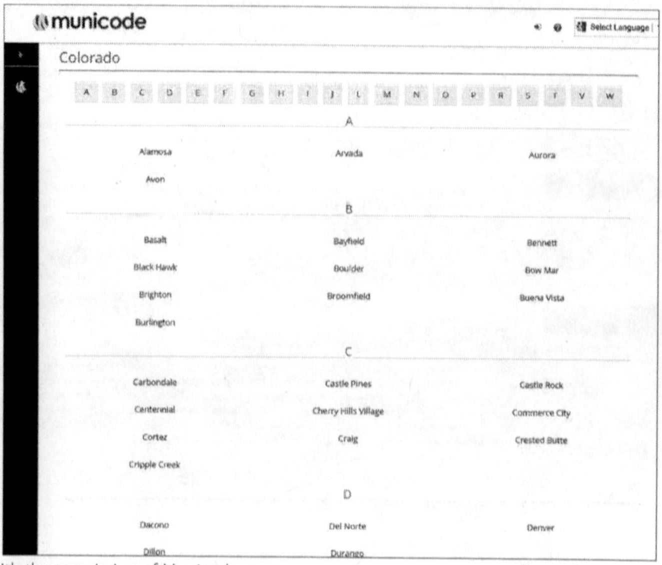


Reprinted with the permission of Municode.

## C. Locating Property and Tax Records

Another function of a local government website is to provide access to real property records including information about appraisals and taxation. Deeds, mortgages, certain easements and other documents need to be filed in the land records of the county in which a property is located in order to give notice to creditors. Historically, these records were available in large, print volumes and also on microfiche. More recently, local governments have digitized these records and are accessible through their websites.

To locate these records, the first step is to find the website for the county in which the land is located. On the local government website, the researcher should search for the assessor's office or real property records. Alternatively, of course, the researcher can search on Google using search terms such as "land records" or "assessor" or even "parcel search" along with the name of the county. See Figure 18-6 for a view of the Douglas County, Colorado Assessor's Office website.

The next step involves entering the property address, property owner's name, or parcel number into the county's property records search engine. On Douglas County's website, the researcher can do this from the homepage using

**Figure 18-4. Municode.com Interface**

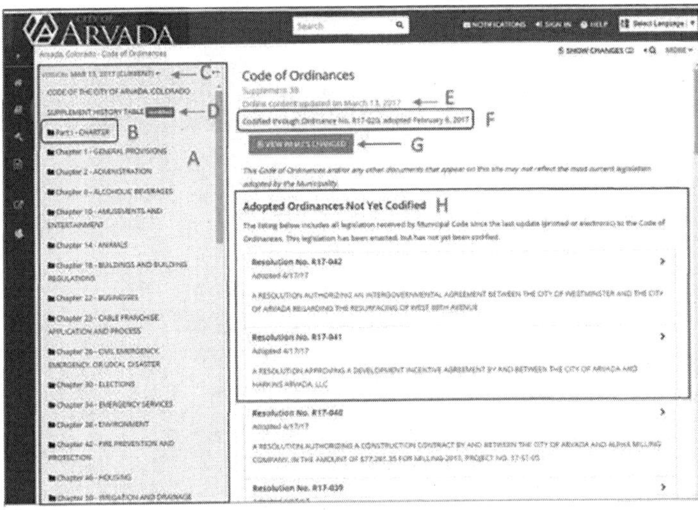


Reprinted with the permission of Municode. https://library.municode.com/co/arvada/code_of_ordinances

the drop-down menu, as noted on Figure 18-6. Typically, the system requires proper postal abbreviations (i.e., Lane as Ln., and Street as St. etc.) but some search engines may be more forgiving in this regard.

**Figure 18-5. Code Section Display on Municode.com**

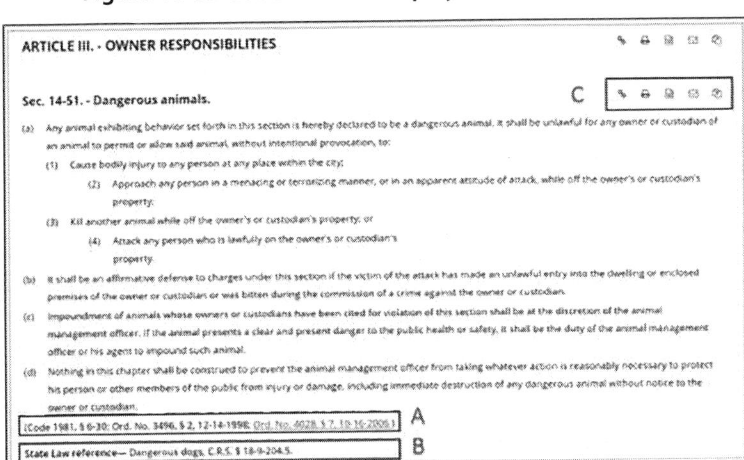

**Figure 18-6. Douglas County, Colorado, Website**

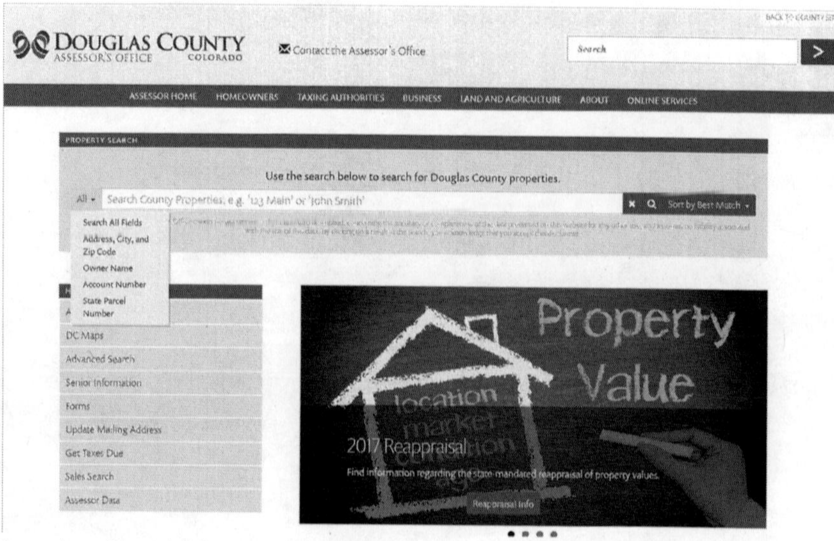


Source: https://www.douglas.co.us/assessor

After a search is entered, the property profile should be returned, as indicated in Figure 18-7. For Douglas County land records, the researcher will find (a) the name and address of the current owner; (b) the sales history including name of the last grantor; (c) the legal description of the property; and (d) the year it was built and information about the structure (i.e., square footage, rooms, etc.).

Importantly, the list will also include the actual and assessed value of the property along with the tax rate and estimated taxes to be paid on the property. Researchers can locate additional details including the various local government taxing authorities levying taxes on the property and the millage rate. These details are available through the "tax authorities" link on the profile, as indicated in Figure 18-8.

Finally, the profile should include a listing of the types of documents recorded for this property, and perhaps provide access to the documents themselves. While these documents may be provided without charge, local governments may also require registration and a fee to access them.

For Douglas County, these documents are available without charge. To find them, the researcher can search the "Recorded Document Search" by name, book, and page or reception number, among other methods. To do this most

**Figure 18-7. Property Record Detail**

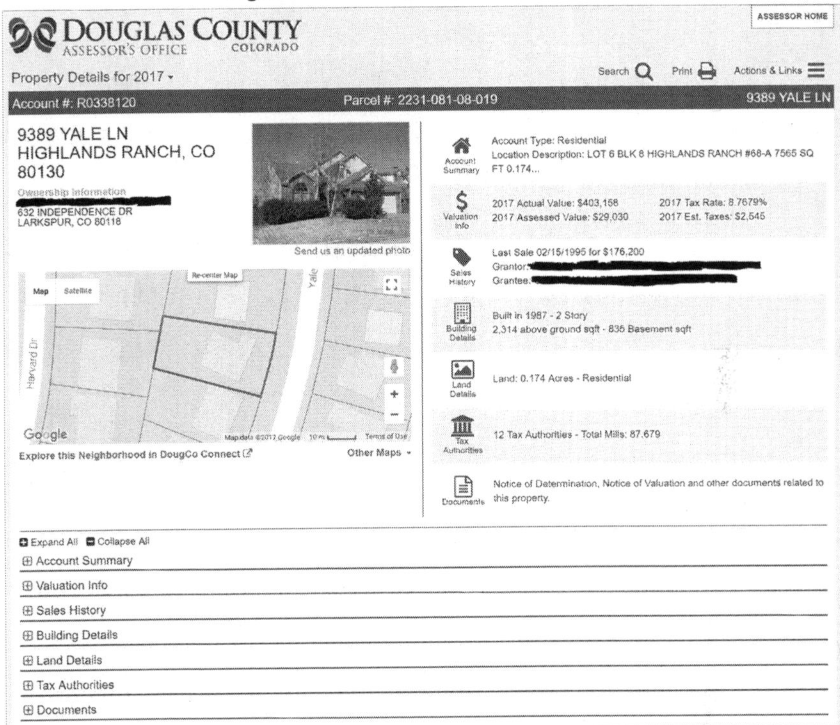


Source: https://www.douglas.co.us/

efficiently, the researcher should find that information under the "Sale History" section in the property profile. (See Figure 18-9.)

In this example, researchers could find the warranty deed executed on February 15, 1995 in Book 1248 at Page 216, or by searching for Reception Number 9508112 in the "Recorded Document Search" application linked in the record. By following this link, the researcher will see a menu of search options, and can use available information to retrieve the document. (See Figure 18-10.) Other property records search systems will vary from that provided by Douglas County and users should review online help provided to most effectively search property records.

## D. Locating Local Government Budgets

Occasionally, researchers will want to find other documents produced by a local government. These can include council meeting minutes, zoning regu-

**Figure 18-8. Tax Authorities**

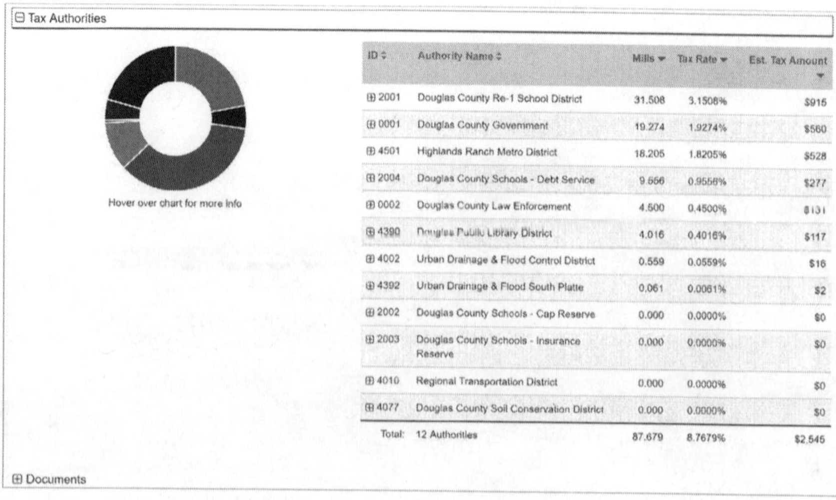


| ID | Authority Name | Mills | Tax Rate | Est. Tax Amount |
|---|---|---|---|---|
| ⊞ 2001 | Douglas County Re-1 School District | 31.508 | 3.1508% | $915 |
| ⊞ 0001 | Douglas County Government | 19.274 | 1.9274% | $560 |
| ⊞ 4501 | Highlands Ranch Metro District | 18.205 | 1.8205% | $528 |
| ⊞ 2004 | Douglas County Schools - Debt Service | 9.556 | 0.9556% | $277 |
| ⊞ 0002 | Douglas County Law Enforcement | 4.500 | 0.4500% | $131 |
| ⊞ 4390 | Douglas Public Library District | 4.016 | 0.4016% | $117 |
| ⊞ 4002 | Urban Drainage & Flood Control District | 0.559 | 0.0559% | $16 |
| ⊞ 4392 | Urban Drainage & Flood South Platte | 0.061 | 0.0061% | $2 |
| ⊞ 2002 | Douglas County Schools - Cap Reserve | 0.000 | 0.0000% | $0 |
| ⊞ 2003 | Douglas County Schools - Insurance Reserve | 0.000 | 0.0000% | $0 |
| ⊞ 4010 | Regional Transportation District | 0.000 | 0.0000% | $0 |
| ⊞ 4077 | Douglas County Soil Conservation District | 0.000 | 0.0000% | $0 |
| Total: | 12 Authorities | 87.679 | 8.7679% | $2,545 |

Source: https://www.douglas.co.us/.

lations, building codes, services and financial assistance programs, road construction plans, and master plans for the municipality. The local government website is the first stop for these sorts of documents.

One such document that researchers may want to locate is the municipal budget. In Colorado, there are two sources for such a document. The first is the local government website. Figure 18-11 shows that part of Arvada's website which provides current and historical budget data including the city's capital improvement plan and other financial transparency documents.

The second source for this data is the Division of Local Government (DOLA) website, a department of the Department of Local Affairs. As noted in Chapter

**Figure 18-9. Accessing Property Documents**

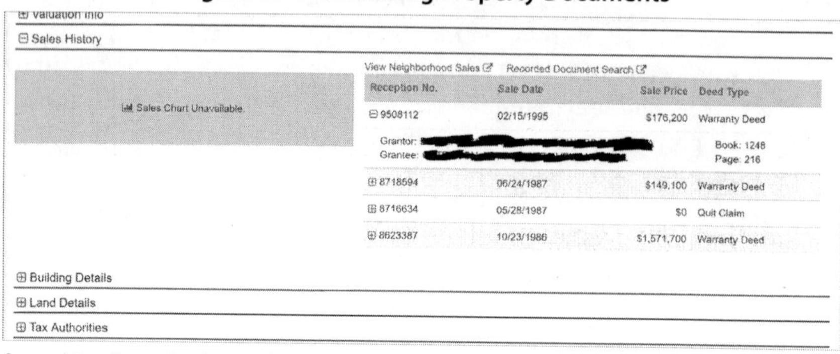


| Reception No. | Sale Date | Sale Price | Deed Type |
|---|---|---|---|
| ⊟ 9508112 | 02/15/1995 | $176,200 | Warranty Deed |
| ⊞ 8718594 | 06/24/1987 | $149,100 | Warranty Deed |
| ⊞ 8716634 | 05/28/1987 | $0 | Quit Claim |
| ⊞ 8623387 | 10/23/1986 | $1,571,700 | Warranty Deed |

Source: https://www.douglas.co.us/.

**Figure 18-10. Accessing the Online Property Records for Douglas County, Colorado**

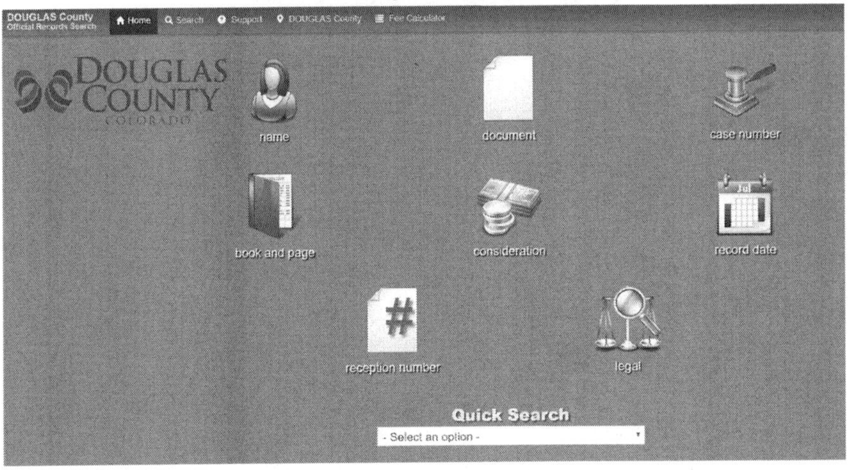


Source: https://www.douglas.co.us/

11, DOLA provides assistance to local governments. As part of their data collection and analysis, the agency maintains a list of active local government's contact information and key documents. Accessible through the "Local Gov-

**Figure 18-11. The City of Arvada Budget Documents on Its Website**

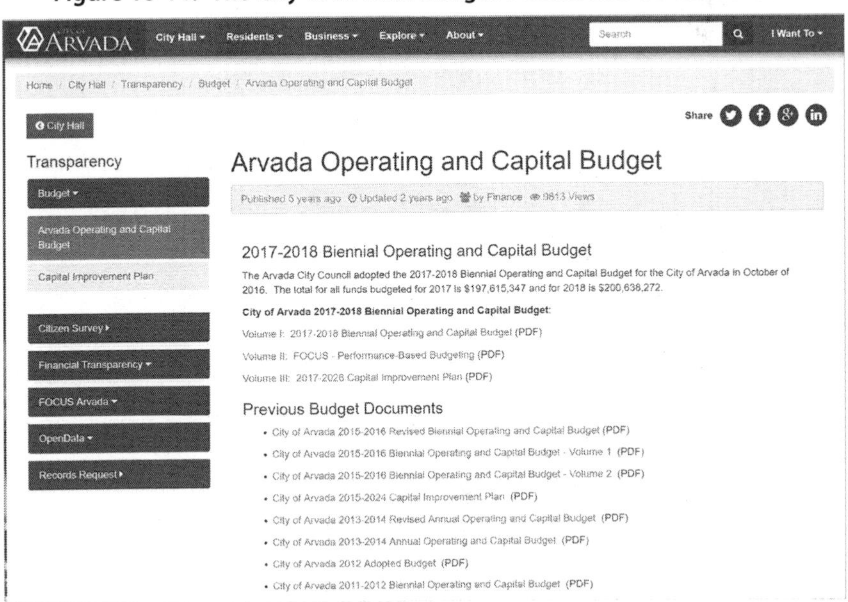


Source: https://arvada.org/city-hall/transparency/operating-and-capital-budget

**Figure 18-12. Researchers Can Access the Most Recent Municipal Budget on the DOLA Website.**

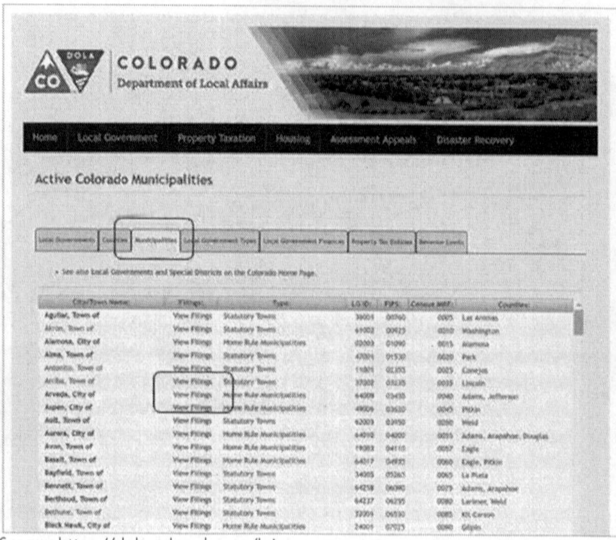


Source: https://dola.colorado.gov/lgis

ernment Information System" under the Local Government website, researchers can locate the municipality's budget and other pertinent information. These are available through the "View Filings" link in Figure 18-12.

**Figure 18-13. Available City of Arvada Documents on the DOLA Website**

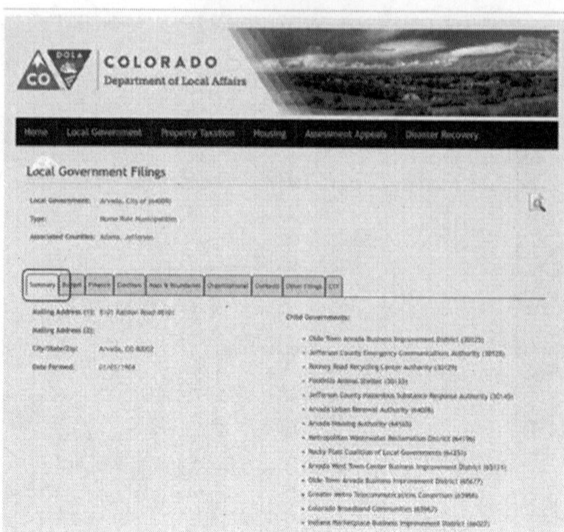


Source: https://dola.colorado.gov/lgis

**Figure 18-14. State Demography Office Website**

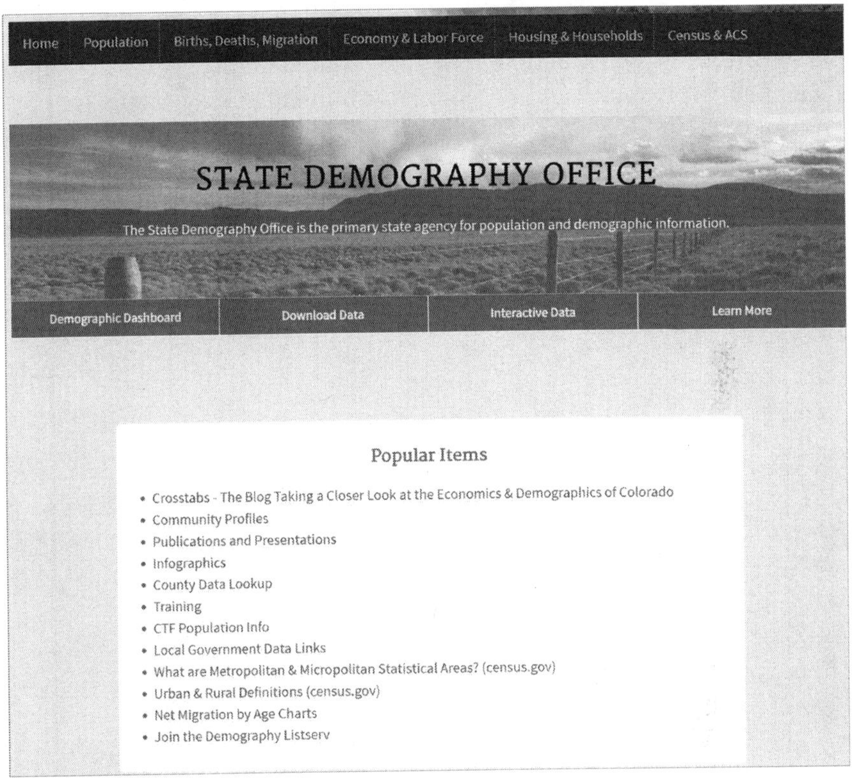


Source: https://demography.dola.colorado.gov

The filings for Arvada include the most recent budget, plus documents related to local governments subject to Arvada, called "child governments" on this page. (See Figure 18-13.)

## E. Locating Demographic Data

The DOLA website also provides demographic data. The State Demography Office publishes reports and data sets on various aspects of local government populations. (See Figure 18-14.) These include census data, economic data, employment data and other information. Reports include community profiles on a select number of Colorado counties, cities and towns. Researchers can generate custom data sets on one or more counties on a variety of statistics dating back to 1985. These data can be downloaded as Comma Separated Values (CSV) documents which can then be imported into a spreadsheet program such as Microsoft Excel. The website even publishes infographics which more clearly illustrate data and trends of various Colorado statistics.

# Chapter 19

# Researching Secondary Authority and Practice Materials

## I. Introduction

This chapter addresses a few issues in researching secondary authority. While these publications typically include a limited selection of research tools, the tools vary widely in how they are implemented by different publishers. For example, one technique to improve search results is to search within an online publication's fields. This allows researchers to narrow search terms to only the title field, for example. However, the step-by-step for this procedure will vary from one database to another, although the concept is the same. Nonetheless, this chapter will highlight some approaches to finding and selecting secondary authority as well as a few different techniques for using secondary authority given different starting points.

## II. Finding Secondary Authority

After the researcher identifies the need for secondary authority, the next question is where can this authority be found. There are five different ways to find secondary authority. These include (1) consulting a library catalog; (2) consulting a publisher's or reseller's website; (3) searching for publications in a vendor's online database; (4) locating a citation from another secondary authority or annotated code; and (5) finally, asking someone for help.

### A. Using a Library Catalog

One place to search for secondary authority is a library catalog. While public libraries may have some legal materials in their collection, the researcher should search the online catalogs of academic and court law libraries. Catalog interfaces will vary from library to library but the principles and approaches of searching will remain constant.

First, the researcher should keep in mind the type of information contained in a library catalog. Library catalogs contains bibliographic records. These are brief descriptions of the book or item itself. Typically, this information includes the title of the item, author(s), subjects addressed by the item, and perhaps a brief description of the contents of the item. Library catalogs do not contain full text of items. Given this type of data in the catalog, researchers should use broad search terms to locate relevant items. For example, if the researcher is looking for materials on Colorado requirements for revocable trusts, the researcher may want to use broad terms such as "trusts," "revocable trusts" or "wills and estates" and also "Colorado." The researcher will then need to parse through the search results to identify titles that likely address the narrower search query.

Next, there are two basic approaches to searching in a library catalog. The first is to search the catalog by keyword. These keywords can search all parts of the catalog record. This would be the broadest search, as it would return results where the keywords appear anywhere in the record.

Researchers can narrow the results by limiting the search to particular fields in the records. Consulting Figure 19-1, these include title, author, subject and call number, among others. The advantage of this approach is to limit the number of results to those that are likely more relevant.

Once the list of search results is obtained, the researcher will need to sift through the results. It is in this process that the researcher can begin to find relevant secondary authority titles. By skimming the titles, and perhaps opening the record to see what the title addresses, the researcher can get an idea of whether the title is relevant to the search. The researcher will need to note the call number of revelant titles to find the title in the library. By going to the bookshelves where these titles are generally located allows the researcher to scan titles and their coverage, and page through books to identify which titles may be most helpful. This technique, the "stand-n-scan" approach, may prove to be the most helpful. This technique works well in large academic libraries and all libraries that organize their materials by a classification system because the titles are organized by subject.

Searching by subject is the second method to identify relevant titles. The electronic equivalent of the "stand-n-scan" is to use the subject identifier fields in the records. If the researcher finds a relevant title, he or she can use the subject field of that record to find additional titles. For example, Figure 19-2

**Figure 19-1. University of Colorado Law Library Catalog**

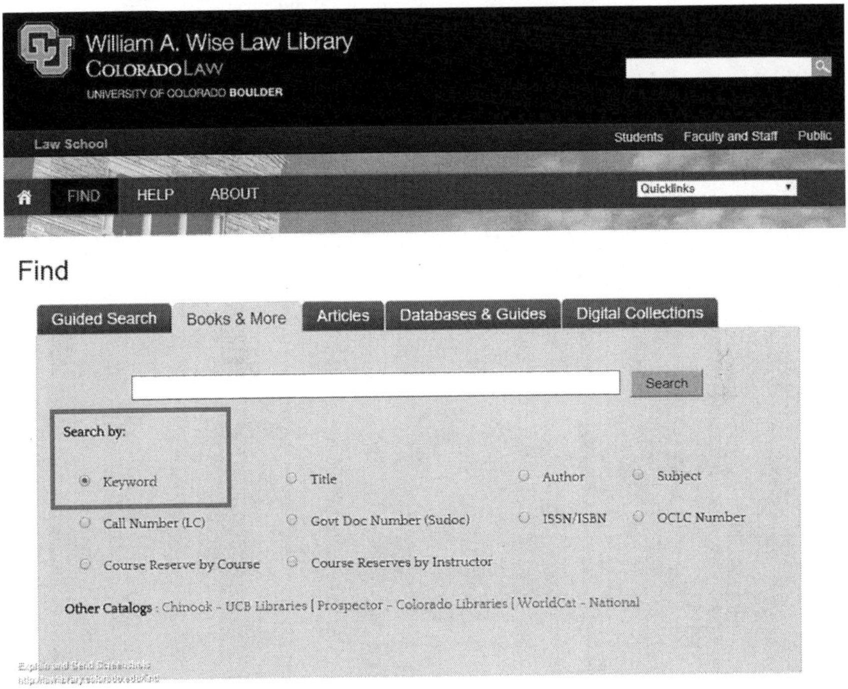


Source: http://lawlibrary.colorado.edu.

shows the record for the title "Funding the Revocable Living Trust." Under the Subject field in this record, the researcher will note that this title covers the subjects "Revocable trusts—Colorado" and "Estate Planning—Colorado" among others. By clicking on the linked subject "Revocable trusts—Colorado" the search engine will return all of the other records in the catalog that are also tagged with that subject heading. The researcher will then need to sift through those results to find titles and publication types are that are most suitable to the research problem.

## B. Consulting a Publisher's or Reseller's Website

Even if the researcher is not in the library to access the print or electronic materials the library provides, the researcher can use the catalog to find relevant titles. In addition to noting the call number or subject, the researcher should also note the publisher of the material. He or she can then search for that publisher (or title) on the Internet to purchase the title and to see also what other relevant materials are available. Of course, the researcher can start

**Figure 19-2. Subject Fields in Bibliographic Record**

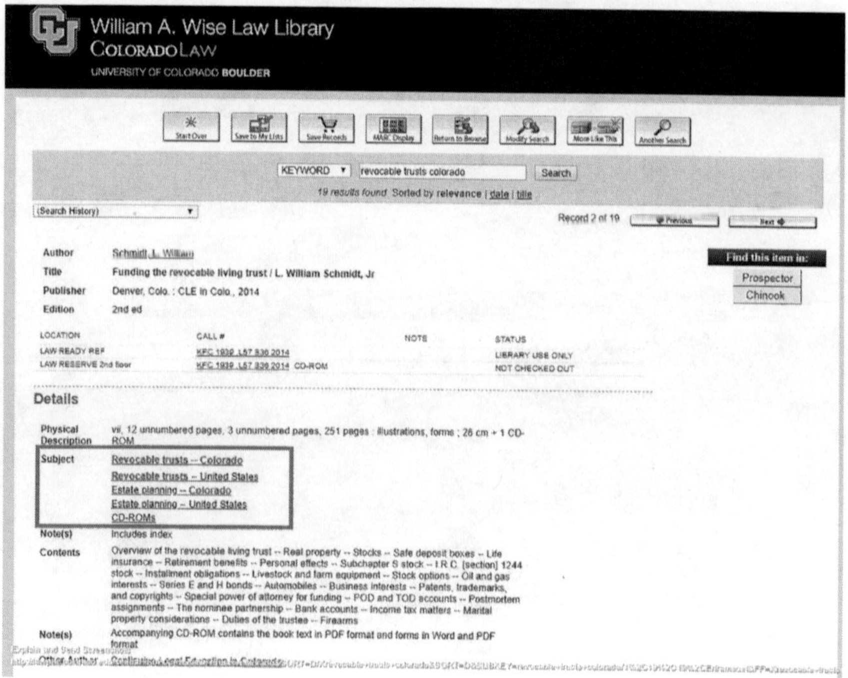


Source: http://lawlibrary.colorado.edu.

with this step either using Google or some other search engine, or use a reseller's website. In this latter instance, Amazon would probably be the best starting point.

For Colorado practice materials, there are only a few publishers. These include Thomson-Reuters, LexisNexis, and most importantly, the Colorado Bar Association's publication arm, the CBA-CLE.[1] By browsing a publisher's website, researchers will see what titles are currently available. The researcher can purchase the title or at least reach out to a law library to locate and use the title. If the library offers a document delivery service, the researcher may be able to obtain the relevant section(s) of the title for a delivery fee.

1. For complete information about publishers of Colorado legal materials, please consult Linz's "Colorado Legal Resources: An Annotated Bibliography" published by the W. S. Hein Company.

**Figure 19-3. Estate Planning Materials on Westlaw**

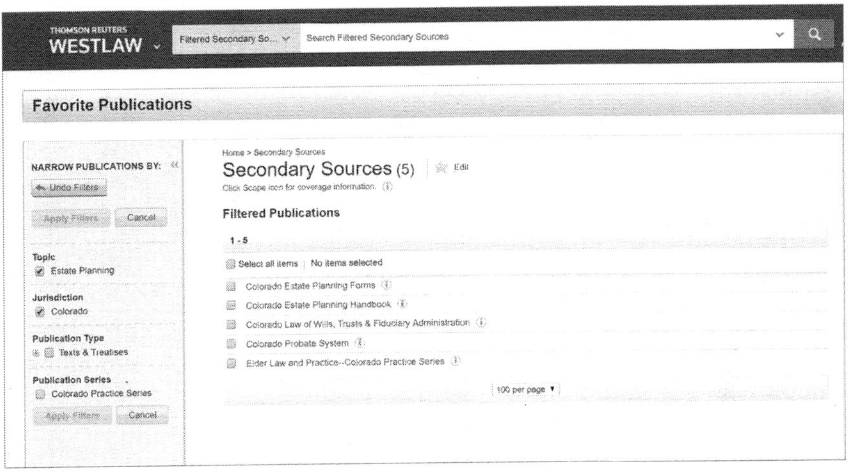




## C. Searching a Vendor's Online Directory

If the researcher is using an online subscription service, such as Westlaw or Lexis Advance, he or she can simply search the database directory to identify what Colorado practice materials and other secondary authority are available through the subscription. If using this method, the researcher should locate the coverage and currency of the title as well as consult any online navigation aids and help. (See Figure 19-3.)

## D. Locating a Title from Another Publication

With this method, the researcher locates a title as reference from another publication. For example, the researcher may find a reference to a wills practice treatise while researching the Colorado probate code in the Colorado Revised Statutes, an annotated code. This technique recalls one of the basic design principles of legal publications covered in Chapter 13—connectivity. The researcher should note these connections wherever possible to save time and conduct thorough research.

## E. Asking Someone for Help

The final technique is simply asking someone for help. Good sources for this sort of advice include practitioners in the area of law and librarians. These individuals will likely know of the major treatise(s) and other types of secondary authority and perhaps have a tip or two about how to use them. They may also direct the researcher to a published directory of Colorado resources, such as "Colorado Legal Resources: An Annotated Bibliography" by Robert Linz.

## III. Selecting Secondary Authority

Chapters 9 and 10 review the variety and types of secondary authority. One overarching consideration is how to know which secondary authority to use. While a researcher may consult a number of different secondary authority while researching a problem, it may prove efficient to start with particular types of secondary authority, depending on the problem to be researched. Secondary authority varies by the types of audiences served, intended use of the information, depth of treatment of a topic, and jurisdictions covered. Researchers should consider these criteria when selecting a secondary authority.

- If a researcher is unfamiliar with a particular area of law, he or she should start research by obtaining a high-level understanding of the area of law. This would include an introduction to the major issues and primary authority as well as the particular jargon used in that area of law. To most efficiently obtain this information, the researcher could start research in a legal encyclopedia, nutshell or hornbook, or a jurisdiction-specific practice treatise.
- If a researcher is familiar with an area of law but is researching a novel application or development in that area of law, he or she should look to more scholarly publications. For example, the researcher would likely use an in-depth, comprehensive academic treatise on the subject, or may even turn to law journal articles which may address a new application or extension of law.
- If a researcher is practicing law in Colorado, then he or she would likely turn to one of the many Colorado practice treatises in their subject area. These treatises will provide sufficient coverage to educate the researcher about the issues and law in Colorado as well as provide checklists, forms, and other tools useful for the efficient practice of law.

Ultimately, researchers will develop a sense for which publications will most likely be helpful to research the legal problems encountered by the researcher.

# Appendix

# Legal Citation[1]

## I. Introduction

Throughout the legal research process, the researcher will encounter and eventually construct legal citations (i.e., references to primary and secondary legal authority). Constructing legal citations for legal memoranda may at first seem daunting, but with practice becomes easier. This chapter describes citation standards in Colorado, provides advice on using *The Bluebook*, and ends with examples of Colorado legal citations.

## II. Why Cite

Legal citations are used to support legal arguments. The citation itself is meant to provide the reader with a gateway to the authority relied upon for that legal argument.[2] More pragmatically, Colorado courts require citations to relevant authority.[3]

## III. Citations Styles

Notwithstanding those practical goals, the strictures of citation manuals can at times seem to value form over function. A helpful question to ask when-

---

1. This chapter was written by Nick Harrell, Student Services and Outreach Librarian at the University of Colorado William A. Wise Law Library in Boulder, Colorado.

2. *See The Bluebook: A Uniform System of Citation* 1 (Columbia Law Review Ass'n et al. eds., 20th ed. 2015) [hereinafter *Bluebook*].

3. *E.g.*, Colo. R. App. P. 56; Statewide Practice Standard § 1-15(3).

ever the researcher crafts a legal citation is: *does the reader have enough information to find this source?* If (1) the researcher can answer *yes* to that question, and (2) the researcher has attempted to conform to an appropriate citation manual, then the researcher's citation is likely in good shape.

The dominant legal citation style manual in the United States is the *Uniform System of Citation: The Bluebook* ("The Bluebook").[4] Recently two other systems have emerged. The Association of Legal Writing Directors ("ALWD") created their own manual with the intent of simplifying legal citation.[5] The ALWD manual, however, is primarily used as a teaching tool and will not be referenced more in this chapter. The third system used in some jurisdictions, including Colorado in some instances, utilizes public domain citations.[6]

Beyond an implied preference to use the public domain citation for Colorado Supreme Court and Colorado Court of Appeals opinions when available, there is no explicit requirement to follow a particular legal citation system when filing legal documents with Colorado state courts. Chief Justice Directive 12-01 permits, but does not require, researchers to use "the public domain citation format"[7] when citing cases. However, it does require that published opinions of the Colorado Supreme Court and Colorado Court of Appeals adhere to that format for opinions issued on or after January 1, 2012.[8] Colorado Appellate Rule 32 et al. require that legal authority be cited to support arguments, but they are silent on what form those citations should take. And because local

4. The Bluebook can be found in all law libraries and some public libraries. The Indigo Book is an attempt to make the citation system freely available here https://law.resource.org/pub/us/code/blue/IndigoBook.pdf.

5. A quick look at the ALWD manual reveals that their efforts may have been in vain; the ALWD manual has ballooned to a comparable length and level of complexity as the Bluebook.

6. Case law citation has historically depended on references to opinions published in commercial case law reporters. Consequently, certain components of those reporters are subject to copyright protection. Beyond copyright concerns, public domain citation improves access to legal information by ignoring the distinction between print and online materials. For those reasons, when given the option between public domain or Bluebook or ALWD citations, public domain citation is typically preferred.

In an effort to promote access to primary legal materials, namely published court opinions, the Supreme Court of Colorado has adopted a vendor-neutral or public domain citation standard for its published opinions since January 1, 2012. Chief Justice Directive 12-01 (Jan. 2012), https://www.courts.state.co.us/Courts/Supreme_Court/Directives/CJD%2012-01.pdf.

7. *Id.*

8. *Id.*

courts can have additional requirements, it is always a good idea to consult local court rules before filing documents with a court. Consult Chapter 8 for a general discussion of local court rules and Chapter 17 for specific techniques for searching for local court rules.

For historical reasons, most legal citations in Colorado follow *The Bluebook*. Citations in opinions from the Colorado Supreme Court and the Colorado Court of Appeals differ from *The Bluebook* in several ways. The examples later in this chapter demonstrate those differences.

## IV. *Bluebook* Usage Tips

*The Bluebook* is divided into two main sections: the blue pages at the front of the book and the white pages.[9] The blue pages should be followed for legal documents to be filed with courts and other legal memoranda; the white pages are primarily used for academic legal writing. Bluebook rule B2 provides a table of the main differences between the blue and white pages. Notably, sometimes the blue pages refer to the white pages for guidance.[10] Legal memoranda, as opposed to academic legal writing, use in-text citations instead of footnotes.

Colorado legal researchers should familiarize themselves with the table of contents of *The Bluebook*. Specifically, page X of the table of contents lists the various sections of the blue pages; this can be used to find relevant citation rules quickly. Another table the researcher should be familiar with is the Colorado section of table T1. That section provides abbreviations for various Colorado-specific authority (e.g., opinions, statutes, regulations). Additionally, the index of *The Bluebook* can direct a researcher to specific citation rules for various primary and secondary sources.

Each *Bluebook* rule begins with an example of a citation for the type of document the rule covers.[11] Following the example, the rule lists the requirements of citations for the particular document and general guidance. Most rules also include subsections that provide additional requirements and exceptions to the main rule. Like interpreting a statute, researchers should rely on the most specific rule or subsection that applies to a given situation.

9. All references to *The Bluebook* in this section are to the Twentieth Edition.
10. *E.g.*, Bluebook, *supra* note 1, at R11.
11. *E.g.*, *Id.* (providing an example of how to cite to constitutions).

# V. Examples of Citations to Colorado Authority[12]

As noted above, Colorado courts do not require a specific citation style. The examples that follow provide citations to Colorado primary and secondary authority as they might appear in (1) opinions of the Colorado Supreme Court; (2) opinions of the Colorado Court of Appeals; and (3) if the citations conformed to *The Bluebook* blue pages. Colorado researchers might prefer to follow the first two categories of examples when filing with those respective courts. However, when in doubt a researcher might follow the third option; for example, a researcher might use *The Bluebook* blue page form for citing materials submitted to a Colorado trial court.

## Examples of Citation to Colorado Primary Authority

### Colorado Constitution

**Colorado Supreme Court:** Colo. Const. art. IX, § 2.

**Colorado Court of Appeals:** Colo. Const. art. IX, § 2.

**Bluebook:** Colo. Const. art. IX, § 2.

### Colorado Statutes

**Colorado Supreme Court:** § 6-1-101, C.R.S. (2016).

**Colorado Court of Appeals:** § 6-1-101, C.R.S. 2016.

**Bluebook:** Colo. Rev. Stat. § 6-1-101 (2016).

- Any of these examples may be preceded by the official title or popular title of the statute; e.g., Colorado Consumer Protection Act, Colo. Rev. Stat. § 6-1-101 (2016).

### Colorado Session Laws

**Colorado Supreme Court:** Ch. 91, sec. 1, § 13-7-60, 1965 Colo. Sess. Laws 333.

**Colorado Court of Appeals:** Ch. 91, sec. 1, 1965 Colo. Sess. Laws 333.

**Bluebook:** Motor Vehicle Financial Responsibility Act, ch. 143, 1969 Colo. Sess. Laws 371.

---

12. The following are for legal memoranda; citation formats differ slightly for academic writing. See *Bluebook*, supra note 1, B3 for a comparison of legal memoranda and academic writing style differences.

### Colorado Legislative Materials

**Colorado Supreme Court:** Hearings on H.B. 06-1326 before the H. Judiciary Comm., 65th Gen. Assemb., 2d Sess. (Feb. 23, 2006).

**Colorado Court of Appeals:** Hearings on H.B. 06-1326 before the H. Judiciary Comm., 65th Gen. Assemb., 2d Sess. (Feb. 23, 2006).

**Bluebook:** *Hearing on H.B. 06-1326 Before the H. Judiciary Comm.*, 65th Gen. Assemb., 2d Sess. (Colo. Feb. 23, 2006).

### Colorado Supreme Court Opinions: 1864 to 1883

**Colorado Supreme Court:** *Coffin v. Left Hand Ditch Co.*, 6 Colo. 443, 447 (1882).

**Colorado Court of Appeals:** *Coffin v. Left Hand Ditch Co.,* 6 Colo. 443, 447 (1882).

**Bluebook:** *Coffin v. Left Hand Ditch Co.*, 6 Colo. 443, 447 (1882).

### Colorado Supreme Court Opinions: 1883 to 2012

**Colorado Supreme Court:** *People v. Cross*, 127 P.3d 71, 73 (Colo.2006).

- **Note:** there is no space in the parenthetical in the Pacific Reporter; however, the slip opinions have a space between Colo. and 2006. Similarly see note below regarding discrepancy in underlining and italics. *https://www.courts.state.co.us/userfiles/file/Court_Probation/Supreme_Court/Opinions/2013/13SC465.pdf.*

**Colorado Court of Appeals:** *People v. Cross*, 127 P.3d 71, 73 (Colo. 2006).

**Bluebook:** *People v. Cross*, 127 P.3d 71, 73 (Colo. 2006).

### Colorado Supreme Court Opinions: 2012 to Present

**Colorado Supreme Court:** *People v. Perez,* 2016 CO 12, ¶ 33, 367 P.3d 695, 702.

- **Note:** slip opinions of both of the Colorado Supreme Court Colorado Court of Appeals underline instead of italicize the cases name; however, cases published in the Pacific Reporter italicize instead of underline cases names. *See e.g., https://www.courts.state.co.us/userfiles/file/Court_Probation/Supreme_Court/Opinions/2013/13SC465.pdf; c.f. https://www.courts.state.co.us/Courts/Court_of_Appeals/Opinion/2016/13CA1680-PD.pdf.*

**Colorado Court of Appeals:** *People v. Perez,* 2016 CO 12, ¶ 33, 367 P.3d 695, 702.

**Bluebook:** *People v. Perez*, 2016 CO 12, ¶ 33.

### Colorado Court of Appeals Opinions: 2012 to Present

**Colorado Supreme Court:** *People v. Ujaama*, 2012 COA 36, ¶ 42, 302 P.3d 296, 304–05.

**Colorado Court of Appeals:** *People v. Ujaama*, 2012 COA 36, ¶ 36, 302 P.3d 296.

**Bluebook:** *People v. Ujaama*, 2012 COA 36, ¶ 36.

### Colorado Court of Appeals Opinions: 1891 to 2012

**Colorado Supreme Court:** *People v. Cooper*, 205 P.3d 475, 478 (Colo. App. 2008).

**Colorado Court of Appeals:** *People v. Cooper*, 205 P.3d 475, 478 (Colo. App. 2008).

**Bluebook:** *People v. Cooper*, 205 P.3d 475, 478 (Colo. App. 2008).

### Colorado Court of Appeals Unpublished Opinions

**Colorado Supreme Court:** *People v. Opana*, No. 10CA1987, slip op. at 1 (Colo. App. May 29, 2014).

**Colorado Court of Appeals:** *People v. Opana*, slip op. at 1 (Colo. App. No. 10CA1987, May 29, 2014) (not published pursuant to C.A.R 35(f)).

**Bluebook:** *People v. Opana*, No. 10CA1987, slip op. at 1 (Colo. App. May 29, 2014).

- **Notes:** Beginning in 2016 the Colorado Court of Appeals opinions began using in paragraph symbols (¶) in its slip opinions. When available, pinpoint citations should be made to those paragraph symbols. If paragraph symbols are not available, pinpoint citations should be made to specific pages of the slip opinion.

### Colorado Rules of Civil Procedure

**Colorado Supreme Court:** C.R.C.P. 26(a)(2).

**Colorado Court of Appeals:** C.R.C.P. 26(a)(2).

**Bluebook:** C.R.C.P. 26(a)(2); or, COLO. R. CIV. P. 26(a)(2).

### Colorado Rules of Criminal Procedure

**Colorado Supreme Court:** Crim. P. 23(a)(5).

**Colorado Court of Appeals:** Crim. P. 23(a)(5).

**Bluebook:** Crim. P. 23(a)(5); or, Colo. R. Crim. P. 23(a)(5).

### Colorado Rules of Appellate Procedure

**Colorado Supreme Court:** C.A.R. 1(d).

**Colorado Court of Appeals:** C.A.R. 1(d).

**Bluebook:** C.A.R. 1(d); or, Colo. R. App. P. 1(d).

### Colorado Rules of Probate Procedure

**Colorado Supreme Court:** C.R.P.P. 25.

**Colorado Court of Appeals:** C.R.P.P. 25.

**Bluebook:** C.R.P.P. 25; or, Colo. R. Probate. P. 25.

### Colorado Rules of Evidence

**Colorado Supreme Court:** CRE 702.

**Colorado Court of Appeals:** CRE 702.

**Bluebook:** CRE 702; or, Colo. R. Evid. 702.

### Colorado Regulations

**Colorado Supreme Court:** 2 C.C.R. 410-1:3.

**Colorado Court of Appeals:** 2 CCR 410-1:3.

**Bluebook:** Colo. Code Regs. § 410-1:3.

## Examples of Citations to Colorado Secondary Authority

### West's Colorado Practice Series

**Colorado Supreme Court:** 2A Cathy Stricklin Krendl et al., *Colo. Prac., Methods of Practice* 214 (6th ed. 2012).

**Colorado Court of Appeals:** Cathy Stricklin Krendl, 2A Colo. Prac., Methods of Practice 214 (6th ed. 2012).

**Bluebook:** 2A Cathy Stricklin Krendl et al., *Colo. Prac., Methods of Practice* 214 (6th ed. 2012).

### Colorado Lawyer

**Colorado Supreme Court:** Robert E. Benson, *Discovery to Nonparties in Colorado Arbitrations*, Colo. Law., Mar. 2016, at 25.

**Colorado Court of Appeals:** Robert E. Benson, *Discovery to Nonparties in Colorado Arbitrations*, Colo. Law., Mar. 2016, at 25.

**Bluebook:** Robert E. Benson, *Discovery to Nonparties in Colorado Arbitrations*, Colo. Law., Mar. 2016, at 25.

### Colorado Jury Instructions: Civil

**Colorado Supreme Court:** CJI-Civ. 41:10 (2016).

**Colorado Court of Appeals:** CJI-Civ. 41:10 (2016).

**Bluebook:** Colo. Supreme Court Comm. on Civil Jury Instructions, *Colorado Jury Instructions Civil*, 41:10 (2016).

### Colorado Jury Instructions: Criminal

**Colorado Supreme Court:** COLJI-Crim. B:04 (2016).

**Colorado Court of Appeals:** COLJI-Crim. B:04 (2016).

**Bluebook:** Model Criminal Jury Instructions Comm. of the Colo. Supreme Court, *Colorado Jury Instructions Criminal* B:04 (2016).

## VI. Conclusion

With time, practice, and the content above, Colorado researchers can learn to cite to Colorado authority quickly and competently. While several citation styles exist in Colorado, researchers can look to the above court-specific examples for guidance; and when those do not cover the authority to be cited, *The Bluebook* should provide enough guidance to lead to a sufficient citation.

### Other Citation Resources

For additional information on Colorado legal citations and legal citations generally, researchers may consult some of the following resources.

- *The Bluebook: A Uniform System of Citation* (Columbia Law Review Ass'n et al. eds., 20th ed. 2015).
- Chief Justice Directive 12-01 (Jan. 2012), https://www.courts.state.co.us/Courts/Supreme_Court/Directives/CJD%2012-01.pdf.
- K.K. DuVivier, *Colorado Citations*, Colo. Law., Mar. 2005, at 39.
- Larry L. Teply, *Legal Citation in a Nutshell* (2d ed. 2016).

# About the Author

Robert Michael Linz is the Associate Director and Head of Public Services for the William A. Wise Law Library at the University of Colorado School of Law in Boulder. In this role, he teaches legal research including Colorado Legal Research and provides research services to library users, among other duties. He has worked in a variety of librarian, technological, and management roles at academic libraries and the Colorado Supreme Court library since becoming a law librarian in 1996. He earned his law degree from the University of Florida, library science degree from Florida State University, and undergraduate degree from Wake Forest University.

# Index